Collective Conflict Management and Changing World Politics

SUNY Series in Global Politics
James N. Rosenau, Editor

Collective Conflict Management and Changing World Politics

EDITED BY

Joseph Lepgold and Thomas G. Weiss

State University of New York Press

Published by
State University of New York Press, Albany

Printed in the United States of America

For information, address State University of New York
Press, State University Plaza, Albany, N.Y., 12246

Production by Diane Ganeles
Marketing by Patrick Durocher

Library of Congress Cataloging-in-Publication Data

Collective conflict management and changing world politics / edited by
Joseph Lepgold and Thomas G. Weiss
p. cm. — (SUNY series in global politics)
Includes index.
ISBN 0-7914-3843-0 (hc : alk. paper). — ISBN 0-7914-3844-9 (pbk. : alk. paper)
1. Security, International. 2. Conflict management. 3. World politics—1989– I. Lepgold, Joseph. II. Weiss, Thomas George. III. Series.
JZ5588.C65 1998
327.1'6—dc21 97-35892
CIP

10 9 8 7 6 5 4 3 2 1

Contents

Tables and Figures

Abbreviations

CCM	Collective Conflict Management
CFE	Conventional Forces in Europe
CINSAC	Commander in Chief of the Strategic Air Command
CJTF	Combined Joint Task Forces
CSCE	Conference for Security and Cooperation in Europe
DHA	Department of Humanitarian Affairs
ECOMOG	Economic Community of West African States Monitoring Group
EU	European Union
GAO	General Accounting Office
HUMPROFOR	Humanitarian Protection Force
ICRC	International Committee of the Red Cross
IFOR	Implementation Force
IGO	Intergovernmental Organization
ILO	International Labor Organization
IMF	International Monetary Fund
INGO	International Nongovernmental Organization
IO	International Organization
MAC	Military Airlift Command
MNF	Multinational Force
NACC	North Atlantic Cooperation Council

NATO	North Atlantic Treaty Organization
OAS	Organization of American States
OAU	Organization of African Unity
ODA	Overseas Development Assistance
ONUC	United Nations Operation in the Congo
ONUSAL	United Nations Observer Mission in El Salvador
OOTW	Operations Other Than War
OSCE	Organization for Security and Cooperation in Europe
PDD	Presidential Decision Directive
PFP	Partnership for Peace
PK	Peacekeeping
PM	Peacemaking
RPF	Rwanda Patriotic Front
SAC	Strategic Air Command
SACEUR	Supreme Allied Commander Europe
SFOR	Stabilization Force
SOP	Standard Operating Procedure
SPD	Social Democratic Party
SSRC	Social Science Research Center
TAC	Tactical Air Command
UN	United Nations
UNAMIR	United Nations Assistance Mission in Rwanda
UNCTAD	United Nations Conference on Trade and Development
UNDP	United Nations Development Programme
UNHCR	United Nations High Commissioner for Refugees
UNICEF	United Nations Children's Fund
UNIFIL	United Nations Interim Force in Lebanon
UNITAF	Unified Task Force

UNITAR	United Nations Institute for Training and Research
UNMIH	United Nations Mission in Haiti
UNOSOM	United Nations Operation in Somalia
UNPROFOR	United Nations Protection Force
UNTAC	United Nations Transitional Authority in Cambodia
WEU	Western European Union
WFP	World Food Programme

Preface

The role and importance of collective conflict management have seen many ups and downs since the late 1980s, and even during the writing of this book. Making sense of these changes has fostered a new generation of studies, some of which have a rather short shelf life. In this collection, we have tried to explain the causes and consequences of multilateral conflict management in a theoretically informed way, but one that will be accessible to students and practitioners as well. All of our contributors have risen ably to this challenge.

Georgetown University's School of Foreign Service funded the conference that began this project through its Walsh Fund, excellently managed by Charlie Pirtle. For this, we owe them our gratitude. We also thank Larry Finkelstein, Doug Stuart, and Richard Betts for serving skillfully as discussants at that conference. Their many insights improved the papers a good deal.

The staff at Brown University's Thomas J. Watson Jr. Institute for International Studies was, as always, extraordinarily dedicated and talented in pulling together the various chapters, standardizing their form and presentation. Fred Fullerton and George Potter of the Communications Department put on the finishing touches after Laura Sadovnikoff had done yeowoman's service in preparing the manuscript. We are very grateful indeed for these efforts that meant the timely appearance of this volume.

Mike Barnett and Marty Finnemore joined this project midstream, and skillfully adapted their contributions to the existing analytic framework. For this we owe them a deep debt of gratitude. We all wish to understand conflict management better and, ideally, contribute to its utility for students, conceptualizers, and policymakers.

J.L. and T.G.W.

Washington, D.C. and Providence, R.I.

Part One

Collective Conflict Management: Theoretical and Historical Perspectives

1

Collective Conflict Management and Changing World Politics: An Overview

Joseph Lepgold and Thomas G. Weiss

> [Collective security requires us] to give up war for all the purposes for which sovereign communities have fought since war has been in existence, but we have still got to be willing to accept the risks and losses of war for a purpose for which hitherto people have never thought of fighting.
>
> —Arnold Toynbee[1]

Major international conflagrations during the last two centuries have regularly spawned hopes about an enhanced multilateral capacity to manage international armed conflicts. Inevitably, they have been quickly dashed—after the Napoleonic Wars, after World War I, and after World War II. The end of the Cold War was no exception.[2] Automatic superpower deadlock seemed a thing of the past by the late 1980s, and the spread of democracy promised to help pacify large regions of the world. The reasoning behind this optimism was familiar: As the interests of states in promoting stability and peaceful change strengthened, they sought common rules and procedures to prevent and respond to armed conflict.

The post-Cold War euphoria, however, was short-lived. Optimism about the possibilities for human development, democratization, and conflict resolution, captured by former President George Bush's "new world order" and by President Bill Clinton's "assertive multilateralism,"[3] ceded quickly to less optimistic assessments. Democratization spread but along with micronationalism, fragmentation, and massive human displacement. The end of the Cold War did not end history, but rather unleashed a more painful epoch than Francis Fukuyama and others predicted.[4]

As part of the longer historical pattern, the onset of the post-Cold War era initially witnessed a reinvigorated United Nations (UN). But bullishness after the Gulf War turned to pessimism following troublesome UN operations in Bosnia, Croatia, Somalia, and Rwanda. After Somalia in particular, Pollyannaish notions about intervening militarily to thwart aggression or thugs and to rescue civilians trapped in war zones or fleeing from them were replaced by more realistic estimates about the limits of such undertakings.[5]

The new bearishness about collective conflict management differs from earlier disillusionments in that the founders of the United Nations, like their predecessors in designing world security orders, imagined that it would help keep the peace among rather than within sovereign states. Yet, since 1990, the UN increasingly has been asked to help out in civil wars.[6] The fact that one out of every 115 humans has been displaced by this type of war, and probably an equal number have remained behind but whose lives are totally disrupted, represents the tragic human consequences of contemporary intrastate wars.[7] Eighty-two armed conflicts broke out in the five years following the collapse of the Berlin Wall, and 79 were civil wars; in fact, two of the three remaining ones (Nagorno-Karabakh and Bosnia) also could be categorized legitimately as civil wars.[8]

Not surprisingly, scholars have had strong opinions about the prospects for multilateral management of international conflict. Since Woodrow Wilson articulated his 14 points, the debate over collective security—the idea that alliances are problematic and that all states should pledge themselves to automatically and instantly aid any state that is a victim of aggression—has been sharply polarized, especially in the United States. Realists have been pessimistic, and idealists and liberal institutionalists have been sanguine.

Whereas much of the recent literature similarly takes dichotomous positions, this book takes a different tack. Contributors ask whether some form of collective conflict management (CCM) is feasible amidst profoundly changing world politics. Rather than setting up a straw man of perfect collective security, they ask the following questions: Under what international and domestic conditions will multilateral security efforts tend to work? What types of operations will tend to work? Their chapters spell out the domestic and international conditions that circumscribe the possibilities. Before summarizing the most salient aspects of individual chapters, however, we first discuss the concept of CCM, objections to it, two alternative paths toward it, and a typology of multilateral security operations.

What is Collective Conflict Management?

We ask these questions about collective conflict management: How might it work? What benefits do states derive from it? How intractable are the political, financial, and organizational obstacles that impede it? Can it work in a world where states still prize autonomy and, at times, a narrow view of their interests? How desirable is it in view of the benefits and obstacles? We define CCM as a pattern of group action, usually but not necessarily sanctioned by a global or regional body, in anticipation of or in response to the outbreak of intra- or interstate armed conflict. CCM includes any systematic effort to prevent, suppress, or reverse breaches of the peace where states are acting beyond the scope of specific alliance commitments, the traditional means of international security cooperation.

CCM covers a wide range of cooperative actions. It includes collective security as a polar type, but is broader and more flexible. Whereas collective security requires reliable procedures for collectively identifying and punishing aggressors, CCM includes a variety of multilateral efforts to maintain or restore order and peace, including those where international decisionmakers have not identified a particular aggressor. It ranges from the relatively nonintrusive monitoring of potentially dangerous situations to military coercion to quell breaches of the peace. Chapters VI and VII of the UN Charter thus circumscribe our concerns.[9] Its essence is coordinated action on the basis of broadly defined group standards or norms, or what many would characterize as elements of "international society" if not "international community."[10] These norms rest on particular confluences of national interests, any state subscribing to them may participate.

By way of contrast, alliances are a form of decentralized international policymaking. They differ from CCM in that they protect only specific groups of states from outside threats. Security within alliances is a private good—that is, divisible and excludable. This differs from CCM, in which the benefits of collective action are at least potentially nonexcludable outside any fixed group. Alliances are not necessarily inimical to collective conflict management, although they are incompatible with classical collective security, where no a priori distinction is made between allies and enemies, and automatic responses against aggressors are a necessity.

Because classical collective security is the broadest security commitment that states can make, it is the least likely. Inis Claude, for example, recently revisited the issue and wrote: "Multilateral resistance to aggression will continue to be, as it always has been, selective, unpredictable, and, therefore, unreliable. This is to say that collective security, in the comprehensive Wilsonian sense, is no less an impossible dream today than in earlier postwar periods."[11] By contrast, such CCM operations as third-party monitoring of elections, preventive deployments in crises, peacekeeping, and even humanitarian intervention may be possible short of the types of commitments required for collective security. Only if a reliable collective security were in place would alliances be superfluous. Short of that, states may need alliance protection. In fact, defensive alliances could supplement a CCM system that was defined in a nonexclusive way.[12]

However, just as CCM cannot replace alliances, alliances often cannot substitute for CCM. The threat or use of force may not be so neatly containable within exclusive groups of states for which security may come to be viewed at least partly as a public good. A CCM regime is one solution for such problems, and the differences between it and more decentralized types of international policymaking are summarized in Table 1.1.

We assume that states act on the basis of self-perceived security interests, not abstract ideals. But this does not preclude participation in CCM operations, which do not require idealism. What is critical to the success of CCM is the definition, breadth, and composition of state interests. Definitions of raisons d'état range from North Korea's isolationism to Sweden's internationalism. If states believe that aggression, civil war, or a breakdown of authority inside a state can affect others, they may act collectively, even if they have no immediate stakes in the situation. It is this broad conception of interests that induces a CCM system.

To succeed, a workable system of collective conflict management must satisfy a critical mass of key states in three ways. First, political leaders must believe that they can protect some of their foreign policy stakes multilaterally. Second, it must satisfy the political needs of critical domestic policy factions in the states that are most likely to contribute significantly to the system; without such domestic support, leaders cannot pursue stable and coherent policies. Third, the system also must be compatible enough with societal norms and the manifest wishes of ordinary citizens so that leaders can be confident that they will enjoy necessary popular support. These conditions are not unique to CCM; foreign, factional, and societal incentives must align for any strategy to work.

Since there exists a wide variety of security regimes, what distinguishes CCM? Broadly speaking, it is characterized by an internationalized rather than a selective response to the threat and use of force. This does not require auto-

Table 1.1
Decentralized and Collective Types of Security Systems

	Decentralized Conflict Management	Collective Conflict Management
state behavior is	unconstrained by general norms	coordinated with others, based on general norms
decision criteria are	individualistic self-help: what particular states think is best	pursuit of broad, group-based self-interest
goal of action is	pursuit of narrowly defined self-interest	what is best for group or system
military forces are	independent: no need to share resources, command, etc.	part of a collective force: resources, command, etc. are joint
action occurs when	state's individual interests are at stake	peace and stability of self or others is threatened

matic war against aggressors. But it does assume that states will try to coordinate policies when peace is in jeopardy or order breaks down, and that their actual response to events will be shaped by common obligations, norms, and understandings of mutual interest. In other words, CCM makes uncoordinated, unilateral behavior in response to the use or threat of force, humanitarian emergencies, or communal violence unattractive more than it mandates any particular multilateral action. States clearly are free to act unilaterally, but the potential value of collective conflict management suggests that they will consider joint action before deciding to go it alone. This is the overarching principle from which specific obligations and rules derive.[13]

Heuristically, it might be useful to consider how a CCM mechanism might have functioned in the Balkans between mid-1991 and the Dayton agreements.[14] Counterfactual history does not have the weight of evidence, but it can help us speculate about the conditions necessary for CCM to work in the kind of conflicts where it will be most needed. We can then judge how far we are from those conditions.

In 1991, the major Western powers failed to work out a common policy to deal with the likely disintegration of Yugoslavia, including recognition of successor states and a constitutional mechanism that potentially could have satisfied the rival claims of Serbs and Croats. These would have been hard to satisfy by multilateral means in any case because the Croatian Serbs were and are determined not to be ruled by a non-Serbian government, and all three ethnic groups inside Bosnia have major irredentist claims. In 1992, before the Bosnian war broke out in earnest, there was deadlock on a partition plan that would have given the Bosnian Muslims more territory than they are likely ever to receive. At this point, and in 1993 when the Vance-Owen plan to partition Bosnia fell apart, the United States was the recalcitrant party. In 1994 and 1995, although the North Atlantic Treaty Organization (NATO) was used sporadically to enforce the protection of safe areas for the Bosnian Muslims, fear that the Serbs would retaliate against British and French peacekeeping troops continually interfered with the execution of air strikes against Serbs. As a result, they repeatedly tested NATO's and the UN's resolve to enforce the so-called safe areas, and the Serbs' opponents occasionally tried to provoke Serbian attacks in order to receive Western sympathy and support.

Each of these episodes marked a failure to define and implement an internationalized response to a breakdown of peace. If the rival communities inside Croatia had been constitutionally protected early on, such guarantees might have been extended to the rest of the Balkans, averting much of the subsequent war. This procedure was recommended by the European Community's Badinter Commission but was ignored as Germany and the United States rushed to recognize new states. Moreover, mechanisms through which to implement a multilateral response did exist: the Organization for Security and Cooperation in Europe (OSCE) (which at the time of the outbreak of the Balkan War was the Conference for Security and Cooperation in Europe, CSCE) was empowered to work out codes of conduct and guarantees. NATO also had agreed on a case-by-case basis to enforce its decisions. The CSCE could have but did not develop a common policy for recognizing independence along with the minority guarantees. Germany's unilateral recognition of Croatia and Slovenia at the end of 1991 emboldened the Croatian and Serbian communities in Bosnia to escalate their demands. Recognizing these states might have averted war if Germany and the European Union (EU) had then tried to enforce multilateral norms about the use of force.

At this point, a UN protectorate or governorship over Bosnia might also have averted a war, but it might have required between 100,000 and 300,000 troops. This was between three and ten times the size of the United Nations Protection Force (UNPROFOR) at its strongest and at least twice as large as the NATO-led Peace Implementation Force (IFOR) after Dayton. There was no support for such a force from France, Britain, or the United States. As a result, nothing was done to stop mass expulsions, massacres of civilians, and other acts of aggression.

Despite this obvious lack of European as well as American resolve to suppress the conflict, President Bush emphatically categorized the Balkans as "Europe's problem." President Clinton effectively agreed until mid–1995. Nevertheless, fearing charges of selling out the Bosnian Muslims, Washington implicitly and sometimes explicitly held out hope that Bosnia would receive American help, thereby prolonging the war. Outside of a maritime embargo against Serbia that was fairly well enforced by NATO and the Western European Union (WEU), there was no effective multilateral response to the conflict until the Croatian-Muslim offensive in September-October 1995 embarrassed NATO into employing sustained air power. After Dayton, IFOR changed the pattern. Missing up to this point was a widely shared belief that this conflict was a serious potential danger and that the best response was collective international action to prevent or suppress it.

Admittedly, this would have been a hard case for any CCM mechanism to handle. Aside from a general lack of Western will to restore peace, the complexity of the conflict itself was daunting. For example, the Serbs were responsible for the highest number of atrocities, but Serbs in regions controlled by Croats also suffered. In fact, the largest involuntary flight in Europe since the 1956 Soviet crushing of the Hungarian revolt took place in the fall of 1995 as 150,000 Serbian civilians and 50,000 soldiers fled from the Krajina.

In any case, the Balkans represent a serious setback for advocates of developing a post-Cold War CCM system. What lessons might be learned from this episode? One of us argued a few years ago that a new "strategic concept" is needed that "would stress forestalling violence and war in addition to dealing with their consequences."[15] Under such a strategic concept, war might have been averted in the Balkans if states had prepared standby forces for CCM operations and had deployed troops preventively at the early stages of the conflict. UN Secretary-General Boutros Boutros-Ghali and Brian Urquhart, who ran the UN secretariat's peacekeeping operations for a generation, have forcefully advocated these ideas.[16] As yet, there has been little concrete support for them, but in fact there has been some genuine hostility.[17]

This suggests that we are far from the kind of CCM mechanism that could have prevented, suppressed, or reversed the Balkan war. Some analysts end the discussion here, concluding that CCM is unworkable. We disagree. Little in the preceding discussion convinces us that CCM is inherently unworkable. Before examining how we could move toward such a system, it would be useful to examine objections to it in more detail.

The Objections to Collective Conflict Management

Critics of collective security have raised five objections that also apply to the broader range of operations that we define as CCM. They are as follows:

1. Because international institutions merely reflect the balance of power, they have no independent impact on mitigating conflict.
2. Free riding jeopardizes CCM by requiring too much of large states.
3. Cooperation on CCM is inherently fragile without an outside threat.
4. By demanding adherence to group goals, CCM is insensitive to states' changing interests in different contexts.
5. CCM works best when it is least needed.

In this section, we discuss and respond to each critique.

Hobbesian Anarchy Makes International Institutions Weak

Realists argue that "what is most impressive about [international] institutions . . . is how little independent effect they seem to have on state behavior."[18] In this view, self-help constrains states to care only about their relative power. Whereas liberal institutionalists see the main problem of international relations as the pursuit of Pareto-superior solutions in situations that could become "win-win," realists see a much more zero-sum, distributional world, in which security is inherently hard to achieve.[19] Realists conclude that this often rules out multilateral agreement on managing conflicts, since states tend to be wary of their potential losses as others gain.

Such arguments assume that states' interests are fixed and unaffected by the institutional context in which choices are made. This proposition assumes that every international relationship turns on the balance of force, which in turn assumes that strong states can get their way regardless of the context.[20] But such views of the utility of force apply only in the most "primitive" or Hobbesian of self-help systems. In these situations, interstate rivalry is at its fiercest. States do not recognize one another's core interests and turn every encounter into a test of strength. As Barry Buzan argues, however, there are more "mature" variants of self-help. In these contexts, borders are generally respected and states coexist virtually free from predation or fear.[21] Realists' pessimism about the prospects for CCM and the ability of institutions to foster it assume that the Hobbesian variant of self-help is the norm. But Hobbesian anarchy is an ideal type, as is the benign version, and the present international system combines aspects of both. In self-help situations other than a Hobbesian one, mutually superior security solutions are thus not impossible.

If institutional solutions to a range of security problems are not impossible, what might this imply for CCM? Institutions can help states realize common objectives by reducing the costs of responding to every problem in an ad hoc fashion, by linking issues so that those who might defect find it more costly to do so, and by allowing policy information to be reliably shared multilaterally.[22] In the security area, institutions are likeliest to be created when leaders share an aversion to war or its potential consequences.[23] This may make institutions particularly useful for the kinds of multilateral operations that fall under the CCM rubric.

Free Riders

A second objection holds that free riding jeopardizes CCM because few states have incentives to do the work that it entails.[24] This is a powerful argument. Unless there is a hegemonic state willing to assume large burdens, a regime must be as rational from the standpoint of individual states as it is from the perspective of the system or region as a whole.[25] One result may be that the great powers with incentives to assume those burdens will be likely to deploy military force in areas of special interest, legitimated at most by vaguely worded support from bodies such as the Security Council.[26] U.S. intervention in Haiti and the respective Russian and French versions in Abkhazia and Rwanda are recent examples.

Another result of the collective action problem may be less collective conflict management than is optimal. This has been evident since the backlash began after the debacle in Somalia. For example, President Clinton used his first speech to the UN General Assembly to say that the UN must know "when to say no" to new involvements. In part, it is difficult to induce lesser powers and especially smaller states into sharing CCM burdens unless—as with Pakistan or Canada, for instance—their military organizations and populations essentially derive national satisfaction from such participation.

Neither of these problems, however, is intractable. The solution to loosely disguised endorsement of big-power hegemony is greater accountability, or an insistence by the members of such bodies as the UN Security Council that intervening states be held to standards that are consistent with general norms. A desire to avoid using the veto excessively may induce the permanent five Security Council members to compromise toward somewhat closer guidance from intergovernmental organizations (IGOs). Moreover, the burden-sharing picture is not entirely bleak. Medium-sized countries and regional powers perhaps can be enticed to contribute with selective benefits as a share in the command of military operations, a major voice in determining policy toward the country or region that is the target of the operation, and so on. Conversely, special military and economic privileges might be suspended to noncontributors. Unless these states discount such future benefits and penalties enormously, this should make them more willing to contribute.[27]

To be sure, subcontracting to selected states for CCM operations is controversial.[28] But ad hoc coalitions of interested states, regional powers, and even hegemons may at times constitute the only constituencies with enough interest to act. William Maynes has called this "benign *Realpolitik*"—a revival of spheres of influence with UN oversight.[29] The Security Council is experimenting with a type of great-power control over decisionmaking and intervention, which the United Nations had originally been founded to end but which is increasingly pertinent in the light of some of the inherent difficulties of multilateral mobilization and management of military force.

An observer might ask, "What is new about this kind of rationalization? Is the secretary-general not grasping at straws in justifying a gun-boat diplomacy for the 1990s? Is this not simply *Realpolitik*?" Boutros-Ghali is aware of the dangers: "Authorization to serve as a surrogate might strengthen a particular power's sphere of influence and damage the United Nations' standing as an organization intended to coordinate security across regional blocs."[30] The difference could be that major powers or their coalitions act on their own behalf as well as on behalf of the Security Council; they thus should be held accountable for their actions by the wider community of states authorizing outside interventions.[31] Although major powers inevitably flex their military muscles when it is in their perceived interests to do so, they do not necessarily agree in advance to subject themselves to international law and outside monitoring of their behavior. The political and economic advantages attached to an imprimatur from the Security Council provide some leverage for the community of states to foster heightened accountability from military subcontractors. However limited, it nonetheless affords the possibility to influence the behavior of would-be subcontractors.

CCM is Fragile without a Common Threat

A third objection from Realists holds that multilateral security cooperation is unreliable and at best fragile without a major outside threat. Realists believe that no shared interest, especially one as vague as promoting stability, induces the same degree of commitment as a common threat. This may be true, but it is not necessarily a devastating argument undercutting collective conflict management. If specific CCM operations are undertaken by ad hoc coalitions, a regime would not need the same overall commitment and cohesion as a defensive alliance. Since participation in ad hoc coalitions entails no long-term obligations, the barriers against forming them are not high. By contrast, if a more institutionalized coalition such as NATO had some collective defense and some broader CCM functions, it could be expected to loosen or tighten as external threats waned or grew, with greater or lesser participation as states' interests changed.[32] NATO's efforts to create the Combined Joint Task Forces, through which states selectively participate in out-of-area contingencies under the umbrella of the core collective defense commitment, is an example of this kind of flexibility. Furthermore, a CCM mechanism may be better than alliances to induce security participation from states that want to remain nonaligned.[33]

CCM is Insensitive to the Political Context

A fourth objection, also mentioned by many Realists, is that multilateral security norms are too inflexible. In a self-help system in which security may be hard to achieve and entail major opportunity costs, security cooperation requires rules and commitments that are sensitive to the context and the interests of individual states. This argument is weak. CCM is not akin to an insurance policy, in which states that uphold their obligations are regularly subject to moral hazard as others exploit them. CCM is implemented through political bodies such as the UN Security Council or NATO that either have weighted voting to protect the key actors from these problems or a unanimity rule. Of course, if no norms governing multilateral security operations shape states' behavior, there can be no CCM regime. Boutros-Ghali originally suggested (somewhat inaccurately with the benefit of hindsight) as much in noting that the world seemed willing to do more about starvation and bloodshed in the "rich man's war" in the Balkans than in Somalia. But the need for legitimate, general commitments can be balanced with the need for flexibility in particular contexts, whether in Europe or Africa or elsewhere. If states collectively intervene in ongoing disputes and internal unrest with "finesse and attention to due process," they will over time make their commitments more precise *and* normatively legitimate.[34]

Expanding the UN Security Council while retaining the veto may be one way to accomplish both objectives.[35]

CCM is Most Effective when it is Least Necessary

A fifth objection to CCM is that it can only work when international security conditions are so benign that collective action is unnecessary.[36] To some extent, this is the case whenever coordinated behavior is called for in the face of risks to individual actors: the lower the costs of unilateral action, the less necessary the coordination with others. But this is not a fatal shortcoming unless one demands that a system provides total security immediately to all actors.

Two arguments support this conclusion. First, confidence in the system can be built gradually, and the degree of commitment that states make to common security norms can grow as confidence grows. Consider the evolution of a pluralistic security community in Western Europe since World War II. In recent years, analysts have tried to think through ways in which confidence in CCM operations could be built, particularly expanding the use of preventive diplomacy. Enforcement action under Chapter VII of the UN Charter, for example, would arguably be more likely and more effective if preventive diplomacy could diffuse more potential conflicts without using force.[37] If insertion of a third-party presence occurred regularly in situations of high tension, states that wished to manage conflicts collectively would have more time to do so before violence got out of hand as well as a clearer indication of when enforcement was truly needed.

Second, there is another reason to think that the risks of building a meaningful CCM mechanism are tolerable. As Charles Kupchan argues:

> Even if all states other than those that are directly threatened fail to uphold their commitment to collective action, the remaining coalition will have essentially the same strength as the alliance that would form through traditional balancing. . . . In terms of deterring and resisting aggression, collective security at its worst is equivalent to traditional balancing at its best.[38]

This view is controversial. Richard Betts, for example, argues that if states expected CCM to work and it then failed, they would be unprepared for conflict when it came.[39] But it is hard to see why this would occur unless the level of armaments in a CCM system was much lower than in a completely decentralized security system, which is unlikely. CCM does not require disarmament; it supplements rather than replaces decentralized self-help.[40] As long as procurement policies and military strategies were sensitive to this fact, states would not run large risks by participating in CCM operations.

In sum, none of the five objections destroys the argument as long as CCM is seen as a partial rather than a complete solution to international security. We now consider two paths by which it can be pursued.

Two Paths toward Collective Conflict Management

An evaluation of collective conflict management requires answers to six questions:

1. Who are the actors involved?
2. What are their expectations about the purposes and obligations of joint action?
3. Who authorizes operations, and how?
4. Who defines the rules of engagement in military operations?
5. How is the burden of CCM operations shared?
6. Who commands collective military operations?

Answers to these questions vary from case to case, depending on how much CCM is institutionalized. In this section, we sketch out the characteristics of both noninstitutionalized and institutionalized paths and speculate about the conditions under which each would be used.

The least institutionalized variant of CCM is a series of ad hoc coalitions. Here, precedents derived from past experience would have only instrumental value for the future; the type of situation and nature of the coalition would determine most of the answers to the six key questions. In the Gulf War, for example, German and Japanese contributions to the Desert Storm coalition were driven largely by Washington's ability to twist arms and by a widespread belief that those who did not fight should subsidize those who did.[41] Under these circumstances, neither the leverage to extract financial resources nor troop-contributing countries will necessarily be the same from case to case.

Such coalitions most likely will be assembled by major powers. A concert system could evolve if the major powers were regularly involved.[42] Concerts have the benefit of flexibility because no treaty specifies when or how the members should act. They concentrate decisionmaking in the hands of the actors best able to support demanding operations. Moreover, because they typically form after major wars, concerts offer a respite from the competitive policies that often characterize the behavior of major powers. But concerts also have disadvantages. If they are used to intervene mainly in the periphery, they will appear to be an instrument of domination by big powers. And if the distribution of power changes, some members may become less attached to the status quo, making the entire system fragile.[43]

A second path is also possible: a more institutionalized set of expectations about collective conflict management that would constitute a formal, however nascent, regime. Here, more of the six questions listed above will be pre-answered. As we argued above, international institutions are valuable because they allow expectations to converge around policy solutions that have become at least informal precedents. The UN Charter regime specifies in principle the content of major international security norms and how they are to be enforced. That NATO, the OSCE, and other regional bodies increasingly share in implementation is not an aberration but the fulfillment of Chapter VIII of the Charter.

Formal institutions are needed when uncoordinated behavior leaves governments worse off than coordinated behavior. In these cases, rules are not self-enforcing because actors prefer that others cooperate while they do not.[44] Several aspects of CCM fall into this category, including preventive diplomacy. States allied to one of the parties to a dispute may have too much at stake to participate in crisis management that calls for neutral, third-party intervention, and other states may not care enough to get involved at all. Left to their own devices, governments are unlikely to create a reliable capacity for intervention. By contrast, either predesignated forces available to the UN for such purposes or a volunteer, standing UN force would be readily available for these missions.[45] Either way, a formal mechanism can help avoid a collective action problem. Guidelines or rules to share the costs of CCM operations would also be more efficient if they were institutionalized. Conceiving and implementing an equitable way to share the burden of these missions is a significant transaction cost when operations are ad hoc.

Institutionalization may also serve other political ends. Because IGOs give small states at least a formal voice, the resulting policies carry enhanced legitimacy in the Third World.[46] Also, conflicts between small countries that are strategically unimportant to the major powers might receive more attention than others in the context of a formal regime because "if they are left to be resolved by ad hoc coalitions, they will probably not be resolved at all."[47]

At the same time, some issues do not involve major conflicts of interest, so the likelihood of uncoordinated behavior once rules are established is limited. In these cases, CCM cooperation can be ad hoc. The command and control of multinational military operations is an example.[48] Once states choose command arrangements, which are likely to vary, depending on who participates in an operation and the scale of those efforts, they have strong incentives to follow those procedures.

For these reasons, different CCM issues probably require different degrees and kinds of institutionalization. We turn next to discussing the various types of CCM operations.

A Typology of Multilateral Security Operations[49]

Collective conflict management encompasses a range of military and nonmilitary activities. These constitute "the entire spectrum of activities from traditional peacekeeping to peace enforcement aimed at defusing and resolving

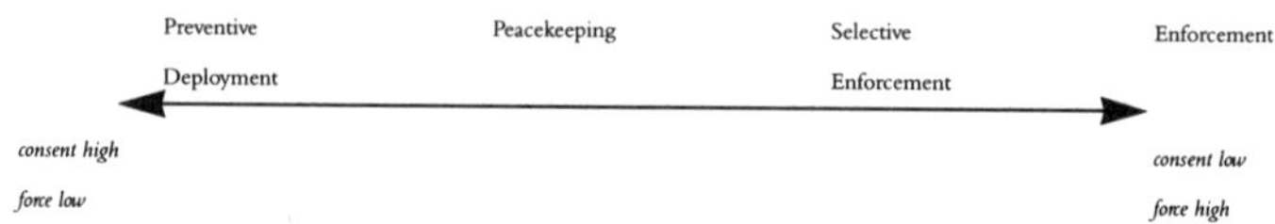

Figure 1.1
The Spectrum of Collective Conflict Management Operations

international conflicts."[50] We highlight the distinction between operations that have the consent of the parties and those that do not; this affects the cost and risk to those who participate and the degree of military professionalism required.[51] In practice, each type of operation exhibits or assumes some specific degree of consent, as illustrated in Figure 1.1:

Degree of Consent from Parties to Dispute and Degree of Force Required

As in virtually any foreign policy decision related to international peace and security, the international stakes and the domestic costs of peace operations are inversely related. Operations on the left end of the continuum are the easiest to justify domestically, since their costs and risks are low, but they are often unimportant in narrow strategic terms to the states that carry them out. Conversely, those toward the right end are harder to justify internally, but if successful carry higher strategic rewards to those that carry them out.

Preventive Deployment

This sits at the far left end of the continuum. It involves stationing observers or troops in an area of conflict before significant force is used by the belligerents. The idea is to provide a tripwire that would discourage recourse to force, as opposed to trying to stop it afterward. Boutros-Ghali contends that this could take place in a variety of instances and ways:

> For example, in conditions of national crisis there could be preventive deployment at the request of the Government or all parties concerned, or with their consent; in inter-State disputes such deployment could take place when two countries feel that a United Nations presence on both sides of their border can discourage hostilities; furthermore, preventive deployment could take place when a country feels threatened and requests the deployment of an appropriate United Nations presence along its side of the border alone.[52]

But just because prevention is desirable in principle does not imply that it is plausible in practice. Preventive diplomacy is the latest conceptual fashion—according to one formulation, "an idea in search of a strategy."[53] Such preventive actions as the symbolic deployment of a detachment of UN blue helmets to Macedonia or the expanded use of fact-finding missions, human rights monitors, and early-warning systems are being discussed and attempted. In addition, economic and social development are generally viewed as essential to help prevent armed conflicts, even if the results from substantial aid and investment in the former Yugoslavia and Rwanda are hardly encouraging for those like the UN secretary-general who wish to make a case for "preventive development" as a "necessary complement to preventive diplomacy."[54]

In terms of forestalling massive human displacement and suffering, potentially the most cost-effective preventive measure would appear to be the deployment of troops.[55] To be a successful deterrent, however, the deployed soldiers must be backed by contingency plans and reserve fire-power for immediate retaliation against aggressors. This would amount to advance authorization for Chapter VII in the event that a preventive force was challenged. Backup would not be easy to assemble either politically or operationally. Yet without it, the currency of preventive UN military action will be devalued to such an extent that preventive action should not be attempted. As such, prevention in practice could move from one end of the spectrum of peace operations to the other.

The rub is, of course, obvious: prevention is cost-effective in the long run but cost-intensive in the short run. Governments that are responsive to electorates rarely can imagine action whose time horizon extends beyond the next public opinion poll, and certainly not beyond the next electoral campaign. On the other hand, the growing preoccupation with saving resources could make a difference to such perspectives. In the former Yugoslavia, the "long run" lasted almost four years, whereas in Rwanda it was reduced to a matter of weeks. The argument that an earlier use of force would have been more economical in the former Yugoslavia runs up against the inability of governments to look very far into the future, and of their consequent tendency to magnify the disadvantages for immediate expenditures and to discount those in the future. In Rwanda, the costs of at least 500,000 dead, over four million displaced persons, and a ruined economy were borne almost immediately by the same governments that had refused to respond militarily only a few weeks earlier. The United States and the European Union ended up providing what is estimated to have been at least $1.4 billion in emergency aid in 1994 alone.[56]

If political leaders decide to invest more in proactive rather than reactive efforts, it is possible that preventive military action may in some cases become more plausible. Reactions to Burundi's ethnic cauldron indicated that the terms of international discourse on this question have changed somewhat, though the willingness to deploy troops preventively lags far behind the rhetoric.

Peacekeeping (Monitoring a Pause)

This is one of the most misused terms in contemporary discussions about multilateral security. It has become common to attach such adjectives as "extended," "aggravated," and so on to the term, as a way to label every type of military undertaking on the spectrum of peace operations.[57] One of the premier training institutes, the Lester B. Pearson International Peacekeeping Training Center in Cornwallis, Nova Scotia, makes a conscious point of including every type of operation under the "peacekeeping umbrella." But this makes "peacekeeping" as a distinct type of operation meaningless.

We define the term narrowly, as was common during the Cold War: peacekeeping refers to either the interposition of neutral forces in a conflict area once hostilities have ceased or observers to verify an actual agreement. Such forces thus monitor a pause. Peacekeeping is undertaken with the consent of the state on whose territory the forces are stationed and, ideally, with the consent of belligerents. The purpose of peacekeeping is to keep the disputants apart, supervise troop withdrawal and disarmament, and provide the opportunity for warring factions to come closer to a negotiating table. In fact, some criticism is that it works so well in places like Cyprus that there is no need for the adversaries to negotiate.

Historically, peacekeeping operations have taken two forms: observation missions and interpositional forces.[58] The former consists of sending a limited group of unarmed observers to an area for purposes of monitoring a cease-fire—the most successful recent example was the UN Observer Mission in El Salvador (ONUSAL). The latter consists of deploying larger and lightly armed military contingents as a kind of buffer—the most controversial earlier ones being in the Congo (ONUC) and Lebanon (UNIFIL), and more recent examples being in the former Yugoslavia (UNPROFOR), Somalia (UNOSOM), and Rwanda (UNAMIR).

In general, blue-helmeted peacekeepers are not only lightly armed, they also are limited to using force in self-defense. It is more the moral backing of the international community than fire-power that is their strength. The UN Charter does not mention "peacekeeping," which is why Dag Hammarskjöld coined the expression "Chapter six-and-a-half" to characterize such operations. PDD 25 does specifically cite Chapter VI of the Charter as the legal basis for such action. Depending on the extent of consent and the need to use military force, however, many recent UN peacekeeping operations have been closer to Chapter VII's coercion than to Chapter VI's pacific settlement of disputes.

The extraordinarily rapid growth in demand for helping hands from UN soldiers meant that there were twice as many operations approved in the last eight years as in the previous forty—which in turn spawned a cottage analytical industry of peacekeeping.[59] Secretary-General Boutros-Ghali wrote in January

1995: "This increased volume of activity would have strained the Organization even if the nature of the activity had remained unchanged."[60] After stable levels of about 10,000 troops in the early post-Cold War period, their numbers jumped rapidly. In the last few years, 70,000 to 80,000 blue-helmeted soldiers have been authorized by the UN's annualized "military" (peacekeeping) budget that approached $4 billion in 1995. Accumulated total arrears in the same year hovered around $3.5 billion—that is, almost equal to this budget and about three times the regular United Nations budget. The secretary-general lamented that "the difficult financial situation . . . is increasingly proving to be the most serious obstacle to the effective management of the organization."[61] Although both the numbers of soldiers and the budget dropped dramatically in 1996, by two-thirds, related financial and professional problems point to a "strategic overstretch" by the UN of the type that Paul Kennedy attributes to empires.[62] Overextension was the diagnosis of the world organization's ills on its fiftieth anniversary.

The UN perennially operates at the margin of solvency, and the secretariat now lacks the technology and enough human resources to monitor a myriad of complex conflicts. Whether states will invest in these resources and entrust them to a multilateral institution are key policy issues. An important question after the Cold War is how and whether the supply of peacekeeping forces can keep up with the demand, even if the United Nations is relegated to fielding only consensual rather than coercive operations. It is to the latter that we now turn our attention.

Selective Enforcement (Imposing a Pause)

Further to the right along the continuum, between peacekeeping and enforcement, is a type of peace operation that might be called "selective enforcement." Although traditional peacekeeping permits the use of force in self-defense, in certain other post-Cold War cases additional force has been authorized for specified purposes. In the Balkans, the UN Security Council authorized "all measures necessary" to protect humanitarian personnel and specifically authorized NATO air strikes to protect safe havens. In Somalia, the Security Council authorized "all necessary means" to ensure humanitarian access.

Selective enforcement constitutes a murky area, one that can be more like consensual peacekeeping or more like nonconsensual enforcement depending on the circumstances. Such operations go beyond traditional peacekeeping, but they do not constitute enforcement because they are not undertaken to defeat an aggressor. In other words, such forces impose a pause in the violence against whomever violates it. Analysts who believe that conflicts end only when the underlying political issues are settled find them so untenable that they may make matters worse.[63] Nevertheless, these operations often appear attractive for a period of time when states are authorized to use force to carry out limited objectives, including the delivery of humanitarian assistance, maintenance of safe havens, and even selective enforcement of human rights and democracy.

As with peacekeeping, selective enforcement is not explicitly provided for in the UN Charter. Nonetheless, authority for doing so can be inferred from Chapter VII—and, in fact, is implicit in mathematically rounding Chapter 6.5 upwards. Under Article 39, the Security Council may determine the existence of a threat to the peace, breach of the peace, or act of aggression, and under Article 42 it may impose non-forcible (economic) or forcible (military) sanctions in any of these situations. If it can authorize force in response to large-scale aggression, it can logically authorize more limited force in situations that fall short of explicit aggression. As Stanley Hoffmann quipped, the interpretation of "threats to international peace and security" constitute an "all-purpose parachute" for Security Council decisionmaking.

Enforcement (Imposing a Solution)

These operations lie at the far right end of the continuum and as a group comprise Wilsonian collective security. They impose a collective solution. As such, they are partisan in nature: a violator of the peace is designated, and the community of states seeks to reverse this behavior. They thus require the most coercion and military professionalism of all CCM operations.

The best recent example of enforcement is the Gulf War, when Iraq committed a clear act of aggression against Kuwait. The Security Council condemned the attack and imposed sweeping economic and diplomatic sanctions. After efforts to reach a negotiated withdrawal failed, the council authorized the use of force. According to that authorization and in spite of questions about proportionality, coalition forces began military operations against Iraq, the first Chapter VII authorization since Korea.[64]

Although Chapter VII of the Charter anticipates that a UN command will be established to carry out enforcement operations, the Security Council may choose to authorize a subcontracted operation, as has occurred in a number of crises. Such decentralization may be the most politically palatable for the states that will likely assume the bulk of the enforcement responsibility. Moreover, the Charter's Chapter VIII specifically empowers the Security Council to employ regional arrangements to undertake enforcement operations.

Advocates for regional institutions, including the UN secretary-general, find them an attractive alternative to an overextended United Nations. As member states of these institutions suffer most from the destabilizing consequences of war in their locales, they have the greatest stake in the management and resolution of regional conflicts. Regional actors also understand the dynamics of strife and cultures more intimately than outsiders, and thus they are in a better position to mediate. Issues relating to local conflict are also more likely to be given full and urgent consideration in regional fora than in global ones where there are broader agenda, competing priorities, and distractions.[65]

This theory contrasts starkly, for instance, with efforts by the Arab League, the Organization of African Unity (OAU), and the Islamic Conference, which were so ineffective that only *cognescenti* of the Somali crisis are vaguely aware of their involvement. The advantages of regional organizations are more rhetorical than real. Most institutions in the Third World have virtually no military experience or resources. Even in Europe, the density of well-endowed and seemingly powerful institutions were of limited use—perhaps even counter productive—for the first four years of Yugoslavia's wars.

Nonetheless, if coercion occurs at all, interventions soon will have to compensate for the military inadequacies of the United Nations. As such, UN decisions may require subcontracting enforcement to regional organizations or ad hoc coalitions of major states. Regional powers (for instance, Nigeria within West Africa and Russia within the erstwhile Soviet republics) could take the lead, combined with larger regional (that is, the Economic Community of West African States and the Commonwealth of Independent States) or coalitions. Perhaps only when regional powers cannot or will not take a lead should more global powers (for example, France in Rwanda or the United States in Somalia) be expected to do so. However, blocking humanitarian intervention, which some powers are willing to conduct when others are reluctant to get involved (for example, the United States vis-à-vis Rwanda between early April and late June 1994), should be ruled out.

The Chapters in this Collection

Part One of this volume, which has one chapter in addition to this introductory overview, sets the context for the more specific discussions by placing CCM in a theoretical and historical context. It asks when collective security, the most demanding type of CCM operation, can work. The four chapters in Part Two examine how political interests among and within states drive the military operations that they are willing to undertake collectively and the preparations that they make to do so. In Part Three, three chapters examine the humanitarian motive for several post-Cold War interventions. Here the authors analyze what animates an apparently new-found interest in collective humanitarian operations, the conditions under which such operations might succeed, and whether they portend any diminution in states' sovereign rights to order themselves internally.

Alan Lamborn's chapter, "Theoretical and Historical Perspectives on Collective Security: The Intellectual Roots of Contemporary Debates about Collective Conflict Management," argues that the success of collective security depends on a number of linked political processes. It can succeed, he claims, when international, domestic factional, and popular agendas align. Where they do align, political leaders are more willing than otherwise to lengthen their time horizons to accept the outcomes generated by multilateral choice procedures. Under these conditions, the associated norms and rules then could take on more weight in policymaking, thereby giving states more of a substantive stake in conflicts that would not otherwise concern them. He concludes that undue pessimism about the prospects for a multilateral security regime is logically and historically unwarranted.

Lamborn emphasizes that collective security is not easily achieved. But neither is highly flexible balancing behavior. Any strategy requires that political leaders make tradeoffs between political and policy risks in a sustainable way. Lamborn thus offers an argument that can be used to think through most of the issues we have discussed so far, and that are discussed in greater detail in the rest of the chapters.

Joseph Lepgold discusses "NATO's Post-Cold War Conflict Management Role" in the opening chapter for Part Two. He analyzes a number of roles that NATO could assume, ranging from "unspecified" collective defense—where NATO members would continue to view security as a private good but would not identify threats in advance—to institutional support for a tight concert of the major powers. Each step away from a traditional alliance will broaden the range of issues that NATO addresses as well as expand the breadth of multilateral rules that it employs. In practice, NATO members will choose its role by answering four key questions: How is pan-European security to be organized, and what is NATO's role in that process? Under what conditions will NATO try to manage out-of-area disputes? How will they alter NATO's military structure to accomplish those interventions? Under what conditions will NATO work with other security organizations?

In "The Limits of Peacekeeping, Spheres of Influence, and the Future of the United Nations," Michael Barnett argues that peacekeeping under UN auspices has at best limited future prospects. This stems directly from the collective action problem discussed in his chapter: UN members, he claims, are reluctant to contribute the required resources unless they have a vested stake in the outcome. As a result, the major powers seem determined to intervene unilaterally in areas that they think of as spheres of influence.

These findings appear to validate one of the key objections to collective conflict management. At the same time, however, Barnett shows that even very powerful states are likely to be held accountable for certain international norms to legitimate certain collective operations and interventions. He sketches out various factors that possibly compel states to look to the United Nations as part of the process by which they further their security stakes.

Robert McCalla examines the "Doctrinal Constraints on Adaptation in the American Military to CCM Missions." He seeks to analyze the transformation of Cold War military forces to those better suited for peacekeeping, humanitarian assistance, and enforcement. Through a close look at U.S. military doctrine and force structure, he claims that national culture and bureaucratic politics make it difficult for the United States to assume new multilateral missions. Even with the political will to do so, major obstacles will remain in Washington. Along with other chapters, McCalla shows that building a capacity to pursue security multilaterally can be politically difficult, albeit not impossible. Various internal as well as external constituencies must be on board, and the linkages among these various groups are complex.

The last chapter in Part Two is Andrew Bennett's "Somalia, Bosnia, and Haiti: What Went Right, and What Went Wrong?" Bennett reviews the experiences of recent CCM operations, focusing both on UN and UN-approved missions in the Balkans, Somalia, and Haiti. In these operations, recurrent difficulties arose in several areas discussed in detail in his chapter. Multilateral coordination among governments and IGOs was highly imperfect. Mandates and missions were often defined in a fuzzy way. Moreover, the domestic politics of these missions was at times very poorly managed.

Nevertheless, Bennett finds that the Haiti mission succeeded in part because lessons were learned from earlier mistakes. This suggests, he contends, that fairly demanding forms of CCM, such as selective enforcement, can indeed work under the right conditions. Success is likely when troop-contributing countries agree on the mission; deploy a mix of forces in which they have a comparative advantage; impartially enforce their mandate but prepare to defeat those who oppose it; deploy sufficient forces that are flexible enough to overwhelm the opponents of that mission; agree on a unified and decisive command structure; and integrate military actions with a viable political strategy in the target country and at home.

Bruce Cronin examines "Changing Norms of State Sovereignty and Multilateral Intervention" in the first chapter for "Part Three: Collective Conflict Management: The Humanitarian Impulse." He argues that the norms of sovereignty determine the range of issues that would fall within the jurisdiction on a CCM regime—that is, the distinction between a domestic and international issue. Many political leaders and commentators tend to employ absolutist notions of state autonomy. But there has been no single notion of what sovereign units are permitted or obligated to do. He shows that as the norms of sovereignty change, the conditions warranting multilateral intervention change correspondingly. Based on this, multilateral institutions have intervened to protect those domestic actors who are viewed as being the legitimate holders of sovereignty. Currently, a multilateral consensus that sovereignty rests with the population may be taking hold, leading to an increase in interventions to protect human rights. Cronin traces out in Chapter 7 the causes and implications of this potentially major set of changes.

Martha Finnemore's "Military Intervention and the Organization of International Politics" explores why we have recently witnessed cases of humanitarian intervention with two distinctive features: their occurrence in places where intervenors have no strategic interests; and their sanction by multilateral bodies. Both of these represent a sharp break from past international practice. She explains these patterns in two ways. IGOs have provided states with some political tools not otherwise available to them. At the same time, international institutions have enmeshed states in webs of multilateral activity that make certain kinds of inaction and withdrawal politically difficult. Finnemore's chapter helps us see how new understandings of state interests in managing conflicts collectively are both a cause and effect of the growth of IGOs in world politics.

Thomas Weiss ends the volume with "Humanitarian Conflict Management: More or Less than the Millennium?" His chapter analyzes the UN's strengths and weaknesses in undertaking humanitarian interventions, and suggests several ways to remedy the weaknesses. Along with virtually every other author, he singles out as the key feature of international responses since the early 1990s, namely the willingness to address rather than ignore emergencies within war-torn states. Weiss calls for a modified form of UN trusteeship for failed states, a prudent subcontracting of humanitarian intervention to interested and capable states, and the creation of a new category of humanitarian workers to deliver relief supplies.

In the end, states retain the policy discretion to act in a decentralized or more multilateral fashion in security affairs. The breadth and definition of their interests may change over time. The chapters in this volume show the implications of and obstacles to such changes, and their effect on the potential for collective conflict management. This suggests that ongoing conversations among scholars and policymakers about CCM are fruitful. We are confident that the chapters constitute at least a modest contribution toward that end.

Notes

1. Arnold Toynbee, *The Future of the League of Nations* cited by Inis Claude, *Swords Into Plowshares,* 4th ed. (New York: Random House, 1971): 252. Claude's chapter 12 remains one of the clearest discussions in the literature about collective security.

2. See Thomas G. Weiss, ed., *Collective Security in a Changing World* (Boulder, Colo.: Lynne Rienner, 1993).

3. For contrasting partisan views, see Warren Christopher, "America's Leadership, America's Opportunity," *Foreign Policy* 98 (spring 1995): 6–27; and Bob Dole, "Shaping America's Global Future," *Foreign Policy* 98 (spring 1995): 29–43, and Jessie Helms, "Saving the U.N.: A Challenge to the Next Secretary-General," *Foreign Affairs* 75, no. 5 (September/October 1996): 2–7. For a bipartisan overview, see George Soros, chairman of an Independent Task Force, *American National Interest and the United Nations* (New York: Council on Foreign Relations, 1996). For a more academic overview, see John Gerard Ruggie, *Winning the Peace: America and World Order in the New Era* (New York: Columbia Univ. Press, 1996). See also Charles William Maynes and Richard S. Williamson, eds., *U.S. Foreign Policy and the United Nations System* (New York: Norton, 1996).

4. Francis Fukuyama, *The End of History and the Last Man* (New York: Free Press, 1992). For a discussion of the phenomenon of fragmentation, see Lori Fisler Damrosch, ed., *Enforcing Restraint: Collective Intervention in Internal Conflicts* (New York: Council on Foreign Relations Press, 1993); Michael E. Brown, ed., *Ethnic Conflict and International Security* (Princeton, N.J.: Princeton University Press, 1993) and *The International Dimensions of Internal Conflicts* (Cambridge: MIT Press, 1996); Ted Robert Gurr and Barbara Harff, *Ethnic Conflict in World Politics* (Boulder, Colo.: Westview, 1994); Gidon Gottlieb, *Nation Against State* (New York: Council on Foreign Relations, 1993); and "Reconstructing Nations and States," special issue of *Dædalus* 122, no. 3 (summer 1993). For discussions of the difficulties of negotiating the end to such wars, see I. William Zartman, ed., *Elusive Peace: Negotiating an End to Civil Wars* (Washington, D.C.: Brookings Institution, 1995), and Fen Osler Hampson, *Nurturing Peace: Why Peace Settlements Succeed or Fail* (Washington, D.C.: U.S. Institute of Peace Press, 1996).

5. See Tom J. Farer, "Intervention in Unnatural Humanitarian Emergencies: Lessons of the First Phase," *Human Rights Quarterly* 18, no. 1 (February 1996): 1–22; and Thomas G. Weiss, "Overcoming the Somalia Syndrome—'Operation Rekindle Hope'?" *Global Governance* 1, no. 2 (May–August 1995): 171–187.

6. See Jarat Chopra, "Back to the Drawing Board," *Bulletin of the Atomic Scientists* 51, no. 2 (March/April 1995): 29–35, and "The Space of Peace Maintenance," *Political Geography* 15, no. 3/4 (March/April 1996): 335–357.

7. For these and other disheartening statistics, see UNHCR, *The State of the World's Refugees 1995: In Search of Solutions* (New York: Oxford University Press, 1995); U.S. Committee for Refugees, *1996 World Refugee Report* (Washington, D.C.: U.S. Committee for Refugees, 1996); International Federation of Red Cross and Red Crescent Societies, *World Disasters Report 1996* (Oxford, U.K.: Oxford University Press, 1996); and Bread for the World Institute, *Countries in Conflict* (Silver Glen, Md.: Bread for the World, 1995).

8. United Nations Development Programme, *Human Development Report 1994* (New York: Oxford University Press, 1994): 47.

9. See Thomas G. Weiss, David P. Forsythe, and Roger A. Coate, *The United Nations and Changing World Politics* 2nd ed. (Boulder, Colo.: Westview, 1997): 1–17.

10. For a discussion, see Oliver Famsbotham and Tom Woodhouse, *Humanitarian Intervention in Contemporary Conflict* (Cambridge, U.K.: Polity Press, 1996).

11. Inis L. Claude, Jr., "Peace and Security: Prospective Roles for the Two United Nations," *Global Governance* 2, no. 3 (Sept.–Dec. 1996): 290.

12. Arnold Wolfers, "Collective Defense versus Collective Security," in Arnold Wolfers, ed., *Discord and Collaboration* (Baltimore, Md.: Johns Hopkins University Press, 1962): 184.

13. Our notion of regime here follows Stephen Krasner's: regimes consist of principles, norms, rules, and decisionmaking procedures. Principles and norms specify the aims and obligations of the joint enterprise; rules and decision procedures implement these. See Stephen D. Krasner, "Structural Causes and Regime Consequences: Regimes as Intervening Variables," in Stephen D. Krasner, ed., *International Regimes* (Ithaca, N.Y.: Cornell University Press, 1983): 1.

14. For a discussion, see Misha Glenny, *The Fall of Yugoslavia: The Third Balkan War* (New York: Penguin, 1994); Susan Woodward, *Balkan Tragedy: Chaos and Dissolution after the Cold War* (Washington, D.C.: The Brookings Institution, 1995); David Owen, *Balkan Odyssey* (New York: Harcourt Brace, 1995); Laura Silber and Allan Little, *Yugoslavia: Death of a Nation* (New York: TV Books, 1996); and Richard H. Ullman, ed., *The World and Yugoslavia's Wars* (New York: Council on Foreign Relations, 1996).

15. Thomas G. Weiss, "UN Responses in the Former Yugoslavia: Moral and Operational Choices," *Ethics and International Affairs* 8 (1994): 10.

16. See, for example, Boutros Boutros-Ghali, *An Agenda for Peace 1995* (New York: United Nations, 1995); Brian Urquhart, "Beyond the 'Sheriff's Posse,'" *Survival* 32, no. 3 (May/June 1990): 195–206, and "Who Can Police the World?," *The New York Review of Books,* May 12, 1994.

17. See, for example, Stephen John Stedman, "The New Interventionists," Foreign Affairs 72, no. 1 (1992–93): 1–16, and "Alchemy for a New World Order: Overselling 'Preventive Diplomacy,'" *Foreign Affairs* 74, no. 3 (May/June 1995): 14–20.

18. For the most extreme statement of the supposedly insuperable problems associated with such efforts, see John J. Mearsheimer, "The False Promise of International Institutions," *International Security* 19, no. 3 (winter 1994–95): 5–49, quote at 47.

19. Stephen D. Krasner, "Sovereignty and Sovereign Lending," paper prepared for the conference on the Changing Nature of Sovereignty in the New World Order, Center for International Affairs, Harvard University (April 22–23, 1995): 2.

20. Robert Gilpin, *War and Change in World Politics* (New York: Cambridge University Press, 1981): 31. We thank George Shambaugh for bringing this point to our attention.

21. Barry Buzan, *People, States, and Fear,* 2nd ed. (Boulder, Colo.: Lynne Rienner, 1991): 174–181.

22. This is the liberal institutionalist argument about the functional utility of regimes. See Robert O. Keohane, *After Hegemony* (Princeton, N.J.: Princeton University Press, 1984), chapter 6.

23. Janice Gross Stein, "Reassurance in International Conflict Management," *Political Science Quarterly* 106, no. 3 (fall 1991): 444–449.

24. The following four sub-sections draw on George W. Downs and Keisuke Iida, "Assessing the Theoretical Case Against Collective Security," in George W. Downs, ed., *Collective Security Beyond the Cold War* (Ann Arbor, Mich.: University of Michigan Press, 1994): 17–39.

25. George W. Downs, "Beyond the Debate on Collective Security," in ibid., 6.

26. See Jarat Chopra and Thomas G. Weiss, "Prospects for Containing Conflict in the Former Second World," *Security Studies* 4, no. 3 (spring 1995): 552–583.

27. Downs and Iida, "Assessing the Theoretical Case," 28

28. See Thomas G. Weiss, ed., *Beyond Subcontracting: UN Task-sharing with Regional Security Arrangements and Service-Providing NGOs* (London: Macmillan, 1997).

29. Charles William Maynes, "A Workable Clinton Doctrine," *Foreign Policy* 93 (winter 1993–94): 3–20.

30. Boutros Boutros-Ghali, "Global Leadership After the Cold War," *Foreign Affairs* 75, no. 2 (March/April 1996): 95.

31. For a discussion of this difference, see Mario Bettati, *Le Droit d'Ingérence: Mutation de l'Ordre International* (Paris: Odile Jacob, 1996): 186–203.

32. Downs and Iida, "Assessing the Theoretical Case," 30.

33. Wolfers, "Collective Defense versus Collective Security," 195.

34. See Downs and Iida, "Assessing the Theoretical Case," 31, emphasis in original.

35. See Bruce Russett, Barry O'Neill, and James Sutterlin, "Breaking the Security Council Restructuring Logjam," *Global Governance* 2, no. 1 (Jan.–Apr. 1996): 65–80.

36. A recent statement of this position is Richard K. Betts, "Systems for Peace or Causes of War? Collective Security, Arms Control, and the New Europe," *International Security* 17, no. 1 (summer 1992): 7 and passim.

37. Joseph P. Lorenz, "The Case for Collective Security," in *Two Views on the Issue of Collective Security* (Washington, D.C.: United States Institute of Peace, 1992): 28; Andrew Bennett and Joseph Lepgold, "Reinventing Collective Security after the Cold War and Gulf Conflict," *Political Science Quarterly* 108, no. 2 (summer 1993): 229; Brian Urquhart, "Learning From the Gulf," *New York Review of Books,* March 7, 1991.

38. Charles A. Kupchan, "The Case for Collective Security," in Downs, ed., *Collective Security*, 45.

39. Betts, "Systems for Peace," 7.

40. To take one example, the U.S. Army Air Force during the last two years of World War II planned for two strategic contingencies, both of which would have required substantial American investment in air power. One was a weak, ineffective United Nations organization, which would mean unilateral American planning for security and a larger national air force; the other was a capable UN that would also require a large American air contingent that would be assigned to the organization. See Perry Smith, *The Air Force Plans for Peace, 1943–1945* (Baltimore: Johns Hopkins University Press, 1970): 45–46. In no sense, then, would participation in CCM have mandated disarmament. We thank Rob McCalla for this reference.

41. See Andrew Bennett, Joseph Lepgold, and Danny Unger, eds. *Friends in Need: Burdensharing in the Persian Gulf War* (New York: St. Martin's Press, forthcoming).

42. See Philip Zelikow, "The New Concert of Europe," *Survival* 34, no. 2 (summer 1992): 12–30 ; Charles A. Kupchan and Clifford Kupchan, "Concerts, Collective Security, and the Future of Europe," *International Security* 16, no. 1 (summer 1991): 114–161; and Bennett and Lepgold, "Reinventing Collective Security."

43. Stephen M. Walt, "Multilateral Collective Security Arrangements," in Richard Shultz, Roy Godson, and Ted Greenwood, eds., *Security Studies for the 1990s* (Washington, D.C.: Brassey's, 1993): 255–256.

44. Robert O. Keohane and Joseph S. Nye, Jr. "Two Cheers for Multilateralism," *Foreign Policy* 60 (fall 1985): 155–157. For an extended discussion of this point, see Arthur Stein, *Why Nations Cooperate* (Ithaca: Cornell University Press, 1990), chapter 2.

45. Richard N. Haass, "Military Force: A User's Guide," *Foreign Policy* 96 (fall 1994): 33–35.

46. See Mohammed Ayoob, *The Third World Security Predicament: State Making, Regional Conflict, and the International System* (Boulder, Colo.: Lynne Rienner, 1995).

47. Lorenz, "The Case for Collective Security," 39–40.

48. See Frank M. Snyder, *Command and Control: The Literature and Commentaries* (Washington, D.C.: National Defense University, 1993).

49. We would like to thank Tony Arend and George Little for having helped to clarify the argument in this section.

50. These were defined as "peace operations" in Presidential Decision Directive 25 (PDD 25), which can be found in "United States: Administration Policy on Reforming Multilateral Peace Operations," reprinted in *International Legal Materials* 33, no. 3 (May 1994): 795–813.

51. For discussions, see John Mackinlay and Jarat Chopra, "Second Generation Multinational Operations," *Washington Quarterly* 15, no. 2 (summer 1992): 113–134; and Thomas G. Weiss, "New Challenges for UN Military Operations: Implementing an Agenda for Peace," *Washington Quarterly* 16, no. 1 (winter 1993): 51–66.

52. Boutros-Ghali, *An Agenda for Peace*, para. 28.

53. See Michael S. Lund, *Preventive Diplomacy and American Foreign Policy* (Washington, D.C.: U.S. Institute of Peace Press, 1994): 27. See also his *Preventing Violent Conflicts: A Strategy for Preventive Diplomacy* (Washington, D.C.: U.S. Institute of Peace Press, 1996).

54. Boutros Boutros-Ghali, *An Agenda for Development 1995* (New York: United Nations, 1995): 99.

55. For a discussion of this problem, see Thomas G. Weiss, "The UN's Prevention Pipe-Dream," *Berkeley Journal of International Law* 14, no. 2 1996: 423–437.

56. See Larry Minear and Philippe Guillot, *Soldiers to the Rescue: Humanitarian Lessons from Rwanda* (Paris: Organisation for Economic Co-operation and Development, 1996); Gérard Prunier, *The Rwanda Crisis: History of a Genocide* (New York: Columbia University Press, 1995); and Joint Evaluation of Emergency Assistance to Rwanda, *The International Response to Conflict and Genocide: Lessons from the Rwanda Experience* (Copenhagen: Joint Evaluation of Emergency Assistance to Rwanda, 1996).

57. See for example, *United Nations Peace Operations: Case Studies* (Washington, D.C.: Library of Congress, 1995).

58. The best historical treatments are Alan James, *Peacekeeping in International Politics* (London: Macmillan, 1990); and the United Nations, *The Blue Helmets* (New York: United Nations, 1996).

59. The best examples of the growing literature are: William J. Durch, ed., *The Evolution of UN Peacekeeping: Case Studies and Comparative Analysis* (New York: St. Martin's Press, 1993) and *UN Peacekeeping, American Policy, and the Uncivil Wars of the 1990s* (New York: St. Martin's, 1996); Paul Diehl, *International Peacekeeping* (Baltimore: Johns Hopkins University Press, 1993); Mats R. Berdal, *Whither UN Peacekeeping? Adelphi Paper 281* (London: International Institute for Strategic Studies, 1993); John Mackinlay, "Improving Multifunctional Forces," *Survival* 36, no. 3 (autumn 1994): 149–173; and Steven R. Ratner, *The New UN Peacekeeping: Building Peace in Lands of Conflict After the Cold War* (New York: St. Martin's, 1995). For a discussion of the literature, see Cindy Collins and Thomas G. Weiss, *Review of the Peacekeeping Literature, 1990–1996* (Providence, R.I.: Watson Institute, 1997), Occasional Paper #28 1997.

60. Boutros Boutros-Ghali, *Supplement to An Agenda for Peace,* document A/50/60-S/1995/1 of January 5, 1995, published in *An Agenda for Peace 1995* (New York: United Nations, 1995), para. 77. References to the 1992 *An Agenda for Peace* and the 1995 *Supplement Agenda for Peace* are taken from this compendium; paragraph numbers are the same as in the original.

61. Boutros Boutros-Ghali, *Report of the Secretary-General on the Work of the Organization, August 1995*, document A/50/1, para. 22.

62. Paul Kennedy, *The Rise and Fall of the Great Powers* (New York: Random House, 1987).

63. Richard K. Betts, "The Delusion of Impartial Intervention," *Foreign Affairs* 73, no. 6 (November/December 1994): 30–33.

64. See Ian Johnstone, *Aftermath of the Gulf War: An Assessment of UN Action* (Boulder, Colo.: Lynne Rienner, 1994).

65. See S. Neil MacFarlane and Thomas G. Weiss, "Regional Organizations and Regional Security," *Security Studies* 2, no. 1 (autumn 1992): 6–37; and "The United Nations, Regional Organizations, and Human Security," *Third World Quarterly* 15, no. 2 (April 1994): 277–295.

2

Theoretical and Historical Perspectives on Collective Security: The Intellectual Roots of Contemporary Debates about Collective Conflict Management

Alan C. Lamborn

Contemporary debates about the prospects for collective conflict management are inescapably colored by the historical experiences and theoretical controversies involving collective security. Analyses of collective security, in turn, usually compare the historical record of the League of Nations and United Nations (UN) with images of the history of the balance of power, the Concert of Europe, and the standing alliances of the Bismarckian and Cold War periods. Consequently, even though collective security is only one form of collective conflict management (CCM), it stands at the juncture of discussions that compare the entire class of collective conflict management systems with more decentralized, self-help security systems.

The extent to which theoretical debates about collective and self-help security systems are entangled in controversies about historical cases creates intellectual baggage and a significant opportunity. If historical systems are to play a crucial role in our analyses of contemporary options, we must ask similar theoretical questions of each period and diplomatic system. Self-contained explanations of the success or failure of different security systems in particular historical periods are not really explanations at all. They are, instead, puzzles in search of explanations. There is a widely shared set of assumptions about the process of strategic interaction in world politics buried underneath the disputes about the relative effectiveness of different security systems.[1] These shared assumptions provide a common lens for different historical and theoretical perspectives on collective security. Moreover, they make it possible to place the analysis of collective security within a larger discussion of alternative security systems.

The ability to compare alternative security systems is crucial to any systematic evaluation of collective security and other forms of collective conflict management. CCM will probably never work as well as early twentieth century proponents of collective security hoped, but the appropriate standard for judging the value of different strategies is their success relative to available alternatives. Success and failure are matters of degree.[2] Too often, critics of collective security have reduced the options to two: if world politics has a community, CCM is irrelevant; if world politics does not have a community, CCM is impossible. But the options before us are not a community characterized by a pure harmony of interests and a Hobbesian world of pure conflict. These stereotypes are the least likely contexts for choice. Conflict management is about the adjustment of differences in mixed-motive situations, ones in which there are some compatible and some competing interests.[3]

There are, moreover, no "default options" in world politics. Anarchy creates only permissive and indeterminate conditions for strategic choice. The strategic incentives for choice vary with actors' foreign policy goals, norms, and perceptions of the international situation confronting them. Indeed, the distinguishing characteristics of the conflict management systems are based on varying assumptions about the "facts"—the substance of actors' values, policy preferences, and perceptions—not on immutable characteristics of politics. To the indeterminacy of anarchy in strategic choice we need to add a second reason for rejecting the notion that there is an automatic or default security system. Foreign policy choice is not driven solely by international incentives. To the contrary, world politics is linkage politics. The strategic incentives generated by international politics are intertwined with the factional politics of policy coalitions and the politics that link those factions to domestic constituencies.

Different security systems make different assumptions about prevailing conditions in the linked international and domestic arenas. Given different initial assumptions about the facts, most competing perspectives on collective and self-help security systems use remarkably similar assumptions about the politics of strategic interaction. Consequently, what separates advocates of different security systems into opposing camps is not so much their theoretical assumptions about the process of strategic interaction in world politics as it is their empirical assumptions about the "facts"—the values of the variables in the same set of theoretical relationships. The best place to begin is with the common assumptions about the process of strategic interaction in politics. With those made explicit, we can review more systematically the principal historical systems and theoretical perspectives that figure in the debates about alternative security systems.

Shared Assumptions about the Politics of Strategic Interaction[4]

Underneath the varied faces of different security systems, there is an enduring process of strategic interaction. The politics of strategic interaction are driven by variations in the compatibility of actors' preferences and their relative power; actors' beliefs about the importance and nature of just relationships; actors' time horizons and their guesses about what the future will bring; the political and policy risks people are willing to run in an effort to achieve their goals; and the linkages that connect international politics, factional politics within policy coalitions, and constituency politics (the relationships between policy factions and their mass and elite constituencies).

Preferences and Power

Politics involves attempts to achieve interdependent outcomes; power involves the ability to increase the probability that preferred outcomes will occur. Actors' preferences and relative power are, therefore, central to the process of strategic interaction. What is less obvious, but absolutely critical to evaluating competing perspectives on the effectiveness of different security systems, is how power and preferences are connected. The strategic significance of differences in actors' relative power varies with the compatibility of their preferences. The more compatible the preferences, the less important is relative power. If policymakers in different countries prefer the same outcome, it does not matter who controls the choice. At the same time, the more incompatible actors' preferences, the more strategically important their relative power positions.

By virtue of the same logic, the strategic importance of differences in actors' preferences varies with the distribution of power. The weaker an actor's relative power position, the more strategically important the more powerful actors' preferences; the stronger an actor's relative power position, the less strategically important the weaker actors' preferences. Those in a weak position know that what really matters in the short run is what stronger actors decide. The other side of the coin is summarized by Thucydides' history of the Peloponnesian War: "For you know as well as we do that right, as the world goes, is in question only among equals in power, while the strong do what they will and the weak suffer what they must."[5]

The relationship between the compatibility of actors' preferences and the strategic significance of their relative power positions is the first step in understanding the politics of strategic interaction. However, the impact of this piece of the process of strategic interaction in politics is contingent on several other theoretical relationships. The second fundamental relationship involves the political significance of actors' beliefs about the importance and nature of just relationships.

The Political Significance of Legitimacy

Values about just procedures and outcomes are important for two reasons. They provide direction for those who hold them by shaping and restricting both their preferences and strategies for achieving them. They also create a larger set of issues about what constitutes a legitimate community or relationship. Strategic interactions within political relationships are embedded within a larger set of interactions about the nature of just relationships and permissible games.

How people react to differences in their preferences and relative power positions varies with the importance that they attach to creating or sustaining legitimate relationships and their perception of how legitimate or just their existing relationships are. The higher the value attached to sustaining legitimate relationships and the more just existing relationships are perceived to be, the more likely it is that they will lengthen the time horizons they use when evaluating the implications of a challenge to their policy preferences and power positions; emphasize the effect of policy choices on the perceived legitimacy of their relationships; and deemphasize the effect of outcomes on their short-term policy preferences and power positions. The less value people attach to sustaining legitimate relationships or the less legitimate relationships are perceived to be, however, the more likely it is that people will shorten the time horizons they use when evaluating the implications of a challenge to their policy preferences and power positions; deemphasize the effect of policy choices on the perceived legitimacy of their relationships; and emphasize the effect of outcomes on their short-term policy preferences and power positions.

The difference between the conjunctions is important and is used when describing the situation in which people care about legitimate relations and believe that existing relations are legitimate. Two demanding conditions must be met before actors' values and perceptions about legitimate relationships are likely to increase the probability that they will accept outcomes that adversely affect their policy preferences and power. Only one condition must be met to increase the probability of a challenge.

Consequently, it is unwise to make sweeping assertions about the importance of shared norms in world politics. Instead, one ought to ask how actors in relevant groups perceive each others' commitments to such norms. The realist tradition in world politics sees norms, shared notions of legitimacy, and values as unimportant because it views states as inherently competitive and mistrustful. Other traditions make the opposite assumptions and therefore come to the opposite conclusions, but neither view is applicable all the time. Actors' commitments to creating or sustaining legitimate relationships—and their judgments about the legitimacy of existing arrangements—are variables.

To assess the full implications of this second aspect of the politics of strategic interaction, we must now consider another: the effect of variations in actors' time horizons and differences in their guesses about what the future holds.

Politics and the Shadow of the Future

People pay attention not only to how power, preferences, and legitimacy are related today but also to how they expect these factors to evolve. The more compatible people expect their substantive aims and norms to be over time, the more cooperative and less power-based their strategic choices are likely to be. Conversely, the more incompatible they expect preferences to become over time, the more competitive and power-based their strategic approach is likely to be. Given the judgment that they will need to rely on power to achieve their goals, the timing of a challenge will vary with how actors expect their power positions to change over time.

How people view the shadow of the future affects more than individual policy choices. It also affects overall bargaining strategies and world views. The longer the time horizons of actors who believe that there is a high probability of creating stable, jointly acceptable relationships, the more likely it is that they will follow a cooperative strategy designed to create a system of diffuse reciprocity. The possibilities for creating diffuse reciprocity depend on people simultaneously having long time horizons, common values, and shared preferences. What happens to bargaining strategies and world views when the length of actors' time horizons shortens? The shorter their time horizons (or the more uncertain actors are about the length of time during which they will be interacting with another actor), the more likely it is that they will resist making concessions that do not produce immediate reciprocal benefits and demand strict reciprocity. When people are unsure about how long a relationship will last, or when they expect the strategic interactions with another person to end sooner rather than later, they are likely to start counting, to keep a running score of who has done what for whom to make sure that they do not end up on the short end when the relationship breaks off.

What happens when the time horizons stay long but the perceived compatibility of the actors' preferences and values drops? The longer the time horizons of actors who believe that there is a low probability of creating jointly acceptable relationships, the more likely it is that they will follow a cautious and skeptical strategy designed to minimize the risks attached to possible defections. If values and preferences are incompatible or perceived as such, trust is dangerous. If preferences are unlikely to grow closer over time, the more dangerous the wait.

Preferences, relative power, and views about the importance and nature of legitimate relationships can vary across individuals, institutions, cultures, and situations; the length of time horizons and guesses about likely futures also can vary. Strategic choices confronting people within a single political arena are a product of how these three sets of political processes combine. The strategic significance of different relative power positions depends on the compatibility of actors' preferences. The strategic implications of that mix depend conversely on actors' views about the importance and nature of legitimate relationships, the length of time horizons, and guesses about the future.

Being able to recognize the underlying strategic situations gives us most of what we need to anticipate choices. However, people vary in how they react to the risks built into a strategic situation, and politics almost always involve links across multiple political arenas. We need, therefore, to add two final sets of political processes.

Risk-Taking Preferences

Strategic choices, by their nature, involve risk. Outcomes are seldom certain, for there is almost always some chance that people will not achieve their goals even if they choose the best option available and implement that choice as effectively as possible. Strategic choices are also risky because policy choices usually involve an investment in resources, time, and political capital. Strategic choices, therefore, carry both policy and political risks. Policy risk refers to the probability that actors' substantive goals will not be achieved, even if their policy choices are implemented effectively. Political risk refers to the probability that policy choices will have adverse effects on actors' political positions—on their ability to make and sustain preferred policy choices.

How people react to the risks that they face can have a major impact on their choices. Some people enjoy chance; others loathe it. But there is more to risky choices than individuals' general feelings about risk-taking. Risk-taking preferences vary with the specific choices and situations. Actors are more likely to make and sustain strategically wise policy when policy and political incentives are reinforcing. But what happens if the political and policy incentives cut in different directions? Other things being equal, the higher the political risks attached to options with a low policy risk, the more likely that actors will be drawn toward options that trade an increase in the level of policy risk for a decrease in political risks. High or escalating political risks also make it more likely that people will not be able to sustain preferred policy choices long enough to maximize their intrinsic probability of success.

But "other things" are often not equal. Sometimes people are willing to run extraordinary political risks to achieve their policy goals. Other times they are so sensitive to perceived threats to their political position that they shy away from political risk. How can we anticipate whether people will run political risks to achieve policy objectives? The general patterns are simple and intuitively reasonable. First, the higher the expected value attached to achieving a policy outcome, the higher the political risks they will be willing to run to achieve it. Second, just as entrepreneurs generally prefer to retain close control over their investments, people usually are averse to running political risks when they have little control over policy choice and how it is implemented. Third, people care more about policy failure when they are visibly responsible for the outcomes. Thus, while people become less willing to run political risks as their control over choice and implementation declines, they also become more indifferent to policy failure—as long as failure is not politically dangerous.

The willingness to run political and policy risks depends, finally, on exactly when the costs and benefits attached to those risks are expected to arrive. People generally prefer to get the benefits of a choice quickly and to defer the costs as long as possible. Consequently, actors typically discount costs (including political risks) and benefits (including preferred policy outcomes) over time, generally preferring current benefits over future ones and future costs over current ones. The exact way in which actors discount costs and benefits, however, varies with the expected value attached to achieving an outcome, the level of political risks attached to options that have a high probability of quickly achieving preferred policy outcomes, and the degree of control over policy choice and implementation. The higher the expected value attached to achieving a specific policy outcome, the less choices will be affected by discounting, and the more incentive will exist to find the best available means for achieving their substantive goals. The higher the immediate political risks of substantively preferred policy options, the more willing actors will be to defer policy benefits in exchange for a reduction in current political risks. The less control over policy choice and implementation, the more actors will prefer future costs over current costs, and the more they will discount future benefits relative to current benefits.

Linkage Politics

World politics also is driven by the interaction of international politics, factional politics within policy coalitions, and constituency politics (the relationships between policy factions and their mass and elite constituencies). The three arenas in world politics are interdependent and mutually constituted. The principal sources of variation are sometimes international and sometimes domestic. But whatever the source of variation, the effects are driven by how the three arenas interact. The connections across these three levels affect the strategic context, choices, and outcomes. Specifically, the strategic situation in each arena depends on the ways in which actors' preferences, power, beliefs about legitimate relationships, and guesses about the future are linked. Choices vary with the mix of international and domestic incentives attached to different options, risk-taking preferences, time horizons, and how costs and benefits are discounted. Outcomes vary with how successfully those choices bridge international, factional, and constituency politics.

The politics of strategic interaction is built on five sets of interconnected theoretical relationships. The impact of each is contingent on the values of the variables in the other four. When the values of the key variables move within stable ranges, these interconnections can reinforce one another and create a striking continuity in the politics of strategic interaction. However, when the values of the variables are close to important thresholds, even small changes in a few key variables can produce dramatic changes in the overall process of strategic interaction and calculation. This potential for both stability and sudden change makes the politics of strategic interaction so dynamic.

Because the values of the variables in these five political processes often move within distinctive ranges, the effectiveness of different security systems varies. Therefore, to evaluate the potential value of any particular security system, we should analyze how well its assumptions about the prevailing conditions fit the strategic incentives in the international arena, the purposes and structure of policy coalitions, and the domestic arenas in which policy factions must satisfy domestic constituents and overcome opposition. Having assessed that fit, the next question is, "compared to what alternative?" A historical data base is required that includes not only collective security systems but also perceived alternatives. The history of alternative security systems is the story of how well their assumptions about the facts fit the prevailing conditions in world politics.

Historical Perspectives on Collective Security

Balance of power is so closely identified with the origins of the European state system that many scholars consider it to be the archetypal security system, the default option that naturally arises in an environment in which there is no central agent to enforce agreements. Although the identification of classical balance of power with Westphalia is correct, thinking of balance of power as the "natural" security system under conditions of anarchy misreads the seventeenth century origins of the state system. Westphalia did not create an anarchic, self-help state system. Europe had been without agreed-upon standards of legitimate rule since the collapse of papal authority at the end of the Middle Ages. But Westphalia stabilized an existing self-help system and moderated the use of force by developing a set of legitimizing principles for the linked international and domestic arenas in world politics.

The distinctive features were anchored in actors' preferences and norms, not structural variables. The signatories at Westphalia agreed that dynastic rulers would receive their legitimacy from one another (hence from interstate not domestic arrangements), that the religion of the country was the ruler's prerogative, and that the settlement of competing territorial claims would be ratified through major power treaties. Westphalia altered the strategic importance of power by increasing the compatibility of actors' preferences, generating an acceptable set of legitimizing principles, and creating opportunities for reciprocity that lengthened actors' time horizons.

Any doubt about the significance for the strategic behavior of increasing the compatibility of actors' preferences and norms can be dispelled by comparing classical balance of power diplomacy with the endemic violence of the Renaissance and the massive destruction of the Wars of Religion. In both cases, the effects of the absence of shared norms were reinforced by structural variables. During the Thirty Years' War, competing legitimizing principles were tied to great military resources. In Renaissance Italy, the distribution of power was fluid and unpredictable, and the small size of the city-states meant that there was little time to respond to unanticipated threats. The resulting short time horizons combined with the absence of shared values to accentuate the stress on power and to reduce radically the perceived possibilities for reciprocity and collaboration. It was these linked dynamics that fueled Machiavelli's distrust of cooperation and alliances.

The alliance behavior characteristic of classical balance of power presupposes more than a state system, for both Machiavelli's diplomacy and the Wars of Religion were creatures of the European state system. The shared norms of Westphalia reduced conflicts of interest, lessened the strategic significance of power differences (including reducing the dangers created by the redistributive effects of cooperating in ad hoc alliances), and lengthened time horizons. Hans Morgenthau argued:

> It [was] . . . common moral standards and a common civilization as well as common interests, that kept in check the limitless desire for power . . . and prevented it from becoming a political actuality. Where such a consensus no longer exists or has become weak and is no longer sure of itself, . . . the balance of power is incapable of fulfilling its functions for international stability and national independence.[6]

Norms do not operate in a strategic vacuum. The effect of Westphalia's legitimizing principles depended on how they interacted with the values of the rest of the variables in the politics of strategic interaction. Classical balance of power operated within a distinctive set of initial conditions, not only in international politics, but also in domestic politics and the factional politics of policy coalitions. The comparatively large geographic size of the major powers lengthened time horizons and facilitated the formation and reciprocity of alliances. The largely agricultural economies made it comparatively easy to measure the resources available to governments and to prevent major changes in military power by preventing, or at least limiting, territorial expansion. The absence of nationalism and the acceptance of dynastic rule reduced ideological differences among elites, supported the norm that legitimacy was a function of interstate agreement, facilitated the practice of reciprocal compensation, and created little domestic resistance to frequent changes in alliance partners or basing policymaking on considerations of power.[7]

The focus on territorial expansion was based on more than the security incentives of self-help systems. It reflected what William Dorn called the "competition for empire."[8] This in turn was anchored, as Paul Schroeder argues, by "understandings, assumptions, learned skills and responses, rules, norms, procedures, etc. which agents acquire and use in pursuing their individual divergent aims within the framework of shared practice."[9] In pre-industrial Europe, empire required the taxation of land and peasants. It was this competition for empire that made military power relevant. Moreover, this diplomatic agenda matched the primary domestic agenda of mercantilist state builders. Centralizing monarchs wanted to extract the resources necessary to increase their interstate power and increase their military capabilities relative to domestic opponents.[10] Given the importance of these reinforcing agendas and the control over policy choice and implementation, policymakers were willing to take political risks.

These conditions changed with the Industrial Revolution, the growth of nationalism, the pressure for democracy, and the increasing involvement first of the upper middle classes and then the mass publics in domestic politics. These changes profoundly weakened both the system's norms and its characteristic forms of diplomacy. Classical balance of power required the ability to measure military power reliably and the ability to prevent significant changes in power by preventing territorial expansion. Classical balance of power also was built on four assumptions about foreign policymaking: decisions based on changes in relative power positions; great flexibility in making and breaking alliances (including no permanent friends or foes); moderation in victory to maintain the number of key actors; and the ability to rebalance the system through reciprocal compensation. Neither the assumptions about power nor those about policymaking survived the social, economic, and political changes of the French Revolution, the Industrial Revolution, and the involvement of more actors in the domestic politics of strategic choice.

The combination of these changes and the costs of the Napoleonic Wars created the conditions for the Concert of Europe, which is central to modern debates about conflict management. Consider the following observations: "the most elaborate attempt at peace preservation prior to the twentieth century;"[11] "the first attempt in peacetime to organize the international order through a system of conferences, and the first explicit effort of the great powers to assert a right of control;"[12] "the most successful postwar settlement of the modern state system;"[13] "the only successful effort at collective security among major powers;"[14] "the Concert of Europe was able to preserve peace in Europe for almost four decades;"[15] the "best example" of the "closest thing" to "a worldwide pluralist security community."[16]

That the Concert of Europe was principally a diplomatic system designed to deter or defeat interstate aggression has historical roots in Castlereagh's understanding of the mechanism. Castlereagh's view lost because he could not overcome domestic resistance within Britain to continental policing and because he could not sell his purely interstate version of the concert to continental policy factions preoccupied with the specter of revolution.[17] As Richard Betts commented, "the moral glue of the concert . . . was monarchical conservatism and opposition to liberalism and nationalism."[18] Henry Kissinger was equally blunt. Metternich sought in the concert "a moral basis for social repression."[19]

The Concert of Europe, however, was not solely a vehicle for social repression. To the contrary, international agendas were important. As Schroeder argues, the concert reflected a consensus that major power war threatened the foundations of the Westphalian system: "the early nineteenth century was . . . the first time [in which the conviction] that war [was] . . . counter-productive, an ineffective and self-defeating instrument of international politics . . . made any durable difference in international politics."[20] Robert Jervis agrees: "The Concert was supported by the shared stake that the major powers had in avoiding war." That shared stake reduced the strategic importance of power differentials among the key members of the concert and, along with the increased value attached to sustaining legitimate outcomes and relationships, lengthened actors' time horizons and increased opportunities for reciprocity.[21] The incentives created by these shifting international dynamics were made even more important by their connection to the primary domestic agenda: the fear of revolution.

From this perspective the Concert of Europe was simultaneously innovative and profoundly conservative. The innovations were in the international arena. They included a shift in policy goals and diplomatic instruments. Schroeder argues that "a fundamental change occurred in the governing rules, norms, and practices of international politics." Eighteenth century diplomacy reflected a "competitive and conflictual balance of power." Post-Napoleonic diplomacy reflected a "concert and political equilibrium." Schroeder finds this diplomatic transformation so striking that he pushes the distinction to the limit: "conservative, legalistic, and peaceful, restrained by treaties and the rules of the essentially co-operative, consensual game."[22]

One could disagree, arguing as does Edward Gulick, that the concert represented an institutionalization of the grand coalition feature of classical balance of power. One also could observe that the desire for peace and cooperation was more instrumental and prudent (a change in preferences over policies) than normative (a change in preferences over outcomes). However, the debate over ultimate objectives versus instruments does not need to be resolved to agree that the forms of diplomacy and strategic interaction changed with the Concert of Europe. Moreover, it is also clear that the domestic agendas of the continental governments were conservative: to save the legitimizing principles of the

Westphalian system. Schroeder prefers to reinforce his interpretation of fundamental change between balance of power and concert diplomacy by separating the diplomatic and domestic features of the Concert of Europe into the Vienna system (which focused on the international arena and was innovative) and the Metternich system (which focused on the domestic arena and was repressive). The perspective presented here suggests a different conclusion. State systems have both a diplomatic and a domestic face. It is an error to frame the analysis of the concert as a debate between international innovation and a reactionary attempt to maintain the old order. It was both.

In the classical balance-of-power period, the stability of domestic arrangements facilitated both the competition for empire and the balancing behavior used to prevent hegemony. In the Concert of Europe, the stability of interstate arrangements facilitated cooperation to quash revolutionary change and preserve the domestic basis of the system. In the earlier period, the principal sources of variation in the level of threat were interstate; in the second, domestic. Charles and Clifford Kupchan's preoccupation with the impact of shared "views of a stable international order" on the concert's ability to preserve the territorial status quo misses this reversal in the links between domestic and international politics.[23] So does Jervis' comment that "states did not play the game as hard as they could."[24] The game for continental policymakers was the perceived connection between social change, regime survival, and war.

The Concert of Europe broke under the weight of Prussian reactions to the rebellions in 1848 and British policy before and during the Crimean War. Westphalia's legitimizing principles died with the wars of German unification. Classical balance of power assumed limited competition within a system as opposed to conflict about a system. Subsequently, the concert reflected a commitment to preserving Westphalia's legitimizing principles by radically reducing major-power conflict and suppressing domestic social and political change. Already coming apart under the pressures created by the underlying social, economic, and political changes that dominated the nineteenth century, including the 1848 rebellions, and the differences over Crimea, the remnants of the legitimizing principles from Westphalia and the concert disintegrated with the wars of German unification. Bismarck's emphasis on nationalism and his refusal to submit his victories for ratification in major-power treaties altered the rules of the game and linkages between domestic and international politics. Perhaps the most immediate effect was on Austria, where the regime lost the international norm that served as the basis for its legitimacy. But the end of Westphalia's legitimizing principles had more general effects. The absence of agreed-upon norms and the stress on *Machtpolitik* increased the strategic significance of any differences in actors' relative power and preferences. Moreover, the question of how the state system should be organized was back on the agenda.

To maintain Germany's now favorable position in the face of these more fundamental conflicts of interest, Bismarck built a new security system. Balance-of-power alliances were reactive, ad hoc combinations formed by states with no permanent friends or enemies. Bismarckian alliances were standing, pre-targeted agreements designed to prevent enduring disputes from escalating into wars by deterring the stronger and restraining the weaker. Classical balance of power was a decentralized security system designed to prevent preponderance. The Bismarckian security system was an organized web of cross-cutting and overlapping alliances designed to prevent the creation of reinforcing grievances and antagonist blocs while preserving German preeminence.

In 1919, 40 years after Bismarck created his first standing alliance, many observers concluded that whatever the proximate causes and catalysts for the outbreak of war in 1914, the structure of the state system was ultimately at fault. Given this interpretation, radical changes were proposed. In the domestic arena, debates over nationalism and democracy were ended by accepting nationality as the basis for drawing interstate boundaries, eliminating the last of the dynastic rulers, and promoting democratic regimes. These changes in the bases of legitimate rule were to be complimented by radical change in the nature of security systems. Arms races, secret treaties, and pre-targeted alliances were to be eliminated. Consultations were to be required before using force and, to enforce it all, a collective security system was created.

The League of Nations was the first security system to establish peace as preeminent and to promise to protect all countries, not simply major powers. On one level, it could not have been more different from the Concert of Europe: in place of an effort to maintain the legitimizing principles of the old order, there was an effort to create a new one; in place of condominium and social repression, there was universality and the promotion of democracy. But on a broader, theoretical level, the same process of strategic interaction was operating. Both levels assumed an intricate connection between international order and the norms and structure of domestic politics. Both assumed that shared values muted the strategic implications of differences in actors' substantive goals and relative power positions. Both also assumed that the strategic significance of power depended on the compatibility of key actors' values and order of preference. All these, in turn, lengthened actors' time horizons and their willingness to trust.

The league's collective security system put the linked dynamics of world politics together in the following way. It assumed that policy factions in autocratic regimes were both more likely to have different interests than the population at large and more likely to be able to pursue those objectives without domestic constraints. Autocratic rulers, said Wilson, building on Kant, "stood to reap the gains of war without paying the price."[25] Given this assumption, foreign policymakers were far more likely to have compatible preferences in democratic than autocratic regimes. The more compatible actors' preferences and their values about legitimate relationships, the less strategically important power. In such an environment, arms races were likely to collapse of their own weight and arms-reduction agreements still to be negotiated. Perhaps even more important, the presumed absence of fundamental conflicts of interest meant that most disputes could be settled through some form of third party fact-finding and mediation. Vulnerable to E. H. Carr's critique of utopianism and the doctrine of the harmony of interests,[26] this view is now supported by more recent academic research on the virtual absence of war between democratic states and the post-Cold War linkage between democracy and peace at the United Nations.[27]

The problem for the league was not that they were wrong about these underlying strategic processes in international politics, but that the assumed initial conditions did not hold. With the United States absent, the majority of the major powers in the league during the crucial 1930–1935 period were both anti-democratic and revisionist. The original permanent members of the league's council were Britain, France, Italy, and Japan. Germany was added in 1926 and the Soviet Union in 1934. Germany and Japan left in 1935, and the Soviet Union was expelled after invading Finland in December 1939. Collective security assumes that the community's security organization can produce preponderant power that will deter most aggressors and can, when deterrence fails, defeat isolated aggressors with relative ease. As the only status quo major powers on the council, Britain and France were far from preponderant. France, moreover, had a special stake in using the league to enforce the Versailles Treaty provisions designed to weaken Germany permanently—hardly the basis for a claim to represent community-wide goals. Indeed, the perceived illegitimacy of the Versailles settlement reinforced the peace movement in Britain.

Once the anticipated initial conditions failed to materialize in the international arena, the cross-level linkages in world politics made it extraordinarily difficult for collective security to work. Collective security requires that governments respond automatically to protect victims of aggression. But such international predictability hinges on governments having enormous policymaking flexibility on such critical issues as going to war or preserving the peace. The foreign policy goals of collective security and classical balance of power could hardly be more different, but the domestic requirements are strikingly similar. Both systems require convincing key domestic policy factions and their constituents to pay substantial, visible, and immediate costs to gain possible future benefits. In the case of classical balance of power, the future benefit was reducing the probability of preponderance; in the case of collective security, it was reducing the probability of war. Moreover, while substantively different, those future benefits would both come in the form of things that did not happen. Given the usual discounts for costs and benefits, a package of certain costs now to achieve uncertain benefits later is hard to sell. High-priced counterfactuals are not big sellers.

Neither international nor domestic preconditions for a collective security system were present when the League of Nations experiment failed. But its performance was better when the conflict management techniques fit the prevailing conditions: fact-finding in the Åland Islands dispute (between Sweden and Finland) and the Greek-Bulgarian crisis; observer forces in the Saar and Upper Silesia. The lessons, as Diehl points out, were that the league could play a useful role in conflicts short of war when the parties were looking for a jointly acceptable peaceful solution. By Possony's count, it helped settle 35 out of the 66 disputes brought before it. The league could not handle incompatible preferences when some of the parties were willing to use force to prevail.[28] In short, it could not make collective security work.

Despite the dismal record of the League of Nations, collective security was given a second chance in the United Nations. The framers showed an understanding both of the politics of strategic interaction and of the crucial role of prevailing conditions in the success of any conflict management system. They assumed that collective security systems could work only if the values and goals of the major powers were compatible. As Inis Claude observes, "The security scheme of the Charter . . . was conceived as an arrangement against relatively minor disturbers of the peace, in cases where the great powers were united."[29] The perceived choice was between an option that would certainly fail—no cooperation and no collective security system—and one that might work—cooperation facilitated by the United Nations.[30] The league had required unanimity while excluding the parties to the dispute from the vote. The UN substituted a special majority for the requirement of unanimity but gave the permanent members a veto even if—one might say especially because—they were parties. As Claude noted in his famous phrase, "The veto is a deliberately contrived circuit breaker."[31]

The framers also were acutely aware of the role of domestic politics, most obvious in the sensitivity to the U.S. and the determination that there be no empty chair. That awareness also appeared in the broadening Wilsonian connection between democracy and peace to include a stronger emphasis on decolonization, human rights, and social and economic justice. Concerns about the ability of foreign policymakers to conduct resource-dependent statecraft quickly enough to aid victims led to the provision for a military staff committee (in UN Charter article 47) and the provision calling for the negotiation of special agreements that would place national forces at the disposal of the Security Council (articles 43 and 46).

Collective security failed during the Cold War because the framers of the UN Charter had been right about the preconditions for success.[32] As Kupchan observed, "The cold war era does not represent a legitimate test of collective security because one of the key preconditions was missing. American and Soviet visions of an acceptable international order were simply incompatible."[33] The Cold War's end removed many of these international impediments, but the resounding lack of enthusiasm that greeted Boutros-Ghali's 1992 suggestion for the creation of a standing force reflected the fact that conflict-management systems must also fit the prevailing domestic conditions. Whether a classic interstate collective security system or a "second-generation" intrastate operation, peace enforcement is expensive in lives and resources. Those costs generate substantial political risks, which are especially difficult to overcome in the absence of a perceived security threat, side-payments of private goods, or some sort of legitimizing principles based on access to the policymaking process or the manipulation of political symbols.[34] Consequently, the debate over the value of collective security and other collective conflict management systems needs to include an assessment of whether policymakers see the value of each system as worth the political risks of creating and sustaining it.

Theoretical Perspectives on Collective Security

There is a wide range of theoretical literature about collective security and its effectiveness. Claude offers the most appropriate beginning:

> Balance of power treats conflict as general and cooperation as exceptional; collective security treats conflict as exceptional and cooperation as an *attainable* general circumstance. . . . The difference is fundamentally a difference regarding the *facts*.[35]

Claude's list of the "subjective" and "objective" requirements reveals factual assumptions about the values of almost all of the central variables in the politics of strategic interaction. Falling under subjective requirements are "conviction of the desirability of peace"; "loyalty to the world community"; the willingness to adopt international goals as national ones; "willingness to fight for the status quo"; and a willingness "to rely [on the system's] . . . effectiveness and impartiality." Claude's objective requirements are the distribution of economic and military power. "Being precariously founded upon [a] . . . psychological and moral paradox [created by the subjective requirements], collective security requires a power situation that permits it to do its job with a minimum of military exertion." Specifically, "considerable diffusion of power"; involvement of all the major powers; technological levels in which mobilization for war can be identified in time for ad hoc defense to work; and "the universality of economic vulnerability."[36]

Factual assumptions about the substance of actors' goals and legitimizing principles—as well as about their relative capabilities—are also central to contemporary assessments of collective security. Kupchan's "case for collective security" in the early 1990s was built on two empirical assumptions: a change in the distribution of power and the existence of "compatible views of a stable international order."[37] Although Betts was far more skeptical, he agreed about the reasons for the "reborn enthusiasm"—the convergence in visions of how the world should be organized, the changed power distribution created by the disintegration of the Soviet Union, and the radically reduced level of perceived threat.[38] As George Downs and Keisuke Iida point out, the Realist preoccupation with the problems generated by power distributions misses the possibility that a group of major powers—and, perhaps, even a hegemonic one—might value the goals of collective security and look to a universal organization to "bestow legitimacy."[39] Assuming that high levels of conflict are an intrinsic feature of interstate politics, Realists also typically set aside the possibility that the importance of differences in power may vary with the degree of shared values and compatible preferences. When weighing the values of the key variables instead of assuming them, one can conclude that collective security and other forms of collective conflict management will succeed or fail depending on the mix of prevailing conditions in the linked domestic and international arenas of world politics.

The difficulty in seeing such a conclusion is largely the result of the historical failures of collective security and the widespread belief that decentralized, self-help balancing behavior is the default model of international politics and the necessary consequence of the structure of international politics. Kenneth Waltz, equating self-help with balancing behavior, has argued that "the enduring anarchic character of international politics accounts for the striking sameness of international life through the millennia."[40] But where in historical systems do we find pure balancing behavior—balancing driven solely by the strategic incentives built into the anarchic structure of the interstate system? Classical balance of power was based on a set of legitimizing principles and had a security norm: compete to gain marginal advantage but cooperate to prevent preponderance. More generally, as Michael Doyle argues, it may not be possible to deduce self-help balancing from structural variables: "The best place to look for classical balancing is when the conditions of the sociological model hold. . . . The orderly results of classical balance in the eighteenth century required the conditions of eighteenth-century balancing: independent states, coherent and similar domestic structures, a shared transnational culture, even a degree of inspired leadership."[41] Furthermore, the argument that decentralized balancing behavior arises automatically requires that one sees fundamental continuity across security systems as different as Machiavellian Renaissance diplomacy, the classical balance of power, the Concert of Europe, Bismarck's crosscutting and overlapping alliances, pre-World War I's antagonistic alliance blocs, and Cold War containment.

Different scholars such as Helen Milner, Bruce Bueno de Mesquita, Richard Betts, and Alexander Wendt agree that anarchy creates a wide range of variation in strategic incentives. "To view anarchy as *the* fundamental background condition of international politics underestimates the ambiguity of the concept."[42] "The loose structural factors of international politics . . . may constrain individual choices, but they do not determine behavior."[43] "Anarchy [creates] . . . necessary but not sufficient causes of war"; to anarchy one needs to add a *casus belli*.[44] "Without assumptions about the structure of identities and interests in the system, . . . the content or dynamics of anarchy [cannot be predicted]."[45]

If anarchy generates indeterminate conditions for strategic choice, the anarchic character of international politics cannot create by itself a default option for responding to security threats and international conflict. The permissive, as opposed to determinate, role of anarchy can be seen in the distinctive strategic approaches that have evolved in different diplomatic and domestic contexts. Europe has had an anarchic, self-help system since the collapse of papal authority at the end of the Middle Ages and the onset of Renaissance diplomacy. Europe's classical balance-of-power system emerged in the seventeenth century, thrived in the eighteenth, and collapsed in the nineteenth. The Concert of Europe reflected a different mix of goals and prevailing conditions, as did the Bismarckian alliance system, the collective security systems of the League of Nations and the United Nations, and the competitive alliances of the Cold War.

In moving from anarchy to power distributions, security incentives are still indeterminate. Whether or not an actor is vulnerable to security threats depends on whether other actors have a positive expected utility for attack. One can link such security threats to specific power distributions only if one looks at the interaction of power with the goals of the actor, beliefs about legitimacy, and expectations about how all the above will change over time.

Finally, even determinate international incentives would not determine foreign policy by themselves. The dynamics of international politics are intertwined with the factional politics of policy coalitions and the politics that link those factions to their domestic constituencies. After comparing the relative value of a pure statecraft interpretation that assumes "foreign policy objectives are determined by the structure of the international context" with a "domestic/constrained" version that assumes "domestic imperatives interact with international structural forces to shape foreign policy outcomes," Bruce Bueno de Mesquita and David Lalman conclude that "the world operates as in the constrained model. . . . None of the evidence for the realpolitik deductions from the theory is consistent with expectations. None of the results for the domestic interpretation of international interactions are inconsistent with the theory."[46]

Whether they are decentralized, self-help systems or collective conflict management systems, evaluating different security systems requires analyzing the strategic goals of key coalitions. If those do not fit, the strategic approach will fail. If world politics is dominated by predatory elites, there is no point in considering collective conflict management as an option. But the substance of policymakers' goals is just the start. The probability of achieving those goals depends on what the international strategic context makes possible and the ability of policy coalitions to make and sustain coherent policy.

Conclusions about Collective Security: Implications for Collective Conflict Management

Historically, collective security systems have been built around three theoretical dilemmas and paradoxes. First, most conceptualizations of collective security define aggression procedurally as the use of armed force. Procedure is one dimension of what makes a political act legitimate, but the other dimension involves the perceived substantive fairness of different outcomes. A dilemma arises in the absence of effective mechanisms for achieving significant changes peacefully because choosing procedural legitimacy over outcome-based legitimacy privileges the status quo. As Claude pointed out, whereas "peace through justice must be the watchword of collective security . . . , its provisional rule of action can hardly be other than peace *over* justice."[47]

Second, collective security assumes that policymakers and their constituents can be convinced that force is so morally reprehensible that they should forgo any individual goals achieved only through force. Collective security simultaneously requires that force be used to achieve peace. The paradox is that peace needs to be so important that it is the only goal worth fighting for.

Third, policymakers must be able to count on collective security to work well. Without reliable community-organized defense, prudence requires that potential victims create their own alliance systems. Individually organized alliance systems designed to counter threats within the community will often undermine community-level obligations. To avoid this dilemma, policymakers must minimize the risks associated with relying on collective security by creating reliable and predictable mechanisms. Predictability requires multinational coordination to identify cases of aggression quickly and to get help to the scene in time to protect the victim. Paradoxically, the solution to the dilemma of predictability creates a dilemma of accountability. The political entities with the resources to fulfill the international obligations of collective security also have domestic moral and political obligations. These obligations historically have led to an insistence that countries decide whether or not to fulfill their collective security obligations on a case-by-case basis. The international requirement that collective security be predictable (or automatic) counters the domestic requirement that national policymakers not delegate responsibility for life-and-death choices.

These issues are compounded because economic and military power is unevenly distributed. Unequal distribution creates acute problems for collective security when, as in the 1930s in Ethiopia and Manchuria, the aggressor is a major power. But even if the aggressor is relatively weak, the burden of enforcing collective security falls disproportionately on those few states that can project enough economic and military power to affect outcomes (while nearby states need less power to get involved, neighbors are more likely to be parties to the dispute and less likely to go home afterwards). The more the success of collective security depends on the choices of a small set of states, the harder it is to demonstrate that the enforcers of collective security are implementing community-wide values. The more the international community attempts to resolve this problem by transferring the choice about whether or not to intervene to supranational institutions, the less likely it is that domestic constituencies in the major powers will be willing to send their fellow citizens in harm's way.

The expansion of peace enforcement beyond collective security to include involvement in civil wars accentuates both the diplomatic and domestic dilemmas, because stopping such armed conflicts is fundamentally harder than reinforcing existing arrangements through deterrence. Civil wars are also less likely to generate visible security stakes commensurate with the costs and political risks generated by involvement. The increasing concerns about the human and financial costs of international and domestic peace enforcement in the post-Cold War era are arising in a changing domestic context, one in which modern communications make it easier for policymakers' constituents to see the costs of involvement and for opponents to organize coalitions that can generate unacceptably high political risks.

This combination of factors creates enormous disincentives for committing national resources in peace enforcement operations. This is not to say, however, that the necessary conditions cannot be met. Instead, it suggests that peace enforcement operations are most likely to be undertaken when community-wide values happen to coincide with the perception of policymakers in powerful countries that national goals are also at stake—such as in the expulsion of Iraq from Kuwait. Moreover, the experience with a wider range of CCM strategies in the 1990s suggests that the enduring domestic and diplomatic dilemmas generated by collective conflict management may be coming together in a novel way. Doing nothing about Bosnia, Somalia, and Haiti, while scenes of horror are televised in constituents' living rooms, also was politically risky for policymakers. Since both doing something and doing nothing involved risks, there was some incentive to innovate. Politicians in Europe began to move toward stronger multinational institutions several decades ago when they found that changing conditions made them politically accountable for economic outcomes that they could no longer control at the national level. In the 1990s, policymakers discovered that they are being held accountable for international outcomes that they are unable to resolve nationally, both because their constituents are unwilling to pay the price and because other countries distrust leaving the definition and implementation of international norms to a small subset of national governments. Consequently, it is becoming increasingly attractive for policymakers to look for innovative ways to handle peace enforcement and other CCM problems.

Whether these incentives to innovate will produce effective collective conflict management will depend on the compatibility of the substantive goals of the principal actors, their beliefs about what is legitimate, and the different domestic contexts within which they have to make choices. To create a CCM system, policymakers in key states must want not only to do so but also be willing and able to absorb the political risks of allocating enough resources. The domestic problem is acute because moving decisions to the international level, while leaving resource extraction to the state, raises fundamental political disconnects. Even if problems are overcome and a CCM system begins, its success will depend on the fit between this particular diplomatic strategy and the strategic situation in the international arena.

Meeting these conditions for peace enforcement operations will be more problematic than for either peacekeeping or preventive deployment. The closer the fit between the prevailing international conditions and those necessary for successful peace enforcement, the harder it will be for policy factions to mobilize against a particular international action. A system to enforce peace is not designed to function in an international arena in which the major powers are divided by visible, immediate, and enduring security threats; governments will have great difficulty in convincing domestic constituencies to allocate substantial resources and send their citizens in harm's way in the absence of a visible threat. This dilemma will be particularly acute in countries with substantial economic and military resources. Major military powers have less incentive to invest in peace enforcement systems than weaker states. The positive incentives for investing in such multilateral arrangements will be stronger in post-colonial societies and militarily weak countries because they provide an opportunity to create more "legitimate" international institutions and to gain access to resources. A multinational conflict management system, with a highly dispersed resource base that places few costly demands on countries with substantial independent military capabilities, would have a higher probability of surviving the domestic politics of strategic choice in the sorts of international contexts in which peace enforcement is best suited to work. This approach, however, carries two important liabilities. The military units are less likely to be well trained and equipped. Visibly sharing decisionmaking with other countries—and, particularly, with international organizations—is likely to raise the level of opposition within the United States.

That all these pieces could be put together in ways that would simultaneously achieve their international and domestic objectives is problematic. But there is no logical reason why it is impossible. The question concerns the relative value and political sustainability of peace enforcement and other collective conflict strategies—that is, collective conflict management compared to what alternative? There is no default system of conflict management that will emerge automatically, without the choices by policymakers about what they value and the political risks they are willing to sustain in an effort to achieve those goals.

Notes

1. Alan C. Lamborn, "Theory and the Politics in World Politics," *International Studies Quarterly* 41, no. 2 (June 1997).

2. For the importance of examining counterfactuals (the effects of alternatives not taken) and assessing the degrees of success or failure attached to different policy outcomes, see David Baldwin, *Economic Statecraft* (Princeton: Princeton University Press, 1985).

3. See Robert Keohane, *Beyond Hegemony* (Princeton: Princeton University Press, 1984).

4. The argument in this section draws on Alan Lamborn, "Theory and the Politics in World Politics." Similar arguments, also based on "Theory and the Politics in World Politics," can be found in Alan Lamborn and Joseph Lepgold, *World Politics into the 21st Century: Unique Contexts and Enduring Patterns* (New York: St. Martin's Press, forthcoming).

5. Thucydides, *The Peloponnesian War* (New York: Random House, the Modern Library, 1982): 351.

6. Hans Morgenthau, *Politics Among Nations*, 2nd edition (New York: Alfred A. Knopf, 1954): 200. Edward Vose Gulick has also argued that "the balance of power was . . . an old and oft-repaired machine that creaked badly enough as it was; without a lubricating homogeneity [of values] it might well have broken down." See his *Europe's Classical Balance of Power* (New York: W. W. Norton, 1967): 24.

7. There was, of course, substantial resistance to the extraction of resources by the state from groups that were adversely effected.

8. Walter Dorn, *Competition for Empire, 1740–1763* (New York: Harper, 1940).

9. Paul W. Schroeder, *The Transformation of European Politics 1763–1848* (Oxford, U.K.: Clarendon Press, 1994): xii.

10. Jacob Viner, "Mercantilism," *Economic History Review* VI (1935–36): 100; see also Eli Hecksher, *Mercantilism* (London: Allen and Unwin, 1935).

11. Stefan Possony, "Peace Enforcement," *Yale Law Journal* 55, no. 5 (1946): 919.

12. Henry Kissinger, *A World Restored* (Boston, Mass.: Houghton Mifflin, 1957): 221.

13. Charles Lipson, "Is the Future of Collective Security Like the Past," in George W. Downs, ed., *Collective Security Beyond the Cold War* (Ann Arbor, Mich.: University of Michigan Press, 1994): 117.

14. Ibid., 106.

15. Charles A. Kupchan and Clifford A. Kupchan, "Concerts, Collective Security, and the Future of Europe," *International Security* 16, no. 1 (summer 1991): 123.

16. Robert Jervis, "From Balance to Concert," *World Politics* 38, no. 1 (October 1985): 58, 59.

17. Kissinger, *A World Restored*, 218, 230–31, 248–49, 323, 326–29.

18. Richard Betts, "Systems for Peace or Causes of War," *International Security* 17, no. 1 (summer 1992): 27.

19. Kissinger, *A World Restored*, 238.

20. Schroeder, *Transformation*, 773.

21. Robert Jervis, "Security Regimes," *International Organization* 36, no. 2 (spring 1982): 365, 364.

22. Schroeder, *Transformation*, vii, 799.

23. See Kupchan and Kupchan, "Concerts," especially 120–23.

24. Jervis, "Balance," 59.

25. Inis L. Claude, Jr., *Swords into Plowshares*, 4th edition (New York: Random House): 51, 221–22.

26. Edward. H. Carr, *The Twenty Years' Crisis*, 2nd edition (New York: Harper Torchbooks, 1964).

27. Michael N. Barnett, "The Politics of Peacekeeping," *Global Governance* 1, no. 1 (winter 1995): 79–97.

28. Paul F. Diehl, *International Peacekeeping* (Baltimore: The Johns Hopkins Press, 1993): 17–21; Possony, "Peace," 929; Gerald J. Mangone, *A Short History of International Organization* (New York: McGraw–Hill, 1954): 143–54.

29. Inis L. Claude, Jr., *Power and International Relations* (New York: Random House, 1962): 162, 164.

30. Claude, *Swords*, 75–76.

31. Claude, *Swords*, 156.

32. Those who call NATO a collective security alliance would disagree with the assertion that collective security failed in the Cold War. However, describing a standing, pre-targeted defense pact as a collective security arrangement eliminates the distinctive within-community-policing characteristic that defines collective security.

33. Charles A. Kupchan, "The Case for Collective Security," in Downs, *Collective Security*, 48.

34. Alan Lamborn, *The Price of Power* (Boston, Mass.: Unwin Hyman, 1991), chapter 4.

35. Claude, *Power*, 146–147, emphasis in original.

36. Claude, *Swords*, 250–260; Claude, *Power*, 194.

37. Kupchan, "Collective Security," 44.

38. Betts, "Peace," 7, 13–15.

39. George Downs and Keisuke Iida, "Assessing the Theoretical Case against Collective Security," in Downs, *Collective Security*, 21.

40. Kenneth Waltz, *Theory of International Politics* (Reading, Mass.: Addison–Wesley, 1979): 65–66.

41. Michael W. Doyle, "Balancing Power Classically: An Alternative to Collective Security," in Downs, *Collective Security*, 148, 162.

42. Helen Milner, "The Assumption of Anarchy in International Relations Theory," *Review of International Studies* 17, no. 1 (January 1991): 83.

43. Bruce Bueno de Mesquita and David Lalman, *War and Reason* (New Haven, Conn.: Yale University Press, 1992): 11.

44. Betts, "Peace," 40.

45. Alexander Wendt, "Anarchy Is What States Make of It," *International Organization* 46, no. 2 (spring 1992): 396.

46. Bueno de Mesquita and Lalman, *Reason*, xi, 269, 275–6.

47. Claude, *Swords*, 254, emphasis in original.

Part Two

Collective Conflict Management: Military Operations and Political Interests

3

NATO's Post-Cold War Conflict Management Role[1]

Joseph Lepgold

Over the last half decade, NATO's role in regional collective conflict management has undergone a major transformation. Just after the Cold War, without a significant threat on the horizon, its days appeared numbered. Even now, from a realist perspective, it is hard to explain why a costly alliance that is difficult to activate for any specific operational mission should persist without such a threat. The puzzle is only partly resolved by focusing on its members' apparent desires to take on new conflict management tasks of the kind laid out elsewhere in this volume.[2] One still needs to ask why NATO is seen as a useful tool for accomplishing these missions and whether it is capable of doing them effectively. This chapter argues that even though NATO has survived its early post-Cold War crisis of relevance, to be useful over the long term it must surmount a collective action problem that is more severe than the one it faced during the Cold War, and one that is endemic to collective conflict management (CCM).

After briefly discussing how NATO survived its first post-Cold War challenge, three problems that its members must address successfully to survive over the long term are examined. First, NATO must manage the enlargement process so as to soothe at least as many insecurities as it creates in Central Europe. Second, it must define and implement a relationship with Russia that softens a deep-seated security dilemma. Third, it must define and begin to fulfill its new mission—the projection of stability in Central Europe by political and, if necessary, military means. This carries two requirements: NATO must devise a workable structure for military intervention in discretionary situations, and it must actually supply those forces with the kind of predictability that an effective CCM regime requires. Unlike the situation during the Cold War, when effective political reassurances within NATO were at times harder to come by than the military means that supported them, it now appears that NATO is fairly likely to succeed politically—virtually every remotely plausible member seems to want to join it. At the same time, it may be unable to supply the kinds of forces required on the ground in politically ambiguous or militarily risky CCM situations. If one believes that these tasks are unlikely to be carried out successfully under United Nations (UN) auspices, and instead must be "subcontracted"[3] to regional groups and organizations, some pessimism about NATO's ability to carry out CCM missions seems warranted.

NATO's Early Post-Cold War Crisis of Relevance

To say that NATO suffered an identity crisis after the Cold War is an understatement: "the questions of mission, membership and methodology place a heavy burden on . . . [its] agenda."[4] One key question—to which enemies would it now be addressed, if any?—had no clear answer. The first two North Atlantic Summits after November 1989 sidestepped this issue and stated NATO's future purposes in vague terms. It would strive "to build the structures of a more stable [European] continent" and maintain "a military capability sufficient to prevent war and to provide for effective defense."[5] To achieve the first purpose, NATO reached out to the former Soviet bloc states with programs that included forums to discuss a variety of political and military problems and joint military training. To achieve the second, nuclear arms were made weapons of "last resort" in NATO strategy and flexible rapid reaction groups of forces were formed to undertake new conflict-management missions.

But such changes could not mask the fact that for many, NATO faced a deep crisis of relevance. Member states were relieved by the end of the Cold War, but they were also confused about what to do next.[6] The relief was understandable. Europe was no longer divided, nuclear tensions had virtually vanished, and military budgets had begun to shrink considerably. As a result, at least until wars began in the Balkans, there was much optimism that Europe could finally build a set of institutions that would promote democracy, the peaceful resolution of competing nationalist claims, and human rights. Such sentiments are common at the end of major wars. Just after the Thirty Years' War, for example, "hopes and expectations ran high; intentions were great. They included the creation of a pan-European diplomatic system based on the principles of sovereignty and legal equality."[7] The confusion within NATO, at least in part, was about the alliance's precise role in this new mix of purposes and activities. NATO had always performed nonmilitary as well as military functions for its members, but the former had long been its raison d'être, especially if one views its core as the integrated command structure. It was not obvious that this edifice would survive, or what new priorities would be.

Two such priorities were gradually defined. One involved broadening NATO's ties with former Warsaw Pact countries through a variety of consultative mechanisms, military-to-military exchanges, and similar programs. Much was made during the 1990s of NATO's intentions and efforts to turn itself into a more overtly "political" and less "military" group, but this was something of a misnomer. NATO will remain primarily a military entity or it has no distinct rationale at all. What did begin to change in the first five years after the end of the Cold War was how NATO treated its former enemies. It now offered them the prospect of joint military missions, exchanges of military and civilian personnel, and even instruction in how to run military organizations under civilian control. NATO members coordinated diplomatic and military strategies during Yugoslavia's wars through the Contact Group and developed closer ties with the United Nations and the Conference, and now Organization, for Security and Cooperation in Europe (OSCE), both of which included Russians. The common thread in these activities was a desire to make NATO less politically threatening and relevant for Central and East Europeans.

NATO also moved during the early 1990s to adjust its military doctrine, criteria of military sufficiency, and organizational ability to confront military problems to post-Cold War conditions.[8] In July 1990 it announced a restructuring of its forces into genuinely multinational units that would be tactically and geographically more mobile than before. At the 1991 NATO Summit, the alliance adopted what was called "A New Strategic Concept." While reaffirming the importance of collective territorial defense, it pointed NATO toward missions outside its treaty area, including crisis management, and involvement in peacekeeping operations. In January 1994, the Combined Joint Task Forces (CJTF) plan was announced. It allowed NATO to organize military operations on an ad hoc basis, with participation by some non-members (ordinarily those involved in Partnership for Peace (PFP) exercises and exchanges) and some abstention by members. The idea was to give NATO the capacity to fulfill the missions in the New Strategic Concept, particularly out-of-area responsibilities, on a more flexible, discretionary basis. What drew these efforts together was a desire to make NATO less militarily muscle-bound and better able to respond to crises and CCM tasks across the spectrum discussed in the front chapter.

By the mid-1990s, NATO seemed to have survived its crisis of relevance. Once it became clear that the West retained a major stake in preserving international stability even after the demise of the Soviet Union, NATO's value in drawing Americans and Europeans together on security issues loomed large. Of course, NATO would not be built from scratch today in its present form.[9] Its members have not, however, concluded that it should be scrapped. Their behavior since the early 1990s suggests a very different logic at work. NATO's mechanisms for intergovernmental consultations and its integrated command structure foster common analysis of problems and a sustained (even if at times difficult) official dialogue that helps keep the centrifugal political pressures generated by the end of the Cold War from leading to a profound breakdown in security cooperation. In addition, the high level of military trust, interoperability, and logistical interconnectedness developed among Western military organizations since the 1950s make it much easier for them to operate together than would otherwise be the case. This was evident in the Gulf War, the Peace Implementation Force (IFOR) in the Balkans, and in its successor, the Stabilization Force (SFOR). To the extent that U.S. forces in Europe plan to continue acting together with NATO allies in CCM operations, such habitual political cooperation and logistical coordination is very helpful.[10]

At the same time, the long-term implications of the end of the Cold War tend to develop other pressures. At bottom, NATO will be relevant only so long as Americans and Europeans do value security jointness more than the "opportunity costs" it imposes—a loss of diplomatic and military flexibility, and the forces and bases they might choose not to procure if they pursued more independent policies. Especially to some Americans, NATO represents a visible investment in an often intangible good. It is often easy to see what it costs (witness the rancor over policy in the former Yugoslavia between 1991 and 1995), but not as easy to see its benefits.

Managing the Enlargement Process

The first of NATO's adjustment problems is to manage the process of enlarging the alliance so as to mitigate as much as possible existing and foreseeable security dilemmas. That this issue is on the policy agenda at all illustrates how much Western views about Central European security have evolved since the early 1990s. Historically, NATO members defined their security as meaning stable and prosperous relations among themselves and defense against a Russian threat. Protection against the East was more important than stability in the East, which in any case was assured by Soviet hegemony. Now the stability of the entire continent is seen as critical. NATO leaders became concerned about stability in the area between Russia and Germany when Soviet control began to loosen, and soon resolved to draw these nations into the Western orbit. This task was seen as important because Moscow's demise left the security status of Central Europe's states ambiguous. This was acceptable as long as most Russian leaders clearly accepted these states' external autonomy. But by 1993, a broad array of Russian elites was strongly suggesting that the entire former Soviet empire be recognized as a Russian sphere of influence. In mid-1995, Russia refused to rule out the use of force to protect ethnic Russians in other areas of the former Soviet Union.[11] At the same time, efforts to tie former Soviet bloc states to the West economically through new association agreements with the European

Union (EU) led to a feeling that the "security West" had to go east as well; otherwise, it was believed that the security vacuum east of Germany would continue to invite worry and instability.[12]

Reflecting these insecurities, Czech President Vaclav Havel and Polish President Lech Walesa made impassioned pleas to join NATO around the time of the 1994 North Atlantic Council (NAC) Summit. Led by the United States, NATO members faced difficult tradeoffs in deciding how to proceed. Absorbing new Central European members too quickly—not to mention Ukraine or the three Baltic republics—could reignite a serious rivalry with Russia. On the other hand, acting too slowly might make these countries still more insecure and perhaps help to empower illiberal elements inside them that could threaten long-term internal reform. To address some of these problems, the North Atlantic Cooperation Council (NACC) was instituted in 1991. It is a wide-ranging program of consultations between NATO and the former Warsaw Pact countries, including seminars on defense-related topics and exchanges among officers and military staffs. It was designed to ease the transition between the Cold War and post-Cold War European security systems. But since it provided no security guarantees, it satisfied none of the former Warsaw Pact countries.

NATO took another step toward integrating these states into its fold at the 1994 NAC Summit by establishing the PFP. PFP grew out of a U.S. attempt to avoid making any immediate decisions about expansion, while taking some steps to broaden NATO's constituency and prepare for possible expansion later. PFP allows former members of the Warsaw Pact to consult with NATO about their security if they feel threatened; such a right, based on Article 4 of the North Atlantic Treaty, was not provided within the NACC. PFP also allows countries to join NATO members in peacekeeping and military planning projects, and to prepare their forces to operate interchangeably with those of NATO members. This aspect of the PFP initiative has already borne fruit—thirteen of its members served in the IFOR peacekeeping force that monitored the Bosnian cease-fire accords.

But none of these programs provides an automatic ticket to NATO membership, which has become the objective of many former Warsaw Pact states. For that reason, PFP has not sufficiently reassured them about their identity in Europe or their security. This realization gradually led NATO governments to reevaluate the benefits of admitting new members. A formal announcement is expected at the 1997 Madrid North Atlantic Summit that the Czech Republic, Hungary, and Poland will be invited to join by 1999.

Two assumptions have driven this policy. First, it is believed that enlargement will help stabilize East-Central Europe. As former NATO Secretary-General Willy Claes said, "the alliance has moved beyond a 'territorial' concept of security towards a more active approach of projecting stability beyond its borders."[13] German Defense Minister Volker Rühe has elaborated on this point:

> [The justification for NATO expansion] . . . is not that Poland is threatened. The point is [that] they need a sense of belonging. . . . What we want is for the German-Polish border to become like the German-French border. When you cross the German-French border you don't know you are crossing it. Today crossing the German-Polish border is crossing a border between safe and not safe. You know it.[14]

How can enlargement help bring Europe closer to this objective? As many observers see it, a desire to join NATO has served both to catalyze internal reform in Central Europe and to pacify it. Several prospective NATO members have instituted greater civilian control over their military organizations, expanded freedoms, and effectively delegitimized extreme nationalist political factions. It is claimed that in these efforts, "support for NATO and its enlargement has become a unifying point among divergent political parties in many of these states. . . ."[15] Similarly, "growing cooperation with NATO and the desire to join the Alliance have provided a powerful impetus for resolving past disputes among Central and East European states," among them Hungary and Romania, Poland and Ukraine, and Germany and the Czech Republic. In each case, the parties have been told that NATO will not tolerate border disputes and ethnic conflicts among its members.[16] To be welcomed, they must act in a way that is consistent with the security community that has developed in Western Europe since the late 1940s.[17] It is also believed that adding new members will help NATO deal effectively with the security threats that have emerged in the wake of the Cold War. Ethnic conflicts, terrorism, and dangers arising from the proliferation of weapons of mass destruction are seen as areas in which "a larger circle of like-minded members can cooperate to build a more stable Europe."[18]

A second assumption is that expansion will project stability back onto the West by solidifying multilateral cooperation and defense integration among current NATO members. In particular, it is seen to further anchor Germany into Western institutions that are linked to the United States: "for many of its advocates, NATO expansion is spurred by concern about the power of a unified Germany as much or more than fears over the reliability of Russia."[19] If NATO takes in new Central European members, Germany would be surrounded by security multilateralism, with less desire or capacity to break free of it.[20]

Major costs come with these benefits—enlargement is likely to make those left out of the first round of expansion feel even less secure than before. NATO member states are taking some steps to soften the blow. Officials, including President Bill Clinton, have said that the first round of expansion will not be the last, and that no country is precluded from membership. Meanwhile, PFP members that will not soon join NATO itself are being invited to become more closely integrated into NATO exercises and CCM operations that fall outside the mutual-defense obligation that applies only to members.[21] To some extent, such measures blur the functional distinction between members and non-members.[22]

Even so, these programs are unlikely to reassure those left out, for reasons that go to the heart of why membership is valued so highly. Those states eager to join NATO have residual (and in some cases more active) fears of Russian expansion, but they also seek membership because NATO for them symbolizes "the West," and "the West" is their reference group. Membership is nearly as much an issue of identity as it is one of security in the traditional sense. These issues come together in the way that many Central and East Europeans view the past. They were abandoned to aggression twice in fairly recent memory by the West—once on the eve of World War II, once just after it—and they do not want history to repeat itself again. Even today, memories of abandonment and partition prominently shape conceptions of security.[23] The international context is different now: there is no aggressor in sight. But people tend to make dispositional rather than situational attributions about the causes of others' behavior—that is, they tend to judge others by who they are, rather than the specific circumstances at hand—and in European eyes the United States has not always been a reliable protector of free countries under threat of aggression.[24] Reports that NATO will move very slowly toward a second round of expansion and leave some countries out entirely in order to pacify Russia can only intensify this anxiety.[25]

How NATO can respond to this problem, while also reassuring Russia about its fears relating to NATO's eastward drift, presents a major challenge. NATO officials say that "by the time NATO acquires a seventeenth member, there must be an agreed definition" of NATO's connection to Russia.[26]

Managing NATO's Relationship with Russia

NATO's relationship with Russia exemplifies what international relations theorists call the security dilemma. Because there is no supranational authority that can enforce binding restraints on states, each is generally free to take whatever measures that it feels are necessary to protect its own security. As part of such "self-help," states at times use offensive means to pursue defensive motives. Consequently, "many of the means by which a state tries to increase its security decrease the security of others," even if the first state does not have hostile intentions toward the other.[27] Nevertheless, other states often take countermeasures, the initiator typically responds to those with behavior that might be deemed to signify aggressive intent, and an insecurity spiral can become self-perpetuating. Once inside such a process, it is hard to break out of it. Because intentions can never be fully transparent to outsiders, verbal reassurances of benign motivation are typically heavily discounted by those who have a history of mutually adversarial relations. For this reason, NATO expansion looks benign to those west of its easternmost member, but may well not appear the same to all of those east of that boundary.

These dynamics make it hard to bring new members into NATO and at the same time calm Russian fears. However often NATO officials say that the North Atlantic Treaty nowhere mentions Russia or the Soviet Union and that NATO does not need an enemy to remain relevant, NATO was created "to keep Russia out" as well as "keep the Germans down" and "keep the U.S. in."[28] It is this history that now feeds deep-seated Russian fears of abandonment and encirclement.[29] From the West's and especially Washington's point of view, the situation looks different. NATO is a defensive instrument that until 1994 never fired a shot in anger. Acting on this belief, leaders in Washington overestimated Moscow's flexibility on the enlargement issue and seemed to believe that the Russians would quietly accept expansion if they repeated pledges of good faith often enough.[30] If Russian leaders nevertheless infer that they must respond in kind, the results could be counterproductive. As mentioned above, those to the east of the NATO's new territory may be less secure after enlargement than before, and Russia may become less inclined to participate in mutually beneficial CCM operations. Moreover, if relations with Russia become significantly strained, NATO members would likely be divided over how to deal with the problem.[31]

Until late 1996, Russian leaders have not dealt publicly with this issue in a way designed to produce a compromise. They angrily denounced NATO expansion, demanded a unilateral right to veto particular candidates for membership or alliance actions, and refused to talk about reasonable measures NATO could take to reassure them. Predictably, this has in some ways simply confirmed the fears of those who most want to join. Such behavior made some strategic sense from Moscow's point of view. There has been a healthy debate about the merits of enlargement in every member state, as NATO's Secretary-General Javier Solana recently acknowledged.[32] And Russian leaders may reasonably have tried to see if they could raise the risks of enlargement high enough to reverse the decision. No Russian leader, moreover, could afford politically to simply accept a bigger NATO without strong protest, especially since Mikhail Gorbachev was specifically promised that NATO would not take any former Warsaw Pact states as members beyond Eastern Germany.[33]

While insecurity spirals tend to be self-perpetuating, states involved in them can try to demonstrate their benign intentions in tangible ways. The more valuable the concession a state makes to another to assuage its fears and the harder it is to reverse, the less easily it is discounted by the target. Janice Stein has argued that such reassurances are appropriate when states are motivated by genuine fear of the other rather than a desire to exploit the other.[34] Although it is difficult to discern from the outside how much of Russia's protest against enlargement reflects genuine worry and how much is driven by domestic politics, NATO officials have tried to offer Russia concrete reassurances that "enlargement need not be a zero-sum game for Russia."[35]

Essentially unilateral reassurances and verbal arguments are easiest for Moscow to discount. NATO governments have made a number of these kinds of offers and pledges. They have asserted that NATO enlargement can stabilize relations among the states on Russia's western periphery, help prevent ethnic conflict within them, and, through NATO's integrated command, essentially preclude these states from adopting unilateral defense strategies that Russia would find hard to accept.[36] They have emphasized that while new members will enjoy NATO's full security guarantees, and that NATO retains the ultimate right to choose its means of mutual defense, "NATO countries have no intention, no plan, and no reason to deploy nuclear weapons on the territory of new members."[37] Russia has sought, and may yet receive, assurances that no permanently stationed foreign forces will be deployed on the territories of the new members.[38]

Formal and institutionalized reassurances represent more visible sunk costs for those that make them, and thus are harder for the target to discount.[39] Two types of measures have been offered. One is a NATO-Russian Charter and Standing Council. The Council would "promote a regular dialogue on major security issues, reach concerted decisions whenever possible, and seize opportunities for joint action."[40] Secretary of State Madeleine Albright proposes that Russian and NATO planners work together at NATO's major military commands, that Moscow plan regularly to work with NATO's CJTFs, and that a joint military brigade be developed.[41]

The participation of a Russian airborne brigade in IFOR and SFOR has set a precedent for future NATO-Russian military collaboration. The command arrangements have been complex: the Russian contingent was placed under the operational command of the Supreme Allied Commander Europe (SACEUR), but in a manner acceptable to Moscow, by naming a Russian General as SACEUR's deputy for Russian forces, with tactical control exercised by the U.S. commander of the Multinational Division (North). What may be most important about this episode over the long run is the degree to which it makes NATO operations transparent to Moscow. Truly unintended security spirals thrive on opaque policy processes and (presumably) wither under open ones. With that in mind, the observations of one official closely involved in NATO's Bosnian operations become significant: "the military command arrangements for Russian forces in IFOR have given Russian military authorities better access to SACEUR through his Russian deputy and thus more influence over the planning and conduct of operations involving Russian forces."[42]

This type of sustained collaboration amounts to a loose major-power concert. In such an arrangement, the major powers consult and cooperate over a broader range of issues than is common in diplomatic practice. What was left of the Vienna system after 1856 exemplifies this; only Austria and Britain of the original Concert of Europe continued to support the status quo, but they did not act as a highly unified entity to protect it.[43] Continued reliance on arrangements like the Contact Group among the major powers for specific crises, as was used in the Balkans, and even maintaining a special quasi-"superpower" aura in the U.S.-Russian relationship, would be consistent with a loose concert. By contrast, in a tight concert the major powers consult over a broad range of security issues, and coordinate specific policies so as to act as a single entity. In effect, each has a veto on the other's major actions. The Vienna system from 1816 through about 1820 illustrates this.[44]

A second kind of formal reassurance would reduce NATO force levels along Moscow's eastern border. NATO is now negotiating to update the Conventional Forces in Europe (CFE) Treaty, which limits forces throughout Europe. Revision is needed, since the Soviet Union (rather than Russia) was a party. Albright argues that lower force levels "can assure Russia that NATO enlargement will not result in any major buildup of NATO forces along its borders. Indeed, it can assure [that] there is no destabilising concentration of military equipment anywhere in Europe."[45]

There are indications that Moscow has realized that NATO enlargement is inevitable and is looking for a face-saving way to accept it publicly.[46] The challenge, as virtually every Western official emphasizes, is to reassure Moscow in tangible ways without giving it a veto, even an implicit one, in any important area of NATO policymaking. This will be a fine line to walk—the more institutionalized the promise, the greater its value to Moscow, but the more it looks like an implicit veto. Over the long run, the best reassurance may be a truly "new NATO" that serves as more of a European crisis management tool than as an anti-Moscow instrument. This is a purpose to which Moscow cannot in principle credibly object.

Defining and Fulfilling NATO's Operational Missions

How can NATO become a flexible instrument for conflict management in Europe and its periphery? Long after any new members join the Atlantic Alliance, this will be its major operational challenge. The problem is significant because NATO was not built to perform CCM missions, even those that tend toward the "hard" end of the crisis management spectrum.[47] IFOR thus constitutes NATO's first real test in this regard and is likely to provide important lessons for the future. In deciding where to intervene and with what resources, NATO governments must work through four issues. First, they must decide what types of CCM operations they will undertake. Second, they must develop a mutually satisfactory relationship with other IGOs that have a shared role in global and regional CCM operations, including the UN and OSCE. Third, they must develop a military structure that is flexible enough to handle a variety of missions in Europe and its periphery. This was not a problem during the Cold War, when defense of NATO territory from a standing threat was the only mission. Fourth, they need to confront what may be a long-term collective action problem of supplying the forces and political will needed for CCM operations.

What Types of Operations Should NATO Undertake?

Rather than prepare for one large war, NATO is now deciding how it will prevent or suppress various small ones, and whether it will regularly assume humanitarian missions. Since future operations will almost certainly take place outside NATO's Article 6 defense perimeter, they imply a broader anticipated area of activity and a quite different military doctrine for the alliance.[40] In the past, out-of-area issues have been very divisive within NATO; but NATO members, especially Europeans, know that threats arising outside the treaty limits can now affect them more than those within. They have declared their willingness to cooperate militarily on a case-by-case basis outside their territories to deal with them.[49] Policing the Dayton Accords is their first major test.

Militaries taught to fight masses of Soviet armor will find that new weapons, doctrine, and training are needed to deal with critical new issues. The key ones center around how massively and quickly military force should be used. Here several distinct kinds of strategic situations should be accurately identified. As discussed in the first chapter of this volume, "peacekeeping," "selective enforcement," and "enforcement" are quite different CCM tasks. It is one thing to monitor a stable pause in a conflict; little firepower is needed and the physical risks are generally low. It is quite another to impose a pause in an ongoing conflict; significantly more firepower and risk are entailed. Imposing a solution to a conflict is still more demanding in both ways.

As Andrew Bennett illustrates in his chapter in this volume, failure to make these distinctions in the United Nations Protection Force (UNPROFOR) mission in the former Yugoslavia and Somalia led to wide swings between optimism and pessimism about the prospects for successful CCM. Selective enforcement constitutes a wide "gray area" between traditional peacekeeping and enforcement, both of which are easily defined. Unlike peacekeeping and enforcement, it entails widely varying degrees of force, depending on the strength of armed factions that oppose a given cease-fire mandate. A dilemma often ensues. While troops may be vulnerable to being ambushed, taken hostage, or overrun, and thus must be adequately armed and present in sufficient numbers, their mandate is to enforce a pause, not a solution to the conflict. As such, force must be used so as to deter or compel adversaries in a measured fashion, without undue escalation. This is a difficult assignment. It prompts some analysts to recommend against such gray-area operations as a matter of policy.[50] But NATO would lose its post-Cold War operational raison d'être if it did so. The types of missions in this gray area—forcible humanitarian assistance, protection of safe havens for threatened groups, forcible disarmament of armed factions, supervision of cease-fire lines where substantial violations may occur, capture of internationally indicted war criminals, and the rescue of hostages or apprehension of terrorists—are precisely the missions for which NATO has a comparative advantage, and for which its services are most in demand.

It remains to be seen whether NATO policymakers can identify these distinct types of situations in a timely fashion and assemble the right mix of forces for particular contingencies. UNPROFOR—with some NATO air cover added in—was a peacekeeping force with no peace to keep before the Dayton Accords in 1995. However, the military components of IFOR and SFOR, are arguably war-fighting forces with no real war to fight.[51] Ironically, at least some officials had the correct conceptual categories with which to diagnose such situations. Early in the Clinton Administration, Secretary of State Christopher offered U.S. backing in the then-ongoing talks that produced the Vance-Owen plan to settle the Balkans conflict. He "confirmed the U.S. refusal to *impose* a solution, but promised U.S. participation in *enforcing* an agreement accepted by the parties."[52] Effective CCM policies will depend on integrating such careful diagnoses of a problem to the tools that may solve it.

As just suggested, the application of force in such gray areas must be nuanced. Yet U.S. forces continue "intuitively" to prefer massive force, a predilection reinforced by successes in Panama and Kuwait, while Europeans are more willing to operate in the zones between peace and all-out war. The practical consequences are important: British officers stress "the relative ease with which a common approach in a demanding and unconventional multinational mission (such as Bosnia) with their French and Spanish colleagues can be and is developed, in contrast to that with other national forces."[53] If U.S. military doctrine offers too blunt an instrument to be effective in some cases, traditional peacekeeping doctrine is at times not coercive enough. Some people recognize the problem. As one U.S. officer put it, "the president and the American public must have options for the use of military power other than a rerun of Desert Storm or cases with a guarantee of no risk and no casualties." Criteria for intervening in these cases and a doctrine for doing so are being developed, but the process needs more central guidance because "both the United Nations and NATO cry out for effective United States leadership to force rationalization across the multinational doctrine development process." These basic doctrinal differences are compounded by a reluctance, especially in the United States, to make the resource tradeoffs and organizational compromises that low-intensity missions require. Units involved in such operations are unavailable for coercive intervention contingencies, those most officers consider vital. Low-intensity missions also have other implications that many officials prefer to avoid. They require "integrated planning with civilian components, organizational tailoring, special equipment training, and the training and education related to coalition formation and multinational operations, which all drive preparatory time."[54] Military organizations that prize their operational autonomy and strategic culture find these unattractive, a point made by Robert McCalla in this volume.

None of these obstacles to multilateral peace operations is insuperable. NATO and non-NATO forces have by now held several years of joint peace operation exercises. Marked differences in military doctrine and tactics across these countries do not seem to have interfered with the success of the IFOR mission.[55] Military organizations at staff colleges, service academies, and joint staffs are gradually being socialized into the vocabulary and concepts of peace keeping, selective enforcement, and related operations. The U.S. State Department and Marine Corps are together trying to retrain military forces to carry out relief operations, demobilize local armed factions, and improve logistics in chaotic internal environments[56]—that is, the problems that bedeviled the early Somalia operation. And virtually every NATO member and would-be member is investing in flexible forces usable in various military contingencies.

Nevertheless, peace operations are seen as politically risky, especially in the U.S. and Germany. In early 1995, Congress passed a bill limiting the President's ability to commit U.S. forces to joint UN operations. NATO was not directly mentioned, but it is not clear that Congress would condone its involvement in more than a very few of the plausible intervention scenarios. U.S. partners thus worry even more about whether America will be available for joint operations than about the differences in national approaches to carrying them out.[57]

Germans are also divided about using force other than for self-defense. On the one hand, many elites see what Rühe calls the "culture of self-restraint" as outmoded, and are ready to help protect international stability. They agree that for historical reasons, Germany will act only with allies, but if it does, it is prepared to do so beyond the Article 6 limits. This permits debate on the merits of specific operations, as in any other NATO member.[58] On the other hand, resistance within the Social Democratic Party (SPD) to such activity remains. Few German citizens have adjusted to a more assertive military role abroad, and the SPD as a whole may do so only when it has policy responsibility. German officials thus expect their country to do little peace enforcement for the foreseeable future.[59]

Neither, it seems, might others. Most governments are looking for excuses not to intervene. As Stanley Hoffman put it, "it is hard, especially after the Yugoslav experience, to imagine NATO's military involvement in civil wars in Eastern Europe."[60] Fundamentally, NATO's future operational role—as opposed to its political roles in containing a united Germany and reassuring the former

Warsaw Pact states that they will be protected from a resurgent Moscow—hinges on how readily it chooses to intervene in out-of-area disputes that call for selective enforcement. If its members will only risk casualties when their core interests are directly threatened, it will remain operationally irrelevant until or unless a major threat emerges.

NATO's Relations With Other IGOs: The "Subcontracting" Issue

Conflict between organizations is likely when they claim some of the same turf, cannot easily divide what is in dispute, and need each other. During the Cold War, NATO operated entirely independently from the UN which, aside from the controversial and highly idiosyncratic Korean operation, ordered no military enforcement. That kind of arm's-length relationship changed as the UN and OSCE have moved toward CCM involvement across the spectrum depicted in chapter one. Since neither the UN nor the OSCE as organizations can enforce their own decisions, moving toward the enforcement end of the spectrum means that they must look elsewhere to implement such choices. This has been called the "subcontracting" of CCM missions.[61] At the same time and as Michael Barnett argues in this volume, NATO needs political legitimation from the UN when it acts out-of-area. The result has been a somewhat uneasy marriage of convenience. In September 1992, NATO agreed to enforce UN resolutions on a case-by-case basis; this built upon a June 1992 CSCE decision to call selectively NATO for enforcement or peacekeeping. By late 1993, various NATO ministerial meetings had laid out principles to govern such activity.

These decisions were soon implemented. In operation SHARP GUARD, NATO, and Western European Union (WEU) ships enforced the UN-mandated embargo against Serbia and Montenegro. In operation DENY FLIGHT, NATO enforced a UN resolution that established a no-fly zone over Bosnian airspace and protected designated Moslem safe havens. Here a coordination problem arose when the UN secretary-general's special representative for the former Yugoslavia clashed with NATO commanders about when to authorize retaliatory airstrikes.

Different military cultures and objectives within the two institutions significantly worsened this problem. The UN's main Bosnian mission was humanitarian, while NATO's was coercive, and the problem was compounded because Britain and France played major roles in Bosnia through both bodies. The major lesson NATO members have learned from the Bosnian operation is that dual-key operational military systems—in which multiple actors must approve the use of force, escalation of force, or particular targets—are unworkable. Even France, which has sought to shrink NATO's role, agrees that "one lesson of Bosnia is that joint authority does not work." There is virtual unanimity within NATO on this point.[62]

It is also agreed that the mandates of all bodies involved in an operation must be clearly defined and integrated in pursuit of a coherent strategy. This did not occur in Bosnia before the Dayton Accords. The Security Council carried out a humanitarian mission and tried during an ongoing war to protect its peacekeeping forces, while NATO in effect enforced repeated cease-fires and exclusion zones on one party to the dispute. Conflicts between two bodies with such different missions were inevitable, and the result was widely seen among NATO governments as UN micromanagement. With the benefit of hindsight, now UN Secretary-General Kofi Annan suggested in 1993 that the Security Council might instead ask the [UN] secretary-general to exercise his responsibility by providing overall political and strategic guidance through his special representative, leaving the tactical and operational decisions to a Theater Commander who would use NATO command structures and assets in leading a force which, in the main, would be composed of NATO troops. This depicts the Gulf War model, wherein a UN-authorized coalition operated largely independently of the Security Council. This model has the advantage of cleanly dividing responsibility for peace operations, but it is not appropriate for every mission. Where a carrot-and-stick strategy is used, more intrusive political direction in military operations is needed, and at times even desirable, than in an all-out war. NATO therefore must consider, in Annan's words, "at what level of its own political and military hierarchy command and control should be submitted to the authority of the Security Council through the secretary-general of the United Nations."[63]

If NATO is to operate militarily out of area, it must consider this issue carefully. The backlash against the United Nations in Washington means that if NATO is seen by American politicians with unilateralist leanings to submit to UN direction too near the operational military level, both institutions might be discredited. This is less of a problem in countries such as France and Germany where the UN's prestige is higher, but seriously mixed signals from multiple institutions during any operation will ruin its execution. Where joint authority of some type is exercised, a visibly coherent strategy is essential. That will not be easy for bodies with such different cultures as NATO and the UN or NATO and OSCE, but strategically coherent and politically viable peace operations demand it.

When NATO performs CCM operations that are closer to the left side of the spectrum (traditional peacekeeping), working with UN personnel becomes easier because the conceptual differences in organizational cultures are smaller or less important. Officials in charge of the IFOR and SFOR operations have worked closely with UN officials in Bosnia on such tasks as repatriation of refugees, joint patrolling of certain key areas, and restructuring and retraining local police forces.[64] These kinds of situations involve significant shared responsibility for many of the tasks involved in cleaning up a war and rebuilding the state and civil society. In practice, then, the pieces of the evolving post-Cold War "security architecture" often fit together better than the tensions involved in "subcontracting" might otherwise suggest.

NATO's Military Structure

Changing military tasks and doctrine implies changes in NATO's military structure. NATO has tried in two ways to create forces suitable for the more numerous, localized conflicts expected in the post-Cold War world. The first of these involved trading some firepower for flexibility. The second involved changes in the way national units are organized.

First, the nuclear weapons committed to NATO's use have been drastically reduced, national conventional forces have been cut significantly, and efforts have begun to make units more mobile and adaptable. Three categories of conventional forces have been designated: "main defense forces," designed to protect members' territories; "reaction forces," to be used for quick response in crises; and "augmentation forces," intended to reinforce either of the others. Since standing troops and reserves have always been used, the main innovation has been to focus more on light forces backed up by adequate lift capacity. Investment in them will significantly reorient the force structures of the major NATO countries, which for years emphasized the troops needed for a set-piece battle.

NATO has also tried to make its formations more flexible by allowing separate national units to mesh more easily. The CJTF plan, which provides for multinational, multiservice groups of forces organized ad hoc for specific jobs, is one response. NATO as a whole could use such task forces, or they could be used by a WEU group that did not include Washington's forces. The premise is that NATO's strategic situation has dramatically changed with the end of the Cold War; the integrated command worked well for Article 5 contingencies, but it is less useful for those outside NATO territory. Striving for unanimity within the group here is counterproductive: "in the post-Cold War world, if you keep NATO this inflexible, it will break."[65] Accordingly, CJTFs facilitate "coalitions of the willing" among NATO and WEU members. This will be achieved through "separable but not separate military forces" that is, those capable of working in different combinations, but still subject to joint planning and able to work together on a large scale if necessary. As one observer put it: "deploying CJTFs will, for the first time, become the primary modus operandi of a standing alliance in peacetime."[66]

Each task force will borrow an existing military headquarters, either national or multinational. If Americans were not involved, it might be run by the WEU; otherwise, it would likely be a NATO CJTF. The possibility of organizing an operation either way, depending on the situation, is seen as a way to give Europeans more autonomy within the transatlantic relationship. But they will depend on U.S. help for some time to come. Non-NATO task forces almost certainly will need to borrow U.S. assets such as airlift, command-and-control systems, and satellite intelligence. Some Europeans worry that Americans will put strings on their use, although Robert Hunter, U.S. Ambassador to NATO, has denied this.[67]

The CJTF's plan was designed largely so France could move back toward NATO without rejoining the integrated command—still politically unacceptable to Paris—and it has worked. French officials in any case have been assuming a less unilateral stance. The thrust of France's 1993 white paper about an alternative defense policy, the first in 22 years, is to Europeanize its security policy. Pierre Lellouche, an adviser to President Jacques Chirac, has laid out the strategic basis for the new thinking: Since NATO does not fear attack and thus need no longer prepare to act on short notice, France has new-found policy discretion within the alliance.[68] French officials have thus been given more leeway to take part in NATO's military committee, and the Eurocorps, organized by Paris and Bonn, will now be made available to NATO even under non-Article 5 contingencies if the other members agree.

Where disagreements arise is in how the task forces would relate to the integrated command, and what this ultimately implies for NATO's overall structure. France's ideas on these points are at odds with those of most other NATO members. It wants non-Article 5 operations to be run by the North Atlantic Council, which comprises heads of government. The NAC would instruct NATO's Military Committee, bypassing NATO's SACEUR, and through the Military Committee issue instructions directly to the specific command running the task force. Paris wants to cut SACEUR out of the chain of command because NATO's current structure is seen to give military commanders (perceived by Paris to be heavily under Washington's influence) too much authority at the expense of political officials. French officials concede that in a true war, soldiers cannot be closely managed by politicians, but they see no reason why other kinds of peace operations cannot be subject to closer political control.[69]

Ultimately, France seeks equality in NATO between the EU and the United States. This is seen as impossible if Europeans are bound tightly to North Americans in defense. For Europe to approach America's weight in security affairs, a tighter European defense pillar and a much looser NATO is needed.[70]

The United States, Great Britain, and several of the smaller NATO members reject this proposition. Germany is torn between the two positions. The Bundeswehr is so linked to SACEUR's organization that Germany can hardly act outside it; as a French official put it, some Germans "are more fanatical in their devotion to the integrated command than SACEUR himself."[71] But Germany is also committed to tighter European integration, including defense, which requires close partnership with Paris. Even Rühe thus wants to enlarge the EU's role in NATO, though he discourages the idea of an alliance between pillars, as opposed to individual countries.[72]

For now, the CJTFs plan usefully facilitates the ad hoc coalitions everyone wants. This pragmatic attitude may prevail over the long run: One British official said that "we get on fine with the French so long as we can stop them from talking about fancy 'architecture.'"[73] The precedents set by IFOR and SFOR may be useful here as well: 20 percent of IFOR's personnel came from non-NATO countries, and PFP states involved in this operation have gained much practical experience in cooperating with NATO.[74] CJTFs also cut political risks for U.S. officials who want to remain engaged in Europe; they can use European task forces as proof that Europeans are doing more for themselves, which will help stem Congressional pressures for fewer U.S. troops overseas. Yet at some point competing long-term designs for Europe could collide. Because France is convinced that the U.S. will eventually leave Europe, it argues that a significantly more independent European pillar is needed. If this becomes a self-fulfilling prophecy and the U.S. loses interest in an increasingly insular Europe, NATO will dissolve.

NATO's Long-Term Collective Action Problem

NATO's fourth major challenge is to supply, on a predictable basis, the forces and political will for CCM operations. Unless it can do so, it will have little operational relevance in the post-Cold War world. Ironically, NATO may be a victim of its own success in this regard. Having contributed to a victory in the Cold War and now facing no likely potential aggressor, it has discretion to choose when and where to intervene. As a result, even if international responsibility is required for forcible humanitarian intervention, protection of safe havens, and enforcement of cease-fires, and even if NATO is best equipped militarily and organizationally to perform these tasks, such needs may represent a public good that neither NATO nor anyone else has an incentive to fulfill. This is NATO's long-term collective action problem.

Third parties intervene in the situations just enumerated for two types of reasons: private, or "interested" reasons; and public, or "disinterested" reasons. Private motives include hegemonic ambitions in a target state (in civil war situations), a concern for regional stability, or sympathy for a particular group that is seen as weak. Public motives include a sense of international responsibility or humanitarianism.[75] Even if international norms that promote intervention for disinterested reasons grow stronger, as some recent literature suggests,[76] there may be strong incentives for actors to ride free on others' benefits. This is likely to occur if there is no private good at stake and especially if the absence of a private benefit occurs in cases where an operation carries high costs and risks. The repeated buck-passing among Europeans and Americans over Yugoslavia's wars between 1991 and 1995 illustrates the problem.

As recent political rhetoric in the United States exemplifies, governments are increasingly less willing to participate in risky operations that are irrelevant to their private security or other interests. This collective action problem is more severe than the one that NATO faced during the Cold War. At that time, U.S. nuclear extended deterrence commitments could cover much of the shortfall in the conventional forces NATO members were willing to provide.[77] By contrast, since forces will now be tested in combat when they participate in selective enforcement or enforcement operations, a premium is put on a willingness to field appropriate kinds of units and risk what may be significant casualties. It is not evident that NATO can reliably guarantee either of these requirements.

As Robert McCalla illustrates in his chapter, for NATO to deal effectively with crisis management and enforcement problems of various types it needs rapidly deployable forces of a kind that it did not procure before the early 1990s. It must now do so with "steadily eroding resources as national defense budgets, equipment inventories, and manpower continue to decline."[78] It is not a question of NATO members procuring the needed equipment, it is because they have fewer private incentives to do so. Absent conflicts which directly impinge on their security, the hardware requirements may be undersupplied.

The political will to run the risks involved in these missions may be in even shorter supply. American leaders have internalized the Caspar Weinberger-Colin Powell criteria for using force. They are so stringent that they rule out many of the CCM operations of the kind discussed in this volume. When political leaders *do* consent to use force, they tend to focus less on a fit between the mission at hand and the tools available and more on having a visible "exit strategy."[79] As Andrew Bennett discusses in some detail, this risks putting CCM operations in the hands of the most recalcitrant party. It also causes politicians to make misleading promises to their publics, as exemplified by the transparent nonsense that IFOR would entail only a one-year obligation for the United States.

NATO's strengths—that it is a voluntary union of free societies—make it difficult to overcome this problem. Domestic politics and especially electoral cycles make it hard to formulate and execute a foreign policy that responds optimally to the strategic circumstances a state faces. Without a clear enemy on the horizon, there seems little way to overcome this problem.

Conclusions

NATO enters the twenty-first century as a highly effective political organization with an uncertain military future. It survived its early post-Cold War crisis of relevance and now stands poised to help integrate at least some former

Warsaw Pact countries into a viable, voluntary security structure. If it can overcome Russian suspicions of its purposes—not least by opening itself up to wide use as a practical stabilizing force within Europe—it may furnish as important a contribution to the post-Cold War system as it did during the Cold War itself.

The major uncertainty is whether NATO is too blunt an instrument to be used for more than a very few or exceptional CCM cases. States that do not face an immediate security threat may be very reluctant to pay in concrete terms for the new security tasks of the post-Cold War world. Whether NATO can overcome this problem, as it has so many others, remains to be seen.

Notes

1. The author wishes to thank Martha Finnemore, Alan Lamborn, Robert McCalla, and Thomas G. Weiss for advice on this paper.

2. Robert B. McCalla, "NATO's Persistence After the Cold War," *International Organization* 50, no. 3 (summer 1996): 445–475.

3. See Thomas G. Weiss, ed., *Beyond UN Subcontracting: Task-sharing with Regional Security Arrangements and Service-providing NGOs* (London: Macmillan, 1997, forthcoming).

4. Stanley Sloan, "Transatlantic Relations in the Wake of the Brussels Summit," *NATO Review* (April 1994): 30.

5. See, respectively, "London Declaration on a Transformed North Atlantic Alliance," (Brussels: NATO Information Service) July 5–6, 1990, 3, and "NATO's Core Security Functions in the New Europe," Statement issued by the North Atlantic Council meeting, Copenhagen, June 6–7, 1991, reprinted in *NATO Review* 39, no. 3 (June 1991): 30.

6. McCalla, "NATO's Persistence After the Cold War," 448.

7. Kalevi J. Holsti, *Peace and War: Armed Conflicts and International Order, 1648–1989* (Cambridge, U.K.: Cambridge University Press, 1991), 26.

8. See McCalla, "NATO's Persistence," 448–449, for a good summary of these changes.

9. For one example of this argument, see Jonathan Clarke, "Replacing NATO," *Foreign Policy* 93 (winter 1993–94): 22–40.

10. Philip H. Gordon, "Recasting the Atlantic Alliance," *Survival* 38, no. 1 (spring 1996): 43.

11. Lee Hockstader, "Moscow Says It May Use Force to Protect Russians in Ex-Soviet States," *Washington Post*, April 19, 1995, A28.

12. International Institute for Strategic Studies, *Strategic Survey 1993–94, Europe: The Search for the True Russia* (London: Brassey's, 1994): 137; confidential interview.

13. Speech by Willy Claes, Secretary-General of NATO, to "The Grande Conferences Catholiques," January 9, 1995, NATO Integrated Electronic Data Service, no pagination.

14. Quoted in Jim Hoagland, "Reaching Out for NATO," *Washington Post*, March 19, 1995, C7.

15. U.S. Department of State, Bureau of European and Canadian Affairs, *Report to the Congress on the Enlargement of the North Atlantic Treaty Organization* [http://www.fas.org/man/nato/wh970224.htm] (Washington, D.C.: U.S. Department of State, February 24, 1997): 6.

16. Ibid.; conversations with U.S. government officials, December 14 and 22, 1994, and April 2, 1995.

17. Karl Deutsch explicates the notion of a pluralistic security community in Deutsch et al., *Political Community in the North Atlantic Area* (Princeton: Princeton University Press, 1957): 32. For an application of this idea to NATO's Partnership for Peace, see Joseph Lepgold, "The Next Step in European Security," *Journal of Strategic Studies 17*, no. 4 (December 1994): 7–26.

18. U.S. Department of State, Bureau of European and Canadian Affairs, *Report to the Congress on the Enlargement of the North Atlantic Treaty Organization*, 6.

19. Hoagland, "Reaching Out for NATO."

20. Given political sensitivities in Europe about past German behavior, this issue is discussed in subtle terms. Nevertheless, the implication that Germany still needs to be enmeshed in a network of multilateral ties is unmistakable. One draft report, produced by a German and two Americans, put it this way:

> in the debate about enlargement the question of the stability-exporting potential of certain Central European countries is often overlooked or superficially addressed. Here one is not merely talking about potential contributions to peacekeeping efforts (though these would certainly be welecomed) but also to the stabilizing influence the integration of certain Central European countries in multilateral structures would have on certain powerful Western countries. This has to do with the general preference for managing security relationships through multilateral, as opposed to bilateral, frameworks.

See "The Enlargement of the Alliance: Draft Special Report of The Working Group on NATO Enlargement," NATO International Secretariat, NATO Integrated Data Service, electronic version, no pagination.

21. Ibid.

22. For an elaboration of this argument, see Lepgold, "The Next Step Toward a More Secure Europe."

23. NATO Secretary–General Javier Solana himself recently acknowledged this. See Speech by the Secretary-General at the Royal Institute of International Affairs, Chatham House, London [NATO Integrated Data Service, http://www.nato.int/], March 4, 1997.

24. This tendency is known as the fundamental attribution error in human cognition. For a good discussion, see Susan T. Fiske and Shelley E. Taylor, *Social Cognition*, 2nd ed. (New York: McGraw–Hill, 1991): 67–72. I thank Victor Cha for pointing this out to me.

25. Jim Hoagland, "Russia's 'Red-Line' Limits," *Washington Post*, March 9, 1997, C7; Michael R. Gordon, "Russia Accepts Eastward Growth of NATO, But Only Inch by Inch," *New York Times*, March 4, 1997, A1, A8.

26. Quoted in R. Jeffrey Smith and Daniel Williams, "U.S. Plans New Tack on Russia-NATO Tie," *Washington Post*, January 6, 1995, A1, A19.

27. For a classic treatment of this issue, see Robert Jervis, "Cooperation Under the Security Dilemma," *World Politics* 30, no. 2 (January 1978): 167–214, quote at 169.

28. Alyson Bailes, "NATO: Toward a New Synthesis," *Survival* 38, no. 3 (autumn 1996): 27–40, quote on 30.

29. For a succinct, informative, interpretation of Russia's historic identity and sense of security, see John M. Joyce, "The Old Russian Legacy," *Foreign Policy* 55 (summer 1984): 32–153.

30. Stephen Sestanovich, "Why the United States Has No Russia Policy," in Robert J. Lieber, ed., *Eagle Adrift: American Foreign Policy at the End of the Century* (New York: Longman, 1997): 174.

31. Bailes, "NATO: Toward a New Synthesis," 30.

32. Speech by the Secretary-General at the Royal Institute of International Affairs, March 4, 1997.

33. Michael R. Beschloss and Strobe Talbott, *At the Highest Levels: The Inside Story of the End of the Cold War* (Boston, Mass.: Little, Brown and Company, 1993): 185.

34. Janice Gross Stein, "Reassurances in International Conflict Management," *Political Science Quarterly* 106, no. 3 (fall 1991).

35. The quote is from "Report to the Congress on the Enlargement of the North Atlantic Treaty Organization," 18.

36. "U.S. Plans New Tack on Russia-NATO Tie," *Washington Post*, January 6, 1995, A1, A19; Stephen Rosenfeld, "Squaring the Circle in Central Europe," *Washington Post*, March 17, 1995, A27.

37. "Report to the Congress on Enlargement of the North Atlantic Treaty Organization," 5.

38. Hoagland, "Russia's 'Red-Line' Limits."

39. Charles Lipson, "Why Are Some International Agreements Informal?," *International Organization* 45, no. 4 (autumn 1991): 495–538; Stein, "Reassurances in International Conflict Management."

40. "U.S. Proposes a NATO-Russia Military Unit," *Today's News: World News Story Page* [http://www.cnn.com/WORLD/9702/18/ albright.nato/index.html], February 18, 1997, 2. At this writing, NATO and Russia still disagree on whether such a charter would be legally binding. See "Russia Accepts Eastward Growth of NATO."

41. Ibid.; Madeleine Albright, "Enlarging NATO: Why Bigger is Better," *The Economist*, February 15, 1997, 23.

42. Gregory L. Schulte, "Former Yugoslavia and the New NATO," *Survival* 39, no. 1 (spring 1997), 32.

43. Gordon A. Craig and Alexander L. George, *Force and Statecraft: Diplomatic Problems of Our Time* (Oxford, U.K.: Oxford University Press, 1990): 36.

44. Bailes, "NATO: Toward a New Synthesis," 31–32.

45. Albright, "Enlarging NATO," 23.

46. United States Information Agency, "NATO Enlargement: Is 'a Compromise in the Offing' with Moscow?" (Washington, D.C.: USIA, February 27, 1997): 1; Hoagland, "Russia's 'Red-Line' Limits."

47. The phrase is Alyson Bailes'. See "NATO: Toward a New Synthesis," 28.

48. *NATO, Peacekeeping, and the United Nations* (London: British American Security Information Council, 1994), 6.

49. Stanley R. Sloan, "The NATO Strategy Review: Negotiating the Future of the North Atlantic Alliance," Congressional Research Service, Library of Congress, 91–379, April 30, 1991, 5–6.

50. Richard K. Betts, "The Delusion of Impartial Intervention," *Foreign Affairs* 73, no. 6 (November/December 1994): 20–33.

51. I thank Thomas G. Weiss for suggesting this formulation. For an argument that the situation facing IFOR and SFOR *does* constitute a war, see Henry Kissinger, "America in the Eye of a Hurricane," *Washington Post*, September 8, 1996. One could argue that the IFOR and SFOR forces, even if over-armed for the situation they confront, are preferable to a force that is too weak.

52. Stanley Hoffmann, "The United States and Western Europe," in Lieber, ed., *Eagle Adrift*, 186.

53. *NATO, The UN, and Peacekeeping: New Context; New Challenges*, draft interim report prepared by the Subcommittee on Defence and Security Cooperation Between Europe and North America, NATO International Secretariat, November 1994, courtesy of NATO Integrated Data Service, electronic version, paragraphs 37 and 38, no pagination.

54. Major General John Sewall (ret.), "Adapting Conventional Military Forces to the New Environment," *U.S. Intervention Policy for the Post-Cold War World: New Challenges and New Responses* (New York: Norton, 1994): quotes on 102 and 92.

55. Pauline Neville-Jones, "Dayton, IFOR, and Alliance Relations in Bosnia," *Survival* 38, no. 4 (winter 1996–97): 53.

56. Barbara Crossette, "After Somalia, U.S. Studies Ways to Improve Relief Operations," *New York Times*, April 9, 1995, A6. This point is also made in "NATO, Peacekeeping, and the Former Yugoslavia," electronic version, no pagination. Support in the U.S. military for nontraditional tasks is rising "with the realization that this is where the Army's bread is going to be buttered." Quoted in Bradley Graham, "New Twist for U.S. Troops: Peace Maneuvers," *Washington Post*, August 15, 1994, A8.

57. *NATO, the UN, and Peacekeeping*, paragraph 45.

58. Conversations with German officials, June 6 and 23, 1994.

59. Conversations with German officials, June 6, 1994 and December 28, 1994.

60. Hoffmann, "The United States and Western Europe," 182; conversations with a U.S. government official, December 14 and 22, 1994.

61. For an extended discussion, see *Third World Quarterly* 18, no. 3 (1997), titled "Beyond UN Subcontracting: Task-Sharing with Regional Security Arrangements and Service-Providing NGOs," especially Edwin Smith and Thomas G. Weiss, "UN Task Sharing: Toward or Away From Global Governance?"

62. For the French view, see "The Defence of Europe: It Can't Be Done Alone," *The Economist*, February 25, 1995, 21; conversation with a U.S. official, December 14 and 22, 1994.

63. Kofi Annan, "UN Peacekeeping Operations and Cooperation with NATO," *NATO Review* 41, no. 5 (October 1993): 6, 7.

64. Schulte, "Former Yugoslavia and the New NATO," 28.

65. Conversation with a U.S. official, July 6, 1994.

66. Charles Barry, "NATO's Combined Joint Task Forces in Theory and Practice," *Survival* Vol. 38, no. 1 (spring 1996): 82.

67. "The Defence of Europe," 20.

68. Pierre Lellouche, "France in Search of Security," *Foreign Affairs* 72, no. 2 (spring 1993): 129. The 1993 white paper on defense alternatives makes similar points;

see Barry James, "France to Increase NATO Cooperation," *International Herald Tribune*, November 26, 1993, 2.

69. "It Can't Be Done Alone," conversation with Robert Grant, U.S.-CREST, December 29, 1994.

70. Hoagland, "Reaching Out for NATO."

71. Carey Schofield, "France as the Wild Card in NATO?," *International Defense Review*, July 1994, 22.

72. Ibid., and conversation with Robert Grant, December 29, 1994.

73. "The Defence of Europe," 19.

74. Schulte, "Former Yugoslavia and the New NATO," 31.

75. David A. Lake and Donald Rothchild, *Ethnic Fears and Global Engagement: the International Spread and Management of Ethnic Conflict*, Policy Paper no. 20 (Berkeley, Cal.: Institute on Global Conflict and Cooperation, University of California, 1996): 38.

76. For examples, see the chapters by Bruce Cronin and Martha Finnemore in this volume.

77. For an extended discussion, see Joseph Lepgold, *The Declining Hegemon: The United States and European Defense, 1960–1990* (Westport, CT: Praeger, 1990).

78. Bailes, "NATO: Toward a New Synthesis," 29.

79. This was strikingly the case in Bosnia, especially in the early stages of NATO's involvement. See Hoffmann, "The United States and Western Europe," 188.

4

The Limits of Peacekeeping, Spheres of Influence, and the Future of the United Nations[1]

Michael N. Barnett

The last few years have not been particularly kind to the United Nations. After so much hope and hype after the end of the Cold War, the world organization quickly fell on hard times. There were plenty of reasons for its declining popularity. And there were more than enough dire speculations concerning the effect of this decline on its potential contribution to international peace and security. But one notable line of argument was that because member states had clearly demonstrated that they would contribute only to those operations in which they had a vested interest, the UN would be increasingly asked to sanction a growing number operations in which a major power took the lead and was a highly interested party to the outcome. The discourse in and around the United Nations shifted from the projection of its independent role in helping foster global security to a concern that it was legitimating the emergence of spheres of influence.[2]

There were good reasons for this observation and corresponding concerns. In 1994, the Security Council authorized Russia, France, and the United States to take a commanding role in the UN operations in Georgia, Rwanda, and Haiti, respectively. Ever sensitive to the appearance of being and becoming little more than a stamp for great power actions and not an expression of the interests of the international community, the council's debates on these operations were fraught with the concern that the UN was no longer contributing to international peace and security but rather to the ambitions of the major powers. On the occasion of the authorization of the Russian peacekeeping operation in Georgia, the Brazilian permanent representative avowed that his country remained committed to the belief "that the United Nations should ultimately continue to play a fundamental role in this and other situations in ensuring multilateral support for the peaceful settlement of conflicts."[3] If those in the Security Council could only hint of their fears of spheres of influence, the media loudly proclaimed that no other conclusion but spheres of influence could be drawn; the *New York Times* editorialized that "having taken its lumps trying to be a world police force, the U.N. has now fallen into the unhealthy habit of licensing great-power spheres of influence."[4] The UN Protection Force in the former Yugoslavia (UNPROFOR) was unceremoniously shunted aside in Bosnia with the establishment of the Implementation Force (IFOR), barely given the courtesy of playing a modest role in the post-UNPROFOR operation. The subtext was clear: the UN was becoming irrelevant once again.

Yet the rumors concerning the UN's imminent death are highly exaggerated. Although the United Nations is unlikely to become the principal forum for combatting threats to peace and security, neither is spheres of influence apt to dominate the security landscape. Major powers will act when it furthers their security interests, but when and how they will do so will be shaped by global forces that provide a strong role for multilateral mechanisms in general and the UN in particular. Such a security arrangement can be better depicted as the "politics of delegation" rather than the "politics of domination." To this end, I 1) survey the limits of peacekeeping and the dynamics that are creating the appearance of spheres of influence; 2) examine the concept of spheres of influence; 3) outline why the more recent operations that have a prominent lead country suggest not the politics of domination but rather of delegation; and, 4) outline some of the domestic, transnational, and global forces that are propelling major power to retreat from embracing spheres of influence and to rely on the United Nations.

The Limits of Peacekeeping

The end of the Cold War triggered an explosion in peacekeeping operations. The reasons behind the explosion are many, including the end of the Cold War that lifted the paralysis from the Security Council; the desire by the great powers to have a place to dump intractable conflicts; and a "CNN" factor that placed greater demands on the "international community;" and hence the United Nations, to respond to the growing number of humanitarian emergencies. However, the result was unquestioned overextension.

Part of the overextension was due not only to the number of crises that were being dumped on the Security Council but also to an expanded notion of security. Whereas during the Cold War many policymakers judged that juridical sovereignty, balances of power, and deterrence underpinned international order, since the late 1980s, there is greater attention to how the lack of empirical sovereignty—that states have some degree of legitimacy and control over their society and within their borders—affects international order. Specifically, by emphasizing that there is a strong relationship between domestic order and international order, member states were moving from the language of deterrence to that of assurance, and recognizing that the assurance that states will not act aggressively is furthered when states do not have the motivation to go to war. This motivation, in turn, is best minimized by preventing conflicts from arising in the first place, which is due in no small measure to some level of domestic stability.[5] Although domestic stability can be effected through democratic and authoritarian means, there is considerable support and sentiment among many member states and the UN secretariat that there is a strong relationship between democratization and peaceful change.[6] In short, not just any domestic order creates the foundations for international order; it is the rule of law at home that creates the rule of law abroad.

Peace operations are a direct extension of the international community's understanding that there is a strong relationship between empirical sovereignty and international order. Articulating this expanded conceptualization of security, Boutros-Ghali's *An Agenda for Peace* identified three stages to the life-cycle of conflict: peacemaking, preventing conflict from turning violent; peacekeeping, limiting and containing conflict once it occurs; and peace building, facilitating the transition from civil war to civil society through post-conflict political and economic reconstruction.[7] This expanded notion of security is particularly obvious in the UN's second-generation peacekeeping operation: whereas once peacekeepers were situated solely between two combatants that had agreed to a cease fire, and rarely if ever engaged in offensive action, now they are involved in a myriad of activities that reflect an expanded definition of security.[8] The UN, Boutros-Ghali asserted, has an important role in all three stages.

This highly ambitious security agenda left the UN highly vulnerable to overextension. Recent events have repeatedly demonstrated that the UN is unable to participate fully and effectively in all phases of peace operations. Three factors drive the limits of peacekeeping. The first concerns the types of actions that peacekeeping forces should include. Perhaps most striking is the retreat from peace enforcement activities. Hindsight illustrates that the Security Council took lightly the idea of peace enforcement, while not fully entertaining the strategic, political, or ethical issues involved.[9] Rather than reserving peace enforcement for those rare moments when the international community could easily identify and mobilize against a genuine threat to regional or international stability, it was sanctioned for internal security threats in the hope of fostering the political reconciliation process and administering humanitarian assistance. The perils of peace enforcement became dramatically clear in Somalia, as the failed attempt at forced disarmament of the militias and the unsightly attempt by the UN and the U.S. to capture Mohammed Farah Aideed caused many to challenge its value and efficacy. In fact, after the death of the U.S. Rangers and President Clinton's announcement of the withdrawal of forces from Somalia by

March 31, 1994, Boutros-Ghali, retreating from his longstanding position of forced disarmament, conceded that: "The United Nations cannot impose peace; the role of the United Nations is to maintain peace."[10] As a consequence of setbacks in Somalia and Bosnia, and the feeling that perhaps one reason why the UN was successful in Cambodia was because the UN Force Commander refused to engage in enforcement activities and instead relied on his diplomatic skills when confronting a noncompliant Khmer Rouge, peace enforcement finds few advocates today.[11]

Not only did the UN retreat from peace enforcement, but the Security Council also began to operate with some basic criteria for deciding whether to approve or extend a peacekeeping operation. Initially, the council appeared so quick to authorize any proposed mission that many observers quipped that "the UN never met an operation it did not like." By Fall 1993, however, many governmental and UN officials grumbled that such automatic authorizations were leaving the UN stretched thin and unable to operate effectively, causing them to clamor for greater self-restraint.[12] The Security Council responded by adopting a list of considerations that would inform its decision to approve or extend a peacekeeping operation, including whether: there is a genuine threat to peace and security; regional or subregional organizations can assist in resolving the situation; a cease-fire exists and the parties have committed themselves to a peace process; a clear political goal exists and is present in the mandate; a precise mandate can be formulated; and the safety of UN personnel can be reasonably assured.[13] Responding to its habit of using peacekeepers to demonstrate its continuing interest in the conflict without any real consideration of the likelihood of success or the long-term damage being done to the United Nations, the Security Council adopted these guidelines as a way to impose some measure of self-restraint.

Second, the UN confronted numerous bureaucratic and organizational weaknesses that limited its ability to manage the myriad tasks it was assigned. To begin, the world organization was overwhelmed by its expanded duties and responsibilities; it undertook more operations since the end of the Cold War than it had over the previous four decades, and these operations were more involved and complex than anything it has tackled since the United Operations in the Congo in the early 1960s. Without the bureaucratic elan or organizational resources to manage these manifold operations, many were beset by poor staffing in the field, bureaucratic delays and red tape at the secretariat, and numerous other logistical and procurement difficulties that prevented them from executing its mandated responsibilities in a timely and effective manner.[14] In some cases, for instance in the police training components of the operations in Somalia, Haiti, and El Salvador, the UN turned to qualified member states because of its own inadequate expertise and capabilities; such instances were a good sign of the coming times.

Third, and most important, the United Nations was largely unable to carry out its mandated responsibilities because it was not given the required money, men, and material. While the member states were approving one peacekeeping operation after another, they are unwilling to contribute the required inputs to ensure the success of these missions.[15] Most notorious, of course, was the shortfall in financing, a product both of the spotty payment record of some of its more powerful members and the snail's pace at which the UN appropriated the funds for a peacekeeping operation once it was approved by the Security Council. The UN fared little better in obtaining the necessary troops. Unlike the peacekeeping of old when troops were positioned between states that had reached a cease-fire and were called upon to monitor the truce, these new operations exposed blue helmets to greater danger and violence. Only those member states that had a stake in the outcome of the conflict were willing to contribute troops to these more dangerous operations. This, of course, threatened to undermine the UN's neutrality. Once it was a time-honored UN principle that only politically neutral states could contribute troops but now, according to Assistant Secretary-General Alvoro de Soto, "Beggars can't be choosers."[16]

Even when the United Nations obtained the required troops, however, it frequently had a difficult time directing them. Nearly all peacekeeping operations that have a hint of danger also have tremendous command and control issues, namely the difficulty of establishing unified command. These problems were particularly notorious in Somalia and in Bosnia.[17] Although governments are understandably quite concerned over whether their troops are being unnecessarily placed in harm's way, I have spoken to numerous U.S. and other military officials who repeatedly stress that they are more fearful of the prospect of decentralized command and control than they are of serving under UN command. The all too apparent dilemma is that what might be rational for each national contingent becomes highly irrational for the entire operation, and potentially exposes peacekeepers to greater danger. In any event, the result is that the UN has a difficult time obtaining, and then directing, its military forces.

Finally, because the UN has no military equipment of its own, it must rely on the willingness of member states to rent or donate the required material. This is a lengthy, costly, and frequently inadequate procedure, leaving the world organization struggling to outfit its troops (often with derelict equipment) to move them into and out of the operation. For example, even when some African states agreed to contribute forces to Rwanda, the UN had no means to transport them to the theater area. In turn, this required the UN to enter into negotiations with member states for direct assistance or leasing the necessary transport planes. Washington, for instance, essentially agreed to underwrite the cost of outfitting and transporting many of the African troop contributors to the operation in Liberia. To complicate matters even further, those troops who arrive often do so without weapons or even boots. If men, money, and material are the currency of military operations, it is no wonder that the United Nations has been less than effective. Although the Security Council has been willing to approve new peacekeeping operations, the member states have been less than ready to contribute the required inputs to ensure the success of these operations.

The dynamics leading to the UN's "overstretch" and overextension can be understood as a collective action problem. To begin, member states were approving one operation after another, but not providing the men, money, and material required for their successful implementation. This fundamental free riding was readily noted by Boutros-Ghali in his *Supplement to An Agenda for Peace.*[18] Although there are eloquent calls for states to back up their moral outrage of ethnic conflict and interstate violence with military muscle, a painful but all too familiar lesson from recent years is that states will contribute only when it is in their interest to do so. And even when states had a mutual interest in confronting an identified security threat or humanitarian disaster, they still failed to contribute to the collective good. Only those states who had the will and the way stepped forward.

From such dynamics emerged the UN's search for burden-sharing and, euphemistically put, subcontracting. Stretched thin and desperate for additional resources, the UN began joining forces (literally) with major powers and regional organizations that are usually dominated by a regional power.[19] Boutros-Ghali's office acknowledged the importance of financial considerations in driving this possible partnership: "The exponential growth in the cost of peace-keeping operations has been a factor in decisions of the Security Council to delegate the task of peace-keeping and peace-enforcement to groups of Member States rather than having the United Nations perform them."[20] Indeed, Boutros-Ghali confessed that a principal reason why he did not insist that the UN be more heavily involved in a Chapter VII operation in Haiti was because of the UN's attending financial straits; he was willing, therefore, to delegate responsibility to a lead country, the United States.[21] The decision to rely more fully on those states that have the capability and the willingness to partake in these security operations is a direct result of the unwillingness of member states to support the operation unless they have a stake in the outcome.[22] No wonder that many began predicting that great powers were now going to dominate the future security architecture and overshadow any independent role for the world organization.

Spheres of Influence

That the prospect of spheres of influence finds few advocates and many adversaries is not surprising. The concept came into popular usage in the late nineteenth century and into vogue with the scramble for Africa and the Conference of Berlin of 1884–85. Regardless of whether the European powers were intent on establishing proprietary claims over various parts of Africa for strategic, economic, or symbolic advantage, they were determined to establish some well-understood areas that were mutually recognized as under another's domain and control.[23] Historically, spheres of influence represent a great power technique to extend their influence over key strategic areas, and to regulate major power rivalry; accordingly, they are consistent with balances of power, closely associated with managing conflict, highly reminiscent of the Cold War, and therefore far from the role of the UN envisioned by many for the post-Cold War era.

Spheres of influence are distinguished by three basic principles. First, and most intuitive, spheres are territorially-based. "All spheres of influence," writes Paul Keal, "have identifiable geographical limits."[24] Consistent with the arguments of the great geopolitical thinkers like Halford MacKinder and Nicolas Spykman, the view here is that the best way to protect the state's national security is to maintain control and influence over other, usually contingent, territories. Because of major changes in military technology and industrial development, states are increasingly vulnerable to direct attack and therefore must create a buffer zone between themselves and other great powers. Spheres of influence, in other words, represent something of a security belt extended outside the state's territorial boundaries.

A second principle is exclusivity, that the major power maintains preponderant control over its sphere, and other major powers do not exercise the same degree of influence over those within that sphere. For much of the Cold War, for instance, there was a tacit agreement that the U.S. would not meddle in Eastern Europe, and the Soviet Union would not actively interfere in Central America. In this respect, spheres of influence can be a stabilizing factor in major power rivalry; by acknowledging that certain policies directed at a rival's sphere will be treated as extremely aggressive and threatening, major powers are able to reduce the possibility of conflict escalation.

Finally, spheres of influence have a distinct hierarchy. The major power maintains, at the least, the ability to veto the security policies of those states within its sphere when they are viewed as contrary to the interests of the major power. Said otherwise, in contrast to the juridical and legal equality of sovereign states, in practice the security (and frequently economic) policies of the influenced states are subject to tremendous regulation and determination by the major power. Again, the United States in Central America and the Soviet Union in Eastern Europe are prime examples; in both cases they held tremendous sway over the foreign, and frequently domestic, policies of the influenced state, in effect overturning the idea of juridical sovereignty and the principle of noninterference. In general, spheres of influence directly counter the initial post-Cold War hope of an international order premised on cooperation rather than managed conflict; incorporating the security interests of all sovereign states regardless of military power; and expressing the security interests of all states rather than only the most powerful. Spheres of influence pander to the basest understanding of international politics: might makes right.

Haiti, Rwanda, and Georgia

Yet to what extent are there creeping spheres of influence in security affairs? A brief examination of the celebrated cases of the U.S. in Haiti, France in Rwanda, and Russia in Georgia suggests otherwise, and, moreover, isolates a number of important domestic, interstate, and transnational forces that are creating an enduring role for the United Nations. There was little mystery to the fact that Washington sought Security Council resolution 940 on Haiti with its "all necessary means" provision as a blessing for a possible intervention. Because the U.S. sought authorization for an intervention in Haiti, a country it had invaded before and claimed to be within its "backyard," and hardly seemed a genuine threat to international peace and security, this led many observers to claim that the action was nothing more than a return to spheres of influence, with UN approval as little more than a fig leaf.

Various factors undermine a strict reading of it as spheres of influence, however. First, while the U.S. had every interest in overseeing the actual intervention in Haiti, it desired to have the UN involved in the lengthier and more complicated post-intervention Haitian political and economic reconstruction. Without the Security Council's approval, however, neither the UN nor other states were likely to participate in any post-intervention operation. Second, U.S. officials wanted to establish the principle that major powers must obtain authorization for a military incursion in their near abroad from the international community, a plan hardly consistent with the notion of exclusivity. Specifically, many U.S. policymakers feared that Russia might attempt to reestablish military control over the post-Soviet states. By seeking UN approval for its intervention of Haiti, Washington sought to exact some measure of influence over Moscow's future military activities in the so-called near abroad. Pointedly, the Russian Permanent Representative stated that "the Russian Federation attaches great importance to the total transparency of the operation authorized by the Security Council for a multinational force in Haiti. Such transparency is essential to ensure complete confidence in the actions of the multinational force by the international community and support by the international community for that operation."[25] As U.S. officials saw it, the same rule would apply to Russian military activities outside its borders.

Third, the U.S. stressed that it was operating on behalf of the international community. Many observers were troubled by the UN's authorization of an intervention in a state that was not a genuine threat to international peace and security, but there was still considerable sentiment that Haiti represented a concern of the international community. A democracy whose election had been monitored by the United Nations had fallen to a coup, and the world organization had patiently attempted to broker a peaceful resolution to the ongoing crisis. According to one U.S. official, Washington saw itself operating as a lead country, acting on behalf of and with the authority of the United Nations.[26] Another suggested that many Latin American and Caribbean governments supported the U.S. intervention because it would send a strong signal to other would-be leaders of military coups that democracies could not be overturned without some cost.[27] That many Washington pundits interpreted the U.S. decision to seek UN approval for its planned intervention as a renunciation of the Monroe Doctrine signifies how little the UN decision resembles a sphere of influence.[28]

Notwithstanding the Security Council's anguish and embarrassment over its inability to respond effectively to the ongoing massacres in Rwanda, it was unenthusiastic about France's proposed intervention. France had longstanding military and political ties to the very Hutu military that was now accused of committing much of the genocide and was being defeated by the Tutsi-led Rwanda Patriotic Front (RPF). Having intervened only a few years before to support its Hutu allies against the RPF, the Security Council was fearful that France would use the pretext of a humanitarian intervention to intervene on behalf of the Hutu military. Because the RPF also stated that they would treat the French force as hostile meant that the intervention would not have the explicit consent of the parties, and could very well lead to a major military confrontation between a permanent member of the Security Council and the army that was defending the victims of genocide.

Despite these very real concerns, the Security Council's lack of alternatives led it to approve reluctantly the French operation by a vote of ten in favor with five abstentions. Most members used the opportunity of the formal vote to remind France that they would be monitoring its activities and ensuring that it did not depart from the stated humanitarian purpose. In fact, soon after the French landing there were reports that France was considering a more active military mission against the RPF, and the Security Council quickly and repeatedly reminded France of its humanitarian mission and political neutrality.[29] While France's intervention was motivated by domestic pressures and its own sense that as a great power it had certain extraterritorial rights in francophone Africa, the UN represented an institutional constraint on its activities.

Russia's proposed peacekeeping involvement in Georgia also alarmed the Security Council. Boris Yeltsin's desire to seek UN approval appears motivated by two primary factors: the hope that a formal UN blessing would mean that the world body would subsidize Russia's military operation, and the desire for domestic and international legitimacy. Moscow repeatedly claimed that it had genuine security interests in its near abroad, including 25 million ethnic

Russians, stemming the drug traffic, and preventing ethnic conflict in neighboring countries from spilling over into Russia. Hence, the Security Council feared that Russian forces that entered under the guise of the consent of the parties and impartiality would soon take sides in the ethnic and territorial conflict.[30] Indeed, because there were strong suspicions that Russian forces had aided the Abkhazi separatist movement against the Georgian government the previous year, the Security Council feared that by authorizing a Russian peacekeeping presence it was, in fact, sanctioning a military invasion. Notwithstanding these concerns, the Security Council authorized about 2,500 Russian troops on the condition of the simultaneous deployment of 136 UN monitors to ensure that Russia adhered to UN standards of behavior and observed strict neutrality.[31] As most saw it, the UN monitors represented an important mechanism to make sure that Russia would be on its best behavior. France, for one, said that it welcomed the decision by Russia to seek authorization from the UN and, therefore, "this operation thus becomes a part of the process of a political settlement that is under the auspices of the United Nations. . . . It emphasizes the regulatory functions that the Security Council has now shouldered for peace-keeping activities carried out by Powers or by regional forums."[32] The UN would provide an important layer of transparency to encourage Russian troops to abide by the principle of neutrality.[33]

These episodes suggest not spheres of influence or the politics of domination but rather the politics of delegation. The politics of delegation is intimately related to the question of accountability:

> Accountability means the ability to ensure that a mission subcontracted by the international community to a powerful state reflects the collective interests and norms and not merely national imperatives and preferences of the subcontractor.[34]

The politics of delegation and the concept of accountability challenges the notion that the decline of the UN is tantamount to the politics of domination and the emergence of spheres of influence. I want to suggest three ways in which the politics of delegation and accountability undermine a spheres-of-influence reading of the post-Cold War security architecture.

First, these episodes suggest an important relationship between the national and the international interest. While the United States, France, and Russia had tremendous stakes in Haiti, Rwanda, and Georgia, this does not translate into spheres of influence. The Security Council had already defined each episode as a threat to international peace and security and as a concern of the international community before the authorization of the proposed operation. The outcomes sought by the major powers and by the international community were generally consistent. There were real fears that Russia and France might depart from their stated intent of political neutrality and take sides in the conflicts, and there was real opposition to a military solution to the Haitian crisis. Yet the stated goals of these operations—humanitarian assistance in Rwanda, conflict resolution in Georgia, and the return of democracy in Haiti—were highly consistent with the international community's objectives. In each instance, the major power stressed that it was acting on behalf of the international community, and the UN emphasized that the major power was acting as a lead country, being delegated the authority and responsibility by the United Nations. By seeking UN authorization, the major powers essentially abdicated exclusivity and acknowledged that the operation was consistent with its interests and those of the international community.[35]

Second, in addition to a discussion about the ends of the operation, there also was a lengthy discussion about the appropriate means to implement Security Council resolutions. Debates concerned the codes of international conduct and explicit discussion of what those standards were and how the lead country was expected to abide by them. In this respect, to act in a proper manner in these multilateral operations concerns not only the ends to which they are deployed but also the manner in which they operated. These norms emerge because of self-interest and self-understanding; that is, the great powers had a mutual interest in acceding to these norms and therefore holding their rivals accountable to some common standards, and these norms were consistent with previously established understandings of what constitutes legitimate behavior for modern states. In this regard, the Security Council represented an important institutional device to enable states to debate and develop the norms that would guide their behavior.

Third, the Security Council established mechanisms to monitor the behavior of the lead state to ensure that it complied with the codes of conduct and adhered to the goals of the mandate. In short, the UN is monitoring the monitors. The UN monitored Russian forces in Georgia as it had the activities of the Economic Community of West African States Monitoring Group (ECOMOG) in Liberia; in this respect, observer missions have become a central instrument in ensuring accountability.[36] Such monitoring arrangements are far from perfect, as experiences in Georgia and Liberia loudly suggest, but the principle is important and provides states and nonstate actors a device to hold states accountable. As the case of Rwanda suggests, member states also can use their private intelligence sources and the forum of the Security Council to keep the lead countries honest. Parenthetically, the UN is not the only one that can monitor lead states; nongovernmental organizations (NGOs), such as Amnesty International, and intergovernmental organizations (IGOs), such as the Organization for Security and Cooperation in Europe (OSCE), also perform this function. To operate as a third-party mechanism to encourage trust and to keep the parties to the agreement honest requires having freedom of movement in the field and the ability to report its findings to regional and international organizations that are not controlled by the lead party.

What sanctions should and could have been meted out to those who violate the established norms and agreements? There is no doubt that the United Nations lacks acceptable enforcement action in this regard because meaningful sanctions are generally dependent on state power. In this respect, the UN's ultimate and perhaps only true enforcement sanction is the power to withhold approval and to embarrass the party that has violated the established expectations. While moral suasion is generally never enough, it is perhaps unrealistic to expect the United Nations (or any regional organization for that matter) to be able to do more; but because it is unable to punish the violators does not mean that it does not shape the behavior of the lead party in various instances.[37] It is important not to automatically discount the possibility that the search for legitimacy might shape the behavior of even the most powerful states, a subject to which I return later.

In general, the politics of delegation, rather than the politics of domination, imprints various features of the UN's most recent peacekeeping episodes. In contrast to the view that the lead country has imposed its will on the Security Council and used the world organization's approval as a fig leaf for its particularistic interests, I argue that the lead country can be seen as operating similarly to an agent of the international community under the following conditions: 1) when its interests and those of the international community are roughly equivalent; 2) when it agrees to carry out the Security Council resolutions in ways that are consistent with accepted codes of conduct; and, 3) when it accedes to the presence of international monitors who have the authority and freedom to survey and report on the lead country's activities to an independent forum. These are variable conditions, with some operations coming closer to the ideal than others, but the recognition that such conditions are in play undermines a spheres-of-influence view.

The Pull of Multilateralism

Much of the force of this argument hinges on the understanding that major powers will continue to have an interest in operating within a multilateral architecture. I now want to speculate about the domestic, interstate, and transnational forces that are causing the major powers to look to the United Nations (and other multilateral mechanisms) and to retreat from any embrace of spheres of influence. Many policymakers operate with a different understanding of what international and domestic arrangements might further international order. At the international level, there is greater acceptance among policymakers that organizations can foster security cooperation. Rather than pursuing unilateral measures such as building militaries, there is greater interest in developing multilateral arrangements and security institutions. Such sentiments provide an important role for UN and other international forums.

As argued earlier, at the domestic level, policymakers assert that for states to be at peace with each other they must be at peace with themselves. The understanding that there is a strong relationship between domestic and international order is evident in these second-generation peacekeeping operations.[38] Although the idea of multilateralism finds many champions and few opponents, many observers are fearful that a stress on the domestic bases of international order will allow powerful and international organizations to violate juridical sovereignty and the principle of noninterference, and to intervene in the state's domestic affairs. Because such interventions represent a radical departure from international law and are frequently made in the name of the international community, they generally must be authorized and legitimated by international forums such as the United Nations.

Second, a growing cosmopolitanism is leaving its mark on security politics in two ways. States seek not only power but also to be viewed as legitimate by other states. Being viewed as legitimate, however, requires that the state convincingly demonstrates that it abides by and respects the norms of the international community. Power and influence, in this respect, are not a function solely of military might and economic wealth, but also whether the state is viewed by others as adhering to the ideals of the international community. "Nations, or those who govern them," writes Thomas Franck, "recognize that the obligation to comply is owed by them to the community of states as the reciprocal of that community's validation of their nation's statehood."[39] In other words, being viewed as a legitimate member of the international community means behaving in certain ways and not in others. To the extent that the state's influence and power is shaped by its ability to abide by these "standards of civilization,"[40] such norms will have a powerful effect on state behavior.

Whereas states will continue to act unilaterally when their national interests are at stake, changing definitions of security, growing interdependence, and expanded boundaries of the community are causing many states to have their military actions legitimated not only by their citizens but also by the international community. This suggests that the state, which derives its authority and legitimacy not only from its citizens but also from the community of states, is embedded in an increasingly dense normative web that is leaving its mark on the use of military force. This is reminiscent of Inis Claude's argument that states desire not only to be powerful but also to be recognized as acting legitimately and in conformity with the norms of the international community.[41] States, in short, seek collective legitimization. Currently the United Nations articulates the norms of the international community so that it best provides this legitimation function.[42]

Moreover, U.S. officials are increasingly seeking the UN's authority and stamp of legitimacy.[43] In a series of interviews with senior foreign policy officials of the Clinton administration, many spoke of Washington's need to have the world organization legitimate its military activities, and stressed that the domestic and international forces that were prodding this development would operate with nonpartisan effect on Democratic and Republican administrations alike.[44] In fact, the first significant post-Cold War instance was Bush's decision in the fall of 1990 to turn to the United Nations to legitimate the forthcoming war against Iraq. Although many in the U.S. criticized him for asking the UN to legitimate an action that they viewed as a prerogative of a great power and a sovereign state (including Kuwait's right to request assistance in its self-defense), without the United Nations' "stamp of approval" it is doubtful that Congress would have supported Bush's decision to initiate war against Iraq. In general, major powers want to be viewed as acting on behalf, and in a manner that is consistent with the norms of the international community, which increasingly demands UN approval. As Paul Schroeder notes, the ability to participate and accrue the benefits from the group is increasingly dependent on abiding by the group's norms and standards of behavior,[45] and these norms increasingly refer to the state's foreign policy and domestic behavior.

Moreover, individuals and leaders are expressing a sense of obligation and responsibility for those who reside outside the state. While the "CNN factor" is usually uttered in a disparaging tone, its very existence signifies that citizens and their governments frequently feel compelled to help those in distress. In other words, the sense of political community does not stop at the state's borders, for frequently state officials and citizens express a strong sense of obligation and responsibility to provide humanitarian assistance to those in need, regardless of their place on the geopolitical map. For instance, in 1994 at a time when the Clinton administration had stated unequivocally that it would not provide any direct military assistance to Rwanda, a top-ranking State Department official boldly predicted that U.S. troops would be in Rwanda within six weeks because of the pressure "to do something." When queried about the source of these pressures, he replied that they derived from a "responsibility of being part of the international community."[46] Another State Department official who was very involved in the drafting of Presidential Decision Directive 25 (PDD25), the May 1994 interagency review on multinational peacekeeping operations, commented that it was critical to strengthen the UN's peacekeeping abilities for humanitarian operations, otherwise the U.S. would have to become more fully involved. Moreover, he said that the U.S. will continue to feel compelled to contribute to humanitarian operations and that it is better to act multilaterally than unilaterally.[47]

Third, major powers are generally seeking ways to defray the costs of their security activities. In other words, being the sole power also means being a single payer, and most major powers are increasingly looking for ways to defray their security costs. Before becoming part of such a coalition, however, states are insisting that the operation be viewed as consistent with the interests and norms of the international community, that is, be blessed by the United Nations. For instance, Washington arguably would have had a more difficult time obtaining coalition partners in its campaign against Iraq had it not received UN support. Burden sharing also has an important functional dimension: although great powers might have a greater interest in those geographical areas that are viewed as related to their traditional foreign policy and security concerns, they are not necessarily interested in monopolizing all phases of peace operations.

Specifically, much of the concern over spheres of influence pertains to direct military intervention by major powers, that is, to peacekeeping operations, and not to either peacemaking or peace building. Yet the major powers appear quite willing to have regional organizations, the United Nations, and other international organizations play a larger role in these other phases of peace operations. For instance, as Washington attempted to assemble a multinational operation for post-invasion Haiti, a chief concern was recruiting the civilian police that was to retrain and monitor the Haitian security forces; it discovered, however, that many of the most likely contributors, notably Canada, were unwilling to participate unless they flew under a UN flag rather than under the "banner of a U.S. led invasion force."[48] In general, because of increasing budgetary pressures at home, major powers will continue to look to the UN and other multilateral mechanisms for financial and security assistance; to entice other states to join a coalition, however, frequently requires a UN stamp of approval.

Finally, the major powers express little enthusiasm for patrolling security waters far from their immediate shores. The notion of spheres of influence connotes that great powers administer those areas that are viewed as inextricably linked to their security, yet one of the prominent features of the post-Cold War period is that they have difficulty discerning when their national interests are truly at stake. This is, of course, most obvious in the United States since the collapse of the Cold War; domestic priorities now overshadow foreign policy concerns, and many senior policymakers concede that defining U.S. national interests adrift from containment is a nearly impossible assignment. In response to the Security Council's authorization of the U.S. invasion of Haiti and much discussion of the possibility of spheres of influence, a senior State Department official commented that he doubted that there would be spheres of influence because the major powers had very little interest in playing that kind of role. The unwillingness by the major powers to become highly active far from home means that no action is taken; regional organizations become more involved (which is highly doubtful given their weakness); or a multilateral coalition is forged and sponsored by the United Nations. In fact, he continued, even if there were spheres of influence, the UN would have an important caretaking role for the many "orphans" that would result from any such arrangement.[49] The discussions over collective intervention in Zaire in the fall of 1996 suggest that such dynamics and considerations have outlasted disappointments in Somalia and Bosnia.

In general, there are centrifugal forces that propel the UN to search for major powers and regional organizations to help with a rather expansive security agenda, and there are centripetal tendencies that pull them back to and defeat any purely and consistently instrumental use of the United Nations. "Much of what the UN can do in the area of international security regime building," James Schear notes, "does not require rigid adherence to the ideal of collective security."[50] In this respect, perhaps one of the most important functions of the UN is to articulate and repeat what constitutes proper behavior. The UN's effectiveness and ability to compel states to abide by the norms of the international community derives from its moral suasion. Such suasion is not always effective, but frequently it is. The UN can be judged effective to the extent to which states change their behavior; "it is not an all-or-nothing proposition."[51]

Conclusion

After the Cold War, many observers hoped that the UN might become a muscular security organization that possessed real enforcement capacities and expressed the interests of all its members rather than just the most powerful. Such visions, however, outstripped either what the UN was immediately capable of accomplishing or what the member states were willing to support. The inevitable malaise that follows unfulfilled expectations caused some to prematurely abandon the UN and others to suggest that its only role is simply to provide a fig leaf for the foreign policies of the powerful. The world organization is becoming irrelevant once again.

This perceived irrelevance is particularly clear in the growing interest in spheres of influence and regional security organizations. There are people who suggest that what is occurring (and perhaps what should occur) are spheres of influence in which major powers patrol particular expanses of real estate and thus help to ensure global stability. Regional organizations, to the extent that they are dominated by a single power, are functionally equivalent to spheres of influence. Most regional organizations that are moderately effective have a small group of states that are willing to contribute disproportionately to the "collective" enterprise. In some instances they might be acting as an agent of the regional community, but in others such an agency is tied to self-interest.

But even those who see some merit in spheres of influence are loath to resurrect the concept at its worst. Famous here is Charles William Mayne's call for spheres of influence (with a layer of accountability) in which the great powers are designated with the authority to help keep the peace.[52] In making this call he recognizes the basic understanding that major powers are likely to commit significant resources only when their interests are at stake, but he hopes to moderate such impulses with an overlayer of recognized norms that suggest what interventions are deemed legitimate and how they should be conducted. He subtly suggests that such norms are created through the United Nations. And many recent studies of regional security organizations suggest that those that are most effective are also those that have established some norms that hold even the most powerful member accountable to the group and restrain its military activities.[53] Because of scarce resources and (something of) a division of labor, sometimes there will be a cop on the beat, sometimes there will be community patrols (regional organizations), and sometimes an outside security service (the United Nations), but in all instances the international community has a strong interest in making sure that all cops operate according to the accepted standards.

Such observations underscore that, as scholars search for the underlying logic of the coming security architecture, they would do well to examine the interplay between transnational norms that govern the conduct of military activities and state power. This lesson can be drawn from the contemporary concern that the United Nations is being by-passed in favor of spheres of influence. There is little doubt that the UN has seen better days and that the major powers have in the past and will continue to have in the future a strong influence over the UN's activities and operations. After all, that was understood by the very design of the Security Council that reserved veto power for the most powerful.

But thus far the UN's security arrangements are better characterized by the politics of delegation than the politics of domination. While the UN might not be the implementing agent in most security operations, it retains an important function. Global and domestic forces are propelling even the most powerful states to look to the UN for legitimacy, to adopt a multilateral posture, and to desire to be seen as operating in a manner that is consistent with international interests and expectations. Such developments continue to assign to the United Nations an important role in security affairs. The world organization remains an important place where states debate and articulate the norms of acceptable behavior and then establish mechanisms of transparency that encourage those operating in its name to adhere to those norms. This function might not be as glamorous as the vision of blue helmets stationed around the world, but it is probably more realistic, perhaps more efficient, and unarguably critical to a more effective and desirable security order.

Notes

1. The research for this article was supported by a Council on Foreign Relations International Affairs Fellowship, where the author resided at the U.S. Mission to the United Nations, and the United States Institute of Peace.

2. "Spheres of Influence," *Financial Times*, August 8, 1994, 12; James Boone, "US and Russia Broker Haiti Invasion Deal," *London Times*, August 8, 1994, 9. Madeline Albright is quoted as saying that these recent authorizations denote "spheres of influence peacekeeping." Robert Manning, "Foreign Policy That Wears Its Heart on the Sleeve," *Los Angeles Times*, September 11, 1994, M1.

3. Document S/PV.3407, July 21, 1994, 8.

5. For an extended discussion of this point, see Michael Barnett, "The New U.N. Politics of Peace: From Juridical Sovereignty to Empirical Sovereignity." *Global Governance* 1, no. 1 (winter 1995): 79–97.

4. "A U.N. License to Invade Haiti," *New York Times*, August 2, 1994, A20.

6. The relationship between domestic and international conflict is an underlying theme of various commissions and reflections on the post-Cold War security architecture. See Boutros Boutros-Ghali, *An Agenda for Peace 1995* (New York: United Nations, 1995); Commission on Global Governance, *Our Global Neighborhood* (New York: Oxford University Press, 1995); Gareth Evans, *Cooperating for Peace* (St. Leonards, Australia: Unwin and Hyman, 1993); and Report of the Independent Working Group on the Future of the United Nations, *The United Nations in Its Second Half-Century* (New York: Ford Foundation, 1995).

7. *An Agenda for Peace*, para.20.

8. Paul Lewis, "The Peacekeeper in Chief Needs More Soldiers," *New York Times*, March 4, 1994, 2. See John MacKinlay and Jarat Chopra, "Second Generation Multinational Operations," *Washington Quarterly* (summer 1992): 113–131, for an extended discussion of this definition.

9. See John Ruggie, "The U.N.: Wandering into the Void," *Foreign Affairs* 72 (November/December 1993): 26–31.

10. Julia Preston, "U.N. Officials Scale Back Peacemaking Ambitions," *Washington Post*, October 28, 1993, A40. Quoted from Thomas Weiss, "UN Responses in the Former Yugoslavia: Moral and Operational Choices," *Ethics and International Affairs*, 8, 1994, 13. The Commission of Inquiry, which investigated the circumstances leading to the attacks on UNOSOM II personnel, concluded that peace enforcement activities should be avoided whenever possible. *Report of the Commission of Inquiry Established Pursuant to Security Council Resolution 885* (New York, February 24, 1994): 40–42.

11. Responding to President Clinton's suggestion that the UN become more active in peace enforcement and battling the Bosnian Serbs, UNPROFOR Force Commander Michael Rose said, "If someone wants to fight a war here on moral or political grounds, fine, great, but count us [the UN] out. Hitting one tank is peacekeeping. Hitting infrastructure command and control, logistics, that is war, and I'm not going to fight a war with painted tanks." Roger Cohen, "U.N. General Opposes More Bosnia Force," *New York Times*, September 29, 1994, A7.

12. President Bill Clinton, "Address to the United Nations General Assembly," September 27, 1993 (U.S. Department of State, Bureau of Public Affairs, 1993).

13. Document S/PRST/1994/22, May 3, 1994.

14. Gillian Tett, "Red Tape Tangles up UN Troops in Bosnia," *Financial Times*, January 21, 1994, 6; Julia Preston, "Supply Office at U.N. Hamstrung by Probe," *Washington Post*, August 20, 1994, A1, A14.

15. Marguerite Michaels, "Blue Helmet Blues," *Time*, November 15, 1993, 45; Lacia Mouat, "UN is Forced to Rethink Peacekeeping Missions," *Christian Science Monitor*, January 18, 1994, 18; and, "United Nations Peacekeeping: Trotting to the Rescue," *Economist*, June 25, 1994, 19–22.

16. Quoted in Lacia Mouat, "Need for Peacekeepers in Balkans May Force UN to Revise Its Rules," *Christian Science Monitor*, March 16, 1994, 3.

17. See, for instance, Paul Lewis, "Allies at Odds with U.S. on Bosnia Command," *New York Times*, September 12, 1993, A22; Roger Cohen, "Dispute Grows Over U.N.'s Troops in Bosnia," *New York Times*, January 20, 1994, A8; Boutros Boutros-Ghali, "Don't Make the UN's Hard Job Harder," *New York Times*, August 20, 1993, A24; Richard Bernstein, "Italian General Who Refused Order in Somalia is Removed," *New York Times*, July 15, 1993, A10.

18. Also see Michaels, "Blue Helmet Blues," 45; Mouat, "UN is Forced to Rethink Peacekeeping Missions," 18; and, "United Nations Peacekeeping," 19–22.

19. See U.N. staff paper, "The United Nations, Regional, and Sub-Regional Organizations." Also see Michael Barnett, "Partners in Peace? The United Nations, Regional Organizations, and Peacekeeping," *Review of International Studies* 21, no. 4 (fall 1995): 411–33.

20. Ibid, iv.

21. Author interview with high-level State Department official, August 2, 1994. Also see Ann Devroy and Julia Preston, "Clinton Still Undecided on Haiti Invasion," *Washington Post*, July 16, 1994, A1, A18.

22. The many "Friends" groups, a handful of states that volunteer to take a strong interest in a particular peacekeeping operation, that have become a nearly institutionalized feature of all peacekeeping operations since the end of the Cold War, are a precursor to, and less formalized response to the same dynamics that are supposedly driving spheres of influence.

23. Paul Keal, *Unspoken Rules and Superpower Dominance* (New York: St. Martin's Press, 1983): 16–18.

24. Ibid., 15.

25. Document S/PV.3413, July 31, 1994, 23.

26. Interview with author in New York City, August 18, 1994.

27. Author interview in Washington D.C., June 8, 1994. Also see Howard LaFranchi, "Why Outcry Not Heard from Latin Neighbors on Haiti," *Christian Science Monitor*, September 22, 1994, 1.

28. Charles Krauthammer, "Good-bye, Monroe Doctrine," *Washington Post*, August 2, 1994, A15.

29. Interview with staff member of the U.S. Mission to the United Nations, August 12, 1994.

30. Andrew Katell, "Motive Doubted as Russian Troops Go 'Near Abroad,'" *The Washington Times*, March 29, 1994, A13.

31. "U.N. Endorses Russian Troops for Peacekeeping," *New York Times*, July 22, 1994, A3.

32. Document S/PV.3407, July 21, 1994, 4. Also see Douglas Hurd and Andre Kozyrev, "Challenge of Peacekeeping," *Financial Times*, December 14, 1993, 14, where they write that any Russian peacekeeping force must abide by basic CSCE and UN principles of consent of the parties and political neutrality.

33. Also see John Thornhill, "U.S. Approves Role of Russian Troops within CIS States," *Financial Times*, September 7, 1994, 16.

34. Jarat Chopra and Thomas G. Weiss, "The United Nations and the Former Second World: Coping with Conflict," in Abram Chayes and Antonia Chayes, eds., *Preventing Conflict in the Post-Communist World: Mobilizing International and Regional Organizations* (Washington, D.C.: Brookings Press, 1996): 529.

35. See Lea Brilmayer, *American Hegemony: Political Morality in a One-Superpower World* (New Haven, Conn.: Yale University Press, 1994) for a political and legal treatment of the idea of hegemony on behalf of the community.

36. Chopra and Weiss, "The UN and the Former Second World," 528.

37. Ibid., 529–30, for a discussion of noncompliance.

38. See Barnett, "The New U.N. Politics of Peace," for an expanded discussion of this argument.

39. Thomas J. Franck, *The Power of Legitimacy Among Nations* (New York: Oxford University Press, 1990): 196.

40. Gerrit Gong, *The Standard of 'Civilization' in International Society* (New York: Oxford University Press, 1984).

41. Inis L. Claude, Jr., "Collective Legitimization as a Political Function of the United Nations," *International Organization* 20 (summer 1966): 367–79.

42. See especially the essays in Laura Reed and Karl Kaysen, eds., *Emerging Norms of Justified Intervention* (Cambridge, Mass.: American Academy of Arts and Sciences, 1993).

43. Ernst B. Haas argues that a rough measure of the legitimacy of the United Nations is the degree to which "member states invoke its purposes and principles . . . to justify national policy." *Beyond the Nation-State* (Palo Alto, Cal.: Stanford University Press, 1964): 133.

44. Not all welcome the increased tendency of the U.S. to go to the United Nations for approval. Congressman Bereuter, for one, remarked: "One of the growing perceptions in this post-cold war era seems to be that we need some sort of multilateral approval, usually the U.N., in order to take action, even though it is clearly in our national interests, and I am, frankly, concerned about that." Committee on Foreign Affairs, House of Representatives, *U.S. Participation in United Nations Peacekeeping Activities* (Washington, D.C.: U.S. Government Printing House, 1994): 50.

45. "The New World Order: A Historical Perspective," *Washington Quarterly* 17 (1994): 33.

46. Interview with author in Washington, D.C., June 27, 1994.

47. Interview with author in Washington, D.C., June 8, 1994.

48. Eric Schmitt with Michael Gordon, "Looking Beyond an Invasion, U.S. Plans Haiti Police Force," *New York Times*, September 11, 1994, A12.

49. Interview with author in New York City, August 2, 1994.

50. James A. Schear, "Global Institutions in a Cooperative Order: Does the United Nations Fit?" in Janne Nolan, ed., *Global Engagement: Cooperation and Security in the 21st Century* (Washington, D.C.: Brookings Press, 1994): 246.

51. Oran Young, "Effectiveness of International Institutions," in James N. Rosenau and E. Cziempel, eds., *Governance Without Governments* (New York: Cambridge University Press, 1992): 163.

52. Charles William Maynes, "A Workable Clinton Doctrine," *Foreign Policy*, 93, (winter 1993): 3–20. Also see Terry Terriff and James Keeley, "The United Nations, Conflict Management, and Spheres of Influence," *International Peacekeeping* 2, no. 4 (winter 1995): 510–35.

53. See Michael Barnett and Emanuel Adler, "Conclusion," in Emanuel Adler and Michael Barnett, eds., *Governing Anarchy: Security Communities in Theory, History, and Comparison* (forthcoming).

5

Constraints on Adaptation in the American Military to Collective Conflict Management Missions[1]

Robert B. McCalla

In the post-Cold War era, the demand for multinational peace operations has grown substantially. One result is that the United Nations (UN) has become involved in a wider range of peace operations in the past five years than ever before. This has been done either through the Security Council issuing resolutions that call on members of the international community to take action (as in operations Provide Comfort and Restore Hope) or through the direct supervision and involvement of UN forces and personnel (as in Bosnia and Cambodia).[2] Regional organizations like the North Atlantic Treaty Organization (NATO) also have become involved (as in the former Yugoslavia) and have stated a willingness to consider the requests of other international bodies like the Organization for Security and Cooperation in Europe (OSCE).[3] The demand for greater multinational peace operations has been accompanied by a growing recognition in the United States and elsewhere that Washington's involvement in such operations is necessary and desirable, politically and practically. Much attention has been focused on the question of when and how the U.S. will participate in such operations, but substantial organizational and political obstacles remain. This chapter addresses the question: What are the organizational and institutional obstacles that affect post-Cold War military adjustments by the U.S. to peace operations?

Current American military strategies, and the force structures to support them, reflect the Cold War's legacy. With dramatically changing world politics, military roles and missions are undergoing major adjustments. The U.S. continues to be well prepared to deal with traditional military threats to interests and allies (like that posed by Saddam Hussein in the Gulf War), but it is less well prepared politically and militarily to deal with contingencies that involve low-intensity conflict (as when the mission to Somalia moved beyond its humanitarian roots) or are essentially noncombat in nature (such as the deployment of U.S. forces to Haiti and Bosnia). The American doctrinal emphasis on heavy forces as a means of winning wars was appropriate to the primary Cold War missions, and remains essential to enforcement operations, but does not suffice for the wider range of peace operations currently discussed.[4]

There are two types of obstacles standing in the way of American adjustment to peace operations under a regime of collective conflict management (CCM). Structural obstacles arise because of the historical legacy of the Cold War and its impact on the orientation and composition of the armed forces. Cold War imperatives resulted in forces primarily trained and equipped to deal with a historically-contingent set of threats. Making adjustments to these forces will be doubly difficult because of the uncertainty about the proper response to a changed international environment and the difficulties of making changes in a military organization comprising four separate branches with unique but generally complementary functions. Organizational obstacles arise from self-interests and identities that have developed within the U.S. armed forces during the Cold War. Force structures and missions benefited certain service subgroups (for example, the Strategic Air Command and carrier-based forces) at the expense of others (close air support and air- and sea-lift). Many that benefited from Cold War missions stand to gain little under most peace operations, increasing the likelihood of opposition to change.

A strength of existing literature is the recognition that organizations are political entities, comprised of competing factions that contest organizational identity, direction, and control over resources.[5] An institution's ability to change is dependent on how much proposed changes affect its power centers, identity, and traditional ways of operating. Peace operations in the post-Cold War world mean significant changes for the U.S. armed services, moving them into areas where there exist little or no past experience or self-identity, thus increasing the cost of such change.[6]

Necessary adjustments in organization, structure, training, and culture can be made, but not without considerable difficulty. With effort, a football team can be retrained to play soccer. The coaches and the players would have to devise new plays under a different set of rules. A different, longer-term orientation to strategy and tactics would be needed, emphasizing skill and finesse rather than brute force. Defensive linemen would have to learn a new type of "tackle;" offensive linemen would have to lose weight and learn to run for more than a few yards at a time; the quarterback, running backs, and receivers would have to learn to share the ball with the rest of the team; players would have to learn to play both offense and defense while adjusting to continuous play with little prospect of relief from the sidelines; and everyone would have to learn that only the goalie is allowed to touch the ball with his hands!

The argument first addresses the nature of organizations and their dual tendencies towards inertia and change. Next, the Cold War missions of the United States armed forces are considered along with the similarities and differences in peace operations. The core of the chapter discusses the structural and organizational obstacles to change, highlighting the interplay between organizational interests and history. Finally, the conclusion examines the opportunities for change as the United States adjusts to international efforts in collective conflict management.

Organizational Stasis and Change

Existing literature about state behavior in response to external change is a source of both insight and puzzlement. Traditional Realists, for example, argue that states will respond to threats in the international environment, either through balancing behavior or internal adjustments in national capabilities.[7] The path that these adjustments take is assumed to be under the control of national leaders who are ultimately responsible for the direction of security policy.[8] As security is the top priority for the state, necessary changes to state policy are assumed because to do otherwise would undermine security.

Missing from many traditional explanations of behavior is how states make changes.[9] There is not a seamless link between the external environment and state responses to that environment. Uncertainty about external threats is compounded by the question of proper responses to threats. In addition, as the literature on bureaucratic and organizational politics makes clear, there are frequently large gaps between security decisions and their implementation.[10] Also missing from the literature is an appreciation of the way that assessment and implementation interact and affect policy outcomes. Past responses to threats are the foundations on which future change occurs. Thus policymakers' response to change is doubly constrained by both the existing security framework and the interests of those actors that are members of that framework.

Analyses about the responsiveness of military organizations to exogenous changes, and the political framework in which they operate, points to contradictions. There is a growing literature that addresses "innovation" within military organizations—how and why changes in doctrine and force structure occur.[11] One line of argument is that military organizations, disliking change, will only make changes in response to a major military failure or significant change in the international threat environment.[12] Left to themselves, military organizations will not develop new doctrines or force structures but will generally keep doing what they have always done.[13] A different line of argument is that innovation in doctrine emerges when the internal power structure of a military organization changes, allowing officers supportive of new doctrines to rise through the ranks.[14] Still another perspective notes that military institutions are attentive to changes in the nature of their opponent's military capabilities and, as a result, will innovate even in the absence of pressure from their political leaders' or military failure.[15] Clearly military organizations will be responsive to international changes—the key question is what direction they will take.

Finally, this literature often uses cases where military organizations must respond to increased threats, not shrinking ones. Under-preparedness in the face of military threats frequently spurs military innovation. Yet the situation facing the U.S. military is that it is over-prepared to deal with military threats in the new international environment and under-prepared to deal with new missions. Existing analyses tell us little about how we might expect military organizations to respond with respect to doctrine and force structure in such situations.[16] Understanding these difficulties of adjusting to a changed international threat environment is key to understanding the adjustment of the U.S. armed forces to the post-Cold War world.

Military Missions

As Joseph Lepgold and Thomas Weiss discussed in the first chapter, the variety of labels and terms associated with peace operations is large. Three key dimensions emerge: the level of military force, the degree of unilateral or multilateral involvement, and the degree of hostility or cooperation among the parties.[17] In addition, many of the different missions can be concurrent, which adds even greater complications.[18] The traditional Cold War missions of the U.S. armed forces are compared below with some of the missions proposed for the new era and summarized in Table 5.1.[19]

Deterrence and Defense

The primary Cold War task was to deter attacks on the United States and its allies. Heavily-armed troops at home and abroad were part of allied commitments, supported ultimately by nuclear weapons. The use of force in the context of regional alliances was allowed under the provisions of Article 52 of the United Nations Charter. Intrastate disputes were largely irrelevant unless they were accompanied by external aggression or an allied government requested American forces. For these missions, the full combat capabilities of each branch were available. Given the known location of major threats, there was little need for the global movement of large numbers of forces except as reinforcements for allied commitments. In the post-Cold War era, the U.S. continues to be concerned about regional threats (for example, Iraq and North Korea) as well as

Table 5.1
Service Roles and Participation in Different Missions

	Army	Air Force	Navy	Marines	Guard/Reserve
Cold War: Deter and defeat enemies; defense if needed; offense preferred; allies; primarily interstate conflicts; military means dominate	Heavy forces; armor and artillery dominant; equipment in key locations; forces in place with reserves to follow	Long-range bombing and fighters; transport secondary; Army troops and reserves moved to meet equipment	Power projection and sea control; aircraft carriers and submarines; transport secondary	Limited amphibious and low-intensity conflict operations	Reinforcement and support units—combat and noncombat play large roles
Enforcement: Deter and reverse aggression; primarily interstate conflicts; military means when diplomacy fails; combat operations	Heavy forces; armor and artillery dominant; transport essential to move force to meet threat	Heavy forces; long and short range bombing; fighters; transport of Army equipment and troops essential	Power projection and sea control; aircraft carriers and submarines; transport of Army equipment and Marines key	Limited amphibious and low-intensity conflict operations	Reinforcement and support units—combat and noncombat play large roles
Selective Enforcement: Protect weak from aggression and oppression; diplomacy key; latent military threat; intrastate with potential external effects; combat and noncombat operations	Light and heavy forces play role; inter- and intratheater mobility of troops and equipment key	Light and heavy forces; air patrol and surveillance; key role in transport of Army equipment and troops	Limited power projection; surveillance; transport and support of Marines; transport of Army equipment	Limited amphibious and low-intensity conflict; noncombat roles; evacuations	Logistics and noncombat support; limited combat roles in long-duration commitments; rotation with regular forces
Peacekeeping: Diplomacy and conflict resolution; lightly armed defensive force; inter- and intrastate; noncombat operations	Lightly armed forces; mobility important; support units greater role; no combat role	Primarily transport and logistical role; surveillance	Primarily transport and logistics for Army and Marines surveillance	Noncombat roles; patrol and evacuations	Logistics and noncombat support
Preventive Deployment: Key role is to deter and reassure; to avoid combat but be prepared for it if needed	Latent combat role but mostly a presence "just in case;" if extended stay, logistics becomes critical	Latent combat role; if extended stay transport and logistical role become more important	Latent combat role; transport and logistical role become more important if extended stay	Noncombat roles intended	Most likely logistics and noncombat support

various nuclear threats (for example, China, North Korea, and a resurgent Russia),[20] but none is as large as the Soviet threat once was.

Enforcement

The idea of an international community coming together to use force against aggression has received much attention since U.N. Secretary-General Boutros Boutros-Ghali published his *An Agenda For Peace.*[21] The reversal of the Iraqi invasion of Kuwait in 1991 illustrates the concept: an aggressor is identified and action is initiated to deal with the threat. Like the traditional Cold War missions, enforcement is primarily interstate. International support in the form of multinational coalitions or U.N. authorization is important but not necessary. In the post-Cold War climate, nuclear weapons play a minimal role, but in all other respects this mission is essentially the same as the traditional Cold War scenarios. One change is that the declining presence of U.S. forces abroad places a much higher premium on mobility than in the past.

Selective Enforcement

The selective use of military force, generally assumed to be under UN or multilateral control, seeks to bring hostile parties to an agreement. The interposition of international forces between warring parties in Bosnia or the use of military force to protect Kurds in northern Iraq are examples. Identification and pursuit of an aggressor are possible, as is neutrality accompanied by diplomacy in pursuit of a peaceful settlement. The level of involvement can be both inter- and intrastate. The need for heavily-armed forces is important in these missions, but their role is usually more latent, with greater emphasis on minimal coercion. The most combat-capable forces are used less often and lighter forces, along with noncombat support units (medical, logistical, food and water, civil affairs), are given greater roles.

Peacekeeping

Traditionally, peacekeeping involves the introduction of impartial, lightly-armed forces in an effort to prevent a recurrence of conflict. Force is used only in self-defense, and prior consent of the parties to the conflict is common. These activities are almost always done under the sanction of international bodies, most often the United Nations, for both inter- and intrastate conflicts. Light ground forces are most important, with air forces providing logistical support, mobility, and surveillance. Sea-based forces can also play a role in providing logistics and mobility. Finally, these actions frequently occur alongside humanitarian efforts.[22] Washington had little involvement in these types of action during the Cold War

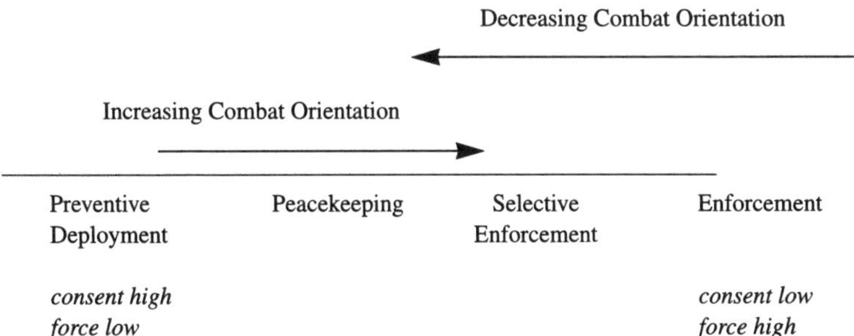

Figure 5.1
Missions and Military Operations

and the possible involvement in these missions has been a recent source of controversy.

Having considered these variables, we see that a key feature is how much combat orientation relates to different missions. In Figure 5.1, the centrality of combat orientation to a mission declines as one moves away from the traditional Cold War missions towards peacekeeping and preventive deployment. Like the Cold War mission, enforcement missions accord top priority to combat skills and power. Recalling our preceding discussion, Table 5.1 illustrates the different roles played by the services for each of these missions, and shows how different elements within each service play more or less prominent roles under different missions. This is a key feature to understanding potential structural and organizational obstacles to new missions.

Structural Obstacles

The overall direction and structure of any organization is the result of a complex dynamic that involves both internal and external factors, as well as past and current activities. Organizational structure is the product of historical processes that interweave external environmental features with internal processes of organizational development and change. Changes in structure and direction necessitate breaks with past practices and alterations in the internal makeup of an organization. Past changes in an organization, for whatever reason, acquire characteristics of both momentum and inertia. The momentum comes from past practices, as organizations tend to do in the future what they have done in the past.[23] This tendency has both practical (change in organizational structure and routine is expensive) and self-serving purposes (it allows the organization to maintain its claim on roles and the resources that accompany them). Inertia is seen in the resistance to change; absent external changes, organizational perspectives, and outlooks are likely to remain stable.

Military organizations are frequently portrayed as being prepared to "fight the last war" and resistant to change, for both doctrinal and self-serving reasons. Change in structure and doctrine comes when there is pressure from above (civilian leaders and resource providers), externally forced changes (defeat on a battlefield or a change in an opponent's capabilities), or shifts in the internal balance of power among factions.[24] The nature of change is well illustrated by the adjustment to peace operations and the obstacles encountered in terms of primary opponent and threat; overall mission and measure of success; strategy, force structure, weapons, and training; and allies, logistics, and support. Examining each of these dimensions, which are summarized in Table 5.2, shows that as American armed forces adjust to new missions, the adjustment is harder the further that they move away from the traditional Cold War missions. The further to the left on the continuum in Figure 5.1, the greater the obstacles to, and difficulties of, change.

Primary Opponent and Threat

A key issue in all military planning and force development is the nature of the perceived threat, which serves as the foundation for all other activities. Organizations of all types function better with a clear sense of mission and purpose. The Soviet threat during the Cold War provided a clarity of purpose and direction to Washington's thinking about national security.[25] Like a spotlight shining in a dark night, the Soviet threat concentrated the attention of U.S. planners in a way that made non-Soviet threats much less noticeable. There were other threats that concerned American policymakers during the Cold War, but none matched Moscow in terms of its impact on U.S. force structure and planning.

In the post-Cold War world, the luxury of having a known and agreed-upon enemy no longer exists. As Les Aspin wrote in the 1994 *Annual Report to the President and the Congress*:

> We no longer have the Soviet threat against which to measure our defense. It is hard today to overestimate how completely the Soviet threat dominated our force structure, our strategy and doctrine, even the design of our weapons. Now, it is gone. What do we need a defense for? For decades we had no reason to ask such fundamental questions about defense. *The Soviet threat supplied the answers.*[26]

The post-Cold War world has created significant uncertainty, and attempts to develop new planning scenarios have attracted considerable controversy.

Table 5.2
Structural Impacts on Changes in Roles and Missions

	Traditional War Missions: Cold War and Enforcement	Peace Operations: Selective Enforcement, Peacekeeping, and Preventive Deployment
Primary Opponent and Threat	*Cold War:* Large, organized, known location, identifiable threat and capabilities *Post-Cold War:* State actors with significant military capabilities, potential locations known	Uncertain and unknown—from terrorists to organized militias to organized armies
Overall Mission and Measure of Success	*Cold War and Post Cold War:* Deter threats to allies and interests; defeat if deterrence or diplomacy fails; measure of success is military victory.	*Peace Establishment:* Intervene in disputes, domestic and interstate, that threaten international peace and nonstate actors, peace and stability is goal *Peacekeeping:* Maintain agreed-upon peace through diplomacy and conflict resolution *Humanitarian:* Relieve suffering, natural and non-natural
Strategy, Force Structure, Weapons, and Training	*Cold War:* Heavy forces, massive firepower, speed; large units, rigid structure, hard to mix and match from services; nuclear weapons underpin strategic position; combat oriented training of forces *Post-Cold War:* Same with decreased or nonexistent nuclear role	*Peace Establishment:* Force and diplomacy crucial; lighter forces, use of firepower very limited; training to emphasize nonforce coercion; longer deployments; emphasis on nonmilitary units *Peacekeeping:* Light forces with defensive mandate; emphasis on constabulary roles and neutrality; longer deployment; interaction with nonmilitary units *Humanitarian:* Light forces if at all; logistical and support units play greater role; greater interaction with nonmilitary units
Allies, Logistics, and Support	*Cold War:* Dominant US role in allied relations; allies play crucial role; few units supporting large fielded forces; forward deployments to match interests; infrastructure generally in place to support interests; prepositioned equipment at most likely battlefield *Post-Cold War:* U.S. dominance less automatic, subject to negotiation; few units supporting large fielded forces; limited forward deployment or infrastructure due to uncertain threats; allies forces and infrastructure of less use; greater reliance on prepositioned equipment	*All missions:* U.S. can act alone or with allies; allies on more equal basis; many units supporting smaller forces; deployments and areas of interest do not always coincide; no assured infrastructure available

Peacekeeping, preventive deployment, and to a lesser extent selective enforcement do not lend themselves to thinking in terms of a "threat" or "opponent." This not only complicates military planning but also constrains efforts to develop public support.

Overall Mission and Measure of Success

A key element of any organization is a conception of "mission" and "success."[27] All armed forces have a similar basic mission: to protect their country and its interests from physical harm and intimidation. During the Cold War, with the threat from Moscow prominent in the minds of policymakers and the public alike, the resulting national security goals were simple and straightforward: containment of the Soviet Union and its allies.[28] To do so, Washington needed to build a military force that was strong enough to deter the Soviet Union and its allies and defeat them if deterrence failed. Measuring the adequacy of national security efforts was conceptually straightforward: identify the threat and assess the adequacy of the response.[29] The Soviet threat was the yardstick against which the U.S. measured the adequacy of its defense efforts. The existence of such a clear external threat provided a sense of mission to the armed forces that increased cohesion and improved the overall level of military effectiveness.

Following the Cold War, U.S. security planning has been in a state of flux. The primary mission of the armed forces remains the protection of American interests. Without a clear threat, however, the specific nature of that mission is subject to considerable debate and discussion. Also without a clear threat, developing and refining priority missions becomes problematic. Politically, the lack of a clear and compelling threat, or the existence of many smaller threats competing for attention, creates problems for the armed forces as they seek resources from Congress or support from allies.[30]

With respect to the various missions described in Table 5.1, the Cold War and enforcement missions lend themselves most easily to thinking in terms of deterrence and defeating an enemy. The peacekeeping and preventive deployment missions clearly are devoid of such thinking. Selective enforcement combines elements of both. Figure 5.1 shows this complication, with the overlapping of combat and noncombat orientations. The enforcement mission requires the least adjustment to the combat-oriented outlook and focus found in the armed forces of the Cold War. With peacekeeping at the other end of the spectrum, combat orientation is explicitly eschewed, lending a certain clarity to the mission. Preventive deployment is potentially the most difficult, as it requires the armed forces to hope for peace but be prepared for war.

Clearly, the perception of threats affects how the overall mission of the armed forces is conceptualized and how success in carrying out those missions is measured. This in turn considerably influences strategy, the force structure, and weapons procurement.

Strategy, Force Structure, and Weapons

The overall strategy of the United States during the Cold War was built on the dual elements of containment and deterrence.[31] The historic reliance on the mobilization potential of the military and economy in time of war was no longer sufficient.[32] The dominance of the Soviet threat meant that the force structure and the equipment procured for them was specifically tailored to that threat. This meant a strong emphasis on heavily-armed forces, tanks and artillery deployed in massive formations supported by sea-borne missile and artillery fire, engaging enemy forces at long distance through air power, and all backed up by tactical and strategic nuclear forces. With the advantage of a known enemy and geography, forces could be supplied and garrisoned in fixed locations near the front lines. Strategic mobility was less of an issue because with the possible battleground known in advance, preparations could be made, and troops transported to join prepositioned equipment.

The strategy and force structure followed from the threat and geography. The Air Force focus on strategic and tactical air power, with a lesser emphasis on mobility, directly resulted from the fact that U.S. forces could be stationed abroad to deal with threats to allies.[33] Prepositioned troops and equipment allowed the Air Force to devote a far larger proportion of its force to combat roles rather than transportation. The Navy was also able to focus relatively more resources on combat capability than on sealift capability.[34] Like the Air Force, the Navy could take advantage of the fact that the U.S. had forces stationed abroad, reducing the need for sealift capabilities and allowing the Navy to emphasize offensive doctrines and strategy over sealift.[35] Even though the Army was, and remains, dependent on the grudging support of the Navy and Air Force for the movement of its troops, it was able to indulge its preferences for heavy forces, even though that limited mobility. Having allies on the frontlines of the most prominent threat allowed the Army to station heavy forces abroad and not have to worry as much about how to move them to trouble spots.

Overall, the Cold War doctrinal emphasis was on the compression of force and time, with defensive operations expected against Soviet forces in Europe and offensive operations elsewhere. Massive force would be applied quickly, with the aim being the overwhelming defeat of the enemy in the shortest period of time with the smallest number of casualties, an approach with deep roots in American military tradition.[36]

In addition to the force structure, strategy and weapons procurement were directly affected. The Cold War versions of the Army's authoritative guide to doctrine, FM 100-5 *Operations*, emphasized the need for heavily armed forces to deal with the Soviet threat. Much less attention was paid to lighter and more mobile forces that might be useful against lesser threats. The Air Force's emphasis on strategic nuclear bombing and air superiority meant that aircraft for close air support and air lift missions received less attention. The Navy similarly developed its naval doctrine and forces with the Soviet threat in mind.[37] In short, the Soviet threat exerted an influence that carried through from threat, to mission, to strategy, to force structure, and finally to weapons system.

In the post-Cold War world, many of these assumptions and certainties are in question.[38] While Operation Desert Storm illustrated the importance of large conventional forces, it also showed the difficulties of moving them to distant crisis points. Had Saddam Hussein moved quickly beyond Kuwait into Saudi Arabia, the situation would have been, in the words of the Pentagon's *Final Report on the Gulf War*, "precarious."[39] Moving troops and equipment will increasingly become an issue in the post-Cold War era as the U.S. reduces its forces deployed abroad and fewer countries allow American troops within their borders.

In addition to mobility, there is a growing mismatch between the goals of peace operations and the means to pursue them. The European context of U.S. force development and deployment, with its well-developed infrastructure of road, railways, and airfields, allowed weapons designers to create 60-ton M1 tanks and fighter aircraft that need long runways. Bosnia has shown some of the limitations of this equipment, as armored vehicles, including "light" armored vehicles, have found roads too narrow, or bridges too weak.[40] And Bosnia's infrastructure is relatively advanced compared with that in many developing countries where such operations are expected to occur most often.

In addition to force structure and weaponry, how the U.S. trains its forces is crucially important to understanding adjustment problems. Making the adjustment to enforcement operations will require the least change in existing training whereas preventive deployment and peacekeeping will require the most.[41] Cold War training assumed that by preparing troops for the most serious contingencies, they were automatically developing capabilities that can be used at lesser levels of conflict.[42] This sentiment is captured by the comment of former Commandant of the Marine Corps General Carl Mundy, "The best peacekeepers are the best warriors."[43] Training a soldier to be a "warrior" imparts a different outlook and set of skills than training to be a "peacekeeper."[44] Taking troops with combat training and asking them to be peacekeepers will be a difficult adjustment:

> The U.S. military organization is organized, trained, and equipped to fight wars in which they inflict the maximum possible violence in the minimum period of time with the lowest possible casualties. They are designed to close with the enemy and kill him.[45]

As former Defense Secretary Les Aspin said: "If a soldier reacts like a policeman in a military situation, he's dead; if he reacts like a soldier in a police situation, he creates an international incident."[46] Or as military sociologist Charles Moskos put it, "Peacekeeping isn't a soldier's job, but only a soldier can do it."[47]

The adjustments required of the Navy and Air Force are also significant. As Table 5.1 outlined, peacekeeping and preventive deployment, with their greater demand for noncombat and transport functions, take the Air Force further away from its traditional Cold War focus on bombers and fighter aircraft. A similar shift is true with the Navy as it focuses on sea control, and to a lesser extent power-projection, which is in less demand than rapid sealift to trouble spots.

Allies, Logistics, and Support

The Cold War structure of U.S. armed forces took advantage of a visible primary threat, the Soviet Union, and of allied willingness to allow American soldiers and equipment in their countries. Washington stationed up to 100,000 troops in Europe where, along with equipment for them and their reinforcements, they were able to train in the most likely scenario for future battles. Being able to focus resources on combat capabilities, rather than having to expend a great deal of resources on mobility forces, was another advantage of known threats and reliable allies.[48]

Allies and logistics were critically important to the Cold War missions and remain so for enforcement missions because of the need for large and heavy forces. As Operations Desert Shield and Desert Storm showed, having U.S. forces deployed in Europe helped shorten deployment time for troops to the Persian Gulf. Key in future scenarios will be stationing of military hardware abroad because moving soldiers is faster and easier than moving their tanks, artillery, and trucks.[49] The need for allied support and logistics becomes less crucial for most peace operations because of the decreased emphasis on combat forces. The problem that faces planners in the post-Cold War era is that many of the places where forces are likely to be needed are distant from American forces and allied resources. An increase in U.S. spending on mobility in the 1980s was offset by weight—even the lightest forces like the 82d Airborne Division and the 101st Airborne Division have increased in physical weight by 29 and 89 percent respectively since 1980.[50]

Support units and training are additional concerns. U.S. combat forces are supported by many different units, from legal support and intelligence, to civil administration and communication. Over the years, these support units have become very efficient, providing support with minimal numbers of personnel to large combat units. Military planners strive constantly to improve the "tooth to tail" ratio by decreasing the number of support personnel ("tail") relative to combat personnel ("tooth") in any given unit. Despite this, a more active role in post-Cold War peace operations will be constrained by the availability of support units. The U.S. Army's deployment of only a portion of the 10th Mountain Division's combat troops (one of two brigades) to Somalia took almost all of the intelligence, aviation, and command units—effectively neutralizing the remaining brigade.[51] The number of support personnel does not decrease proportionately with the number of troops deployed. Sending a quarter of a unit's combat troops does not mean that one can send a quarter of the support units. This is less of a problem for enforcement roles because whole division-sized units are likely to be sent to trouble spots, but more likely when smaller units, or portions of units, are sent on preventive deployment or peacekeeping missions.[52]

The pressures of ever-shrinking numbers of troops and support leave little room for the traditional combination of deployment and stateside training intervals. Because of the rotation policies generally used for forces deployed on noncombat missions (deployment for four to six months, followed by six to eight months training and refitting), two units will usually be unavailable for each unit deployed.[53] A General Accounting Office (GAO) study found that "it can take up to six months for a combat unit to recover from peace operations and become combat ready."[54] Units that could normally expect to return to their home base for extended periods of training and refurbishment find themselves coming home, only to be sent off promptly to the next trouble spot. A study released in August 1994 by the Department of Defense noted that the frequent deployment of Marine units was having very serious consequences for Marine readiness and morale.[55] In short, post-Cold War cuts in forces are creating constraints on carrying out peace operations while at the same time still being prepared for military operations.[56]

Organizational Obstacles

The obstacles discussed to this point would be difficult to overcome, even with determination from political and military leaders. Other obstacles to making the transition to peace operations relate to the organizational identity and self-interests of various players. Military organizations, like others, resist change and innovation that results from outside pressure because it erodes their autonomy and freedom of action. Those innovations that are preferred will be those that expand service autonomy and resources.[57] In addition, military officers have internalized the view that the military has been given a special role in defending the state and as a result will resist any innovation or change that, in their view, undermines security.[58] A parochial incentive to protect the institution combined with the professional ethos to protect the state, results in substantial resistance to changes in military missions.[59] Cold War history shows a number of significant battles that emerged when outsiders tried to influence the direction of the U.S. military, both with respect to what it did and the power relationship among the services.[60] There is no reason to think that similar responses would not emerge in response to efforts to move away from major emphasis on the Cold War missions to more peace operations.

Organizational identity and self-interest on the part of the U.S. armed forces creates obstacles to change that are summarized in Table 5.3.

Services' Core Mission and Weapons Systems

All organizations develop an identity that relates to the organization's primary mission and the agreed-upon means of carrying it out. Those parts of the organization that are most closely tied to the primary mission benefit from

Table 5.3
Organizational Impacts on Changes in Roles and Missions

	Traditional War Missions: Cold War and Enforcement	Peace Operations: Selective Enforcement, Peacekeeping, Preventive Deployment
Service's Core Mission and Weapon System	*Air Force:* Long-range attack and air superiority—bombers and fighters; ICBMs and bombers in deterrent role *Navy:* Power projection, sea control and strategic deterrence—carrier, attack submarine; ballistic missile submarine in deterrent role *Army:* Attack and hold ground—tank and artillery *Marines:* Amphibious power projection	*Air Force:* Transport and air patrols for PM, PK and Humanitarian *Navy:* Transport and air patrols for PM, PK and Humanitarian *Army:* Ground presence and show of force for PM and PK, noncombat support for others *Marines:* Ground presence and show of force
Organizational Center of Power and Flexibility	*Air Force:* SAC early, TAC later *Navy:* Carrier and Submariners *Army:* less clear—artillery and armor *Marines:* Does not exist	*Air Force:* More likely transport (Air Mobility Command, not Air Combat Command) *Navy:* "Brown shoe Navy"—surface ships and transports *Army:* Logistics and mobility Forces *Marines:* All?
Civil-Military Relations and Decisionmaking	Deter known opponent; defeat if deterrence fails. Fits U.S. CM thinking—politicians decide on priorities, military carries out task; less of role for White House and State once operation underway	Prevent conflict, restore peace, contribute to stability—confounds civil-military tradition because cannot use military criteria for military role—are essentially political criteria that military is asked to deliver on; more role for State Department, with greater potential for clashes (e.g. Somalia)

increased resources and status. Challenges to the centrality and status of those missions will be resisted by those whose interests will be affected.[61] Those whose Cold War roles are not as prominent under peace operations stand to lose organizational prestige and support.

During the Cold War, the primary task of the Air Force was the delivery of nuclear weapons on the Soviet Union through the use of long-range strategic bombers and later, ballistic missiles.[62] Conventional missions (air superiority, close air support, interdiction) were of secondary importance, while airlift was at the bottom of the Air Force priority list. Of the armed services, the Air Force received the largest portion of the peacetime defense budget through most of the Cold War; and within the Air Force, the Strategic Air Command (SAC) was the most favored recipient because its main focus was deterring the Soviet Union (and later China) with the threat of nuclear attack.[63] The Commander in Chief of the Strategic Air Command (CINCSAC) was also in charge of the overall U.S. strategic nuclear weapons planning programs, further tying the Air Force to the Soviet threat. The Air Force's other main elements, the Tactical Air Command (TAC), and the Military Airlift Command (MAC), were tied to roles that were less dependent on the Soviet threat. TAC was in charge of fighter and ground attack aircraft, carrying mainly conventional weapons. Its role developed primarily in response to conventional war scenarios in NATO. MAC was always the poor cousin of the Air Force's three branches. Its main function was to provide transportation for troops and equipment, including Army rapid reaction forces such as the 82d and 101st Airborne in their role of moving quickly to trouble spots.

In terms of Cold War budget, missions, and identity, the core of the Navy was its aircraft carriers and submarine forces (both attack submarines and ballistic missile submarines).[64] While the Navy also had devoted a significant portion of its forces and planning to countering the Soviet threat, it had other responsibilities including power projection in the Third World and sea control. Navy responsibilities were truly worldwide, both because of their support of the principle of freedom of the seas as well as needing to provide secure sea lanes of communication to U.S. allies and interests.

Army Cold War strategy emphasized heavy armor formations and heavy artillery support as the key to the Soviet threat. To the degree that mobility was emphasized, it was a peripheral support function that was secondary to heavy forces, or only a small portion of the overall force, like the 82d Airborne.[65] Making the transition to lighter and more mobile forces will be difficult because supporters of heavy forces have been dominant in the upper echelons of the Army since the mid-1970s.[66]

In the post-Cold War era, enforcement operations will likely generate the least resistance, because they require the least change in the power structure among, and within, the services.[67] Peacekeeping (and to a lesser extent preventive deployment) missions potentially entail greater organizational conflict, as these operations are inherently ground-based, which will greatly favor the Army and Marines. Within the Air Force and Navy, those elements with the most to contribute to these operations (air- and sealift, as well as close air support and surveillance) have historically been the weakest actors, yet they will be called on most often in, and benefit from likely post-Cold War scenarios. The Army and Marines have a much longer history of operations similar to peace operations, especially humanitarian efforts, both at home and abroad, than do either the Air Force or Navy (outside of transport units) and are likely to find the transition easier to make. Some observers have suggested making greater use of National Guard-type training, and even National Guard units, in ÒOperations Other Than War" (OOTW) rather than deploying troops whose primary role is combat. The Posse Comitatus Act notwithstanding, National Guard troops are used for domestic problems, including restoration of public order, rather than Army troops because their training and general orientation is more attuned to these types of roles.[68]

Organizational Center of Power and Flexibility

Closely related to the issue of the prevailing doctrine within an organization is the center of power and how that affects organizational flexibility. Organizational flexibility, or the degree of responsiveness in responding to both internal and external changes and pressures, has two elements. The first is how much internal rigidity, or how much the well-being of an organization (particularly with respect to resources) is tied to a particular organizational subgroup. The more closely the health of an organization is tied to a particular subgroup, the less flexibility the organization will have in responding to changes that negatively affect that subgroup. When the fortunes of an organization are closely tied to a dominant subgroup, the organization will have less flexibility among its different parts as they respond to changes.[69] An example of this internal rigidity is found in the Air Force, making it difficult for the organization to respond flexibly to new or nontraditional missions because it would undermine SAC, a dominant subgroup highly dependent on Cold War roles and missions.[70]

A second element of organizational flexibility is "doctrinal flexibility"—the "tightness" of an organization's attachment to a particular doctrine or technical means of following the doctrine. An organization's doctrine influences organizational behavior and structure and becomes a reference point for organizational decisionmaking. An example of a doctrine pervading an entire organization is that of the Marine Corps, where the dominant organizational theme is amphibious assault—a central theme defended in the face of claims that it is outmoded and anachronistic.[71] A narrow doctrine tightly held can hurt an organization and severely degrade its performance when it no longer applies. For example, the Air Force's narrow task conception of strategic air power, reflecting SAC's dominance, had little application outside of the Cold War context, and its performance in Vietnam suffered as a result.[72] As the Cold War ended, the Air Force was left without much room to maneuver because of its historically narrow definition of its task conception. The Army, by contrast, had a less constrained view of its doctrine and organizational essence. Its AirLand Battle doctrine, first announced in 1982 with the Soviet threat in mind, proved to be sufficiently flexible to have application beyond that context.[73] Subsequent efforts by the Army to modify its doctrine and strategy in light of changing world events have shown similar flexibility.[74] The lack of dominance of any one branch of the Army has meant that Army doctrine has been able to shift over time as needed, without running into entrenched interests, or supporting a single doctrine or mission, a point taken up below.

The end of the Cold War has called into question the Air Force's historic primary mission. Outside enforcement missions, forces central to the Cold War Air Force, especially long-range bombers and fighter aircraft, play virtually nonexistent roles in other peace operations. The relative utility of long-range Air Force bombing compared to carrier-borne bombing remains hotly contested, and the Navy currently occupies a stronger position than the Air Force. Its primary fighting platform, the aircraft carrier, was flexible enough that the Navy could adapt in the post-Cold War era to a growing nonnuclear role and a growing role outside the context of NATO. Nonetheless, the Navy's role in most peace operations will be less on the high seas, where carriers and submarines are most free to operate, and more in coastal and littoral waters where these forces are more constrained and traditional surface ships and marine forces play a much greater role.[75]

The key point here is that the organizational centers of gravity, corresponding to the core missions, are in areas that are less useful to the needs of most peace operations, particularly within the Air Force and Navy. So, in an odd twist of fate, those functions that traditionally have received the least attention and resources within the Air Force and Navy (air- and sealift) now are the most important contributions that these two services can make as peace operations replace traditional Cold War missions. Overall, the addition of organizational self-interest to structural obstacles make for a formidable challenge to change.

Conclusion

Of all the military services, the Army has had the least difficulty in adjusting its organizational repertoire to include peace operations. The Cold War Army never developed a central strategic doctrine tightly linked to platforms and missions, like strategic bombing or the Navy's maritime strategy.[76] During the Cold War, no branch within the Army emerged as dominant as SAC or carriers and submarines in the Navy.[77] The Army has not been as dependent on a type of weapon system as either the Air Force (long-range strategic bomber) or the Navy (aircraft carrier), making the Army less vulnerable to changes in the threat for which a weapons system is particularly suited.[78] The Army focused its attention in the post-World War II era on a particular mission, that of defending against the Soviet threat to Western Europe. This focus has meant that the Army simply changed its approach to this mission as the threat (or perception of threat) changed.[79] Thus when the threat that the Army was prepared to defend against changed, the Army changed as well, seeking out new threats that it could prepare for. It is no coincidence that of the various professional military journals, Army publications (particularly *Military Review* and *Parameters*) have dealt the most with these issues in the past five years.

The Navy has been able to adapt as well because of the relatively greater flexibility of Navy weapons systems and doctrine. The Navy could argue that its forces were prepared to deal with a wide range of combat and noncombat contingencies, especially nonnuclear contingencies, without straining credibility; the Air Force, dominated by the Strategic Air Command for over a quarter-century, could not.[80] The Navy has less to offer for peacekeeping (an essentially ground-based operation for the transport of Army and Marine units) but more for preventive deployment and enforcement missions, where the early application of military force or military presence from globally-deployed forces could make a difference.[81] The Navy's *From the Sea* document, which outlined its thinking about post-Cold War roles and missions, emphasizes the need for greater coastal and littoral operations and calls for greater Navy support of Marine operations.[82]

The implications of this review are significant for our understanding of states and their security needs, as well as our understanding of military organizations. The traditional assumptions of realist and neo-realist theories about the adjustment of states to changes in their external environment need to be leavened with a greater sensitivity to the problems of internal adjustment. Security actors within states are not neutral responders to their environment. They actively seek to shape and interpret the environment in ways that are beneficial to them and their views of the world. In addition, the legacy of past responses by states to security threats acts as a brake on adjustments to a changing environment. The degree of doctrinal and institutional development in response to threats will be greater when there is a larger threat or when the threat is longstanding. Both of these conditions were met in looking at Washington and its response to Moscow. The Soviet Union was seen as a mortal and enduring threat, resulting in an institutional response on the part of American armed forces that had great organizational depth and complexity. Changes in such institutions do not come easily, even with the best of intentions.

In addition to understanding the historical legacy of the Cold War, this chapter also has made clear that organizational adjustment will face resistance and challenge as elements within the armed forces find that new roles and missions are not as rewarding as old ones in terms of prestige and resources. The existing literature on organizational and bureaucratic politics treats this issue well but largely overlooks the intersection of structural and organizational obstacles to change.

This chapter also emphasizes another commonly ignored element of organizational adaptation and innovation: How do military organizations adjust to a shrinkage of external threats? History has examples of the successes and failures of states adjusting to new or increased threats in their external environment. Examples of stasis are hard to find, yet that is what the United States and its armed forces have confronted with the end of the Cold War. The United States has found itself simultaneously over-prepared and under-prepared for its new environment. It is over-prepared for its traditional security roles because there is simply no current threat that requires the massive military structure that was necessary for the Cold War. As at the end of previous wars, American armed forces have fought among themselves over who has to take the cuts and how much the overall cuts should be. Yet, unlike the end of World War II when the Soviet threat quickly loomed, or the end of Korea and Vietnam, where regional conflicts ended against a backdrop of ongoing concerns about the Soviet threat elsewhere, the current situation has doubly-challenged the armed forces. Downsizing has happened before, and the interservice rivalries that occurred as a result are readily understood. However, the second challenge, that of organizational innovation and adaption in the absence of significant external threat, is inadequately analyzed within the existing literatures. This chapter has shown how such change and adaptation can be understood.

Notes

1. Many thanks to my research assistant, David Green, for his work on this project.

2. The United Nations and NATO are the significant actors involved thus far. See John Mackinlay and Jarat Chopra, "Second Generation Multinational Operations," *Washington Quarterly* 15, no. 3 (summer 1992): 113–131; and British American Security Information Council, *NATO, Peacekeeping, and the United Nations*, Report 94.1 (London/Washington, D.C., September 1994); William J. Durch, ed., *The Evolution of UN Peacekeeping: Case Studies and Comparative Analysis* (New York: St. Martin's Press, 1993) and *UN Peacekeeping, American Policy and the Uncivil Wars of the 1990s* (New York: St. Martin's Press, 1996).

3. A contentious series of meetings within the alliance resulted in a decision in June 1992 to allow the OSCE to call on NATO forces for peacekeeping activities, and a

decision in September 1992 to consider similar UN requests. See John Kriendler, "NATO's Changing Role: Opportunities and Constraints for Peacekeeping," *NATO Review* 41, no. 3 (June 1993): 16–23.

4. Many within the defense community use the phrase "Operations Other Than War" (OOTW). This includes all uses for military forces outside of traditional combat operations but does not exclude the use of military force at lower levels. For a discussion of the variety of terms and their implications for the U.S., see William W. Allen, Antoine D. Johnson, and John T. Nelsen, II, "Peacekeeping and Peace Enforcement Operations," *Military Review* 73, no. 10 (October 1993): 53–61; Horace L. Hunter, Jr., "Ethnic Conflict and Operations Other Than War," *Military Review* 73, no. 11 (November 1993): 18–24; and Richard N. Haass, *Intervention: The Use of American Military Force in the Post-Cold War World* (Washington, D.C.: Carnegie Endowment, 1994): 49–65. An early discussion is Richard H. Taylor, "What Are These Things Called 'Operations Short of War'?" *Military Review* 68, no. 1 (January 1988): 4–7. For a comparison of different labels for the spectrum of operations and their different impacts on security in different countries, see John Mackinlay, "Improving Multifunctional Forces," *Survival* 36, no. 3 (autumn 1994): 157.

5. See Peter M. Blau, and Marshall W. Meyer, *Bureaucracy in Modern Society,* third edition (New York: Random House, 1987); John R. Kimberly, "Environmental Constraints and Organizational Structure," *Administrative Sciences Quarterly* 20, no. 1 (1975): 1–9; William A. Lucas and Raymond H. Dawson, *The Organizational Politics of Defense* (Occasional Paper, no. 2 of the *International Studies Association,* 1974); Charles Perrow, *Complex Organizations: A Critical Essay,* third edition (New York: Random House, 1986); J. Guy Peters, *The Politics of Bureaucracy*, third edition (New York: Longman, 1989); and James Q. Wilson, *Bureaucracy: What Government Agencies Do and Why They Do It* (New York: Basic Books, 1989). Edward Rhodes, "Do Bureaucratic Politics Matter? Some Disconfirming Findings From the Case of the U.S. Navy," *World Politics* 47, no. 1 (October 1994): 1–41, argues that bureaucratic politics does not play as much of a role as commonly believed.

6. For an insider's look at the difficulty of these types of missions, see John P. Abizaid, "Lessons for Peacekeepers," *Military Review* 73, no. 3 (March 1993): 11–19.

7. See James D. Morrow, "Arms versus Allies: Trade-offs in the Search for Security," *International Organization* 47, no. 2 (spring 1993): 207–37; Eric J. Labs, "Do Weak States Bandwagon?" *Security Studies* 1, no. 3 (spring 1992): 383–416; Robert G. Kaufman, "To Balance or Bandwagon? Alignment Decisions in 1930s Europe," *Security Studies* 1, no. 3 (spring 1992): 417–47; Stephen M. Walt, "Alliance, Threats, and U.S. Grand Strategy: A Reply to Kaufman and Labs," *Security Studies* 1, no. 3 (spring 1992): 448–82; Robert G. Kaufman, "The Lessons of the 1930s, Alliance Theory, and U.S. Grand Strategy: A Reply to Stephen Walt," *Security Studies* 1, no. 4 (summer 1992): 690–96; and Barry R. Posen, *The Sources of Military Doctrine: France, Britain, and Germany Between the World Wars* (Ithaca, N.Y.: Cornell University Press, 1984): 59–67.

8. Stephen D. Krasner, "Are Bureaucracies Important? (Or Allison Wonderland)," *Foreign Policy* 7 (summer 1972): 159–71; Leslie H. Gelb and Richard K. Betts, *The Irony of Vietnam: The System Worked* (Washington: Brookings Institution, 1979).

9. Kenneth N. Waltz, *Theory of International Politics* (Reading, Mass.: Addison-Wesley, 1979): 7–74. He is very clear that he is not attempting to create a theory of foreign policy but rather to show that the international system will favor those states that are responsive to it over those that ignore it. Although this is certainly the case with Waltz's nuanced argument, his structural realist framework has little room for variations in the degree of responsiveness, both desired and actual, of states to changes in the international system. See also Joseph Lepgold, *The Declining Hegemon: The United States and European Defense, 1960–1990* (New York: Praeger, 1990): 72–73.

10. Graham T. Allison, *Essence of Decision: Explaining the Cuban Missile Crisis* (Boston: Little, Brown and Company, 1971). For a recent update, see Jonathan Bendor and Thomas H. Hammond, "Rethinking Allison's Models," *American Political Science Review* 86, no. 2 (June 1992): 301–22. Posen, *The Sources of Military Doctrine*, assesses the strength of these two competing strands of argument while Rhodes, "Do Bureaucratic Politics Matter?" is a recent, critical addition to this debate.

11. Kimberly Marten Zisk, *Engaging the Enemy: Organizational Theory and Soviet Military Innovation, 1955–1991* (Princeton: Princeton University Press, 1994), builds on but does not completely accept Posen's argument in *The Sources of Military Doctrine*. For contrary views, see Stephen Peter Rosen, *Winning the Next War: Innovation and the Modern Military* (Ithaca, N.Y.: Cornell University Press, 1991), and "New Ways of War: Understanding Military Innovation," *International Security* 13, no. 1 (summer 1988): 134–168.

12. Posen, *Sources of Military Doctrine*, 222–226.

[12]Rosen, *Winning the Next War*, is critical of this line of argument, suggesting instead that military organizations can and do innovate without the pressures of external intervention by political leaders or failure on the battlefield.

13. Posen, *The Sources of Military Doctrine*, 18–22.

14. Zisk, *Engaging the Enemy*, 26.

15. An initial effort is Robert B. McCalla, "Coping with Uncertainty: How the United States Armed Forces Respond to a Changing World" (Paper Presented at Southern Political Science Association Meetings, Atlanta, Georgia, November 5–7, 1992); and Robert B. McCalla, "'When Johnny Comes Marching Home:' Organizational Response of the United States Armed Forces to a Changing World," (Paper presented at the International Studies Association, Vancouver, British Columbia, March 19, 1991).

17. Richard N. Haass also has identified twelve different types of peace operations, as well as discussion of the conceptual and policy complications that arise in trying to sort these out in his *Intervention*, 49–65; Martha Bills, Robert Butto, John Culclasure, Marvin Hall, Roberto Marrero-Corletto, and John Scales, *Options for U.S. Military Support to the United Nations* (Washington, D.C.: Center for Strategic and International Studies, December 1992); Allen, Johnson and Nelsen, "Peacekeeping and Peace Enforcement Operations;" James H. Baker, "Policy Challenges of UN Peace Operations," *Parameters* 24, no. 1 (spring 1994): 13–26; John B. Hunt, "Hostilities Short of War," *Military Review* 73, no. 3

(March 1993): 41–50; Mackinlay and Chopra, "Second Generation Multinational Operations;" Taylor, "What Are These Things Called 'Operations Short of War'?"; Edward E. Thurman, "Shaping An Army for Peace, Crisis, and War: The Continuum of Military Operations," *Military Review* 72, no. 4 (April 1992): 27–35; and Henk Vos and James Bilbray, "NATO, Peacekeeping and the Former Yugoslavia." Draft Interim Report of the North Atlantic Assembly, International Secretariat, Sub-Committee on Defence and Security Co-Operation Between Europe and North America, May 1994. (Document AL 78: DSC/DC (94) 2). Available in electronic form from NATO via NATO's Gopher.

18. Thurman, "Shaping an Army for Peace, Crisis, and War," 31–35.

19. A review of the match between UN missions and U.S. military capabilities is Bills, et al., *Options for U.S. Military Support to the United Nations*.

20. See Les Aspin, *Annual Report to the President and the Congress, January 1994* (Washington, D.C.: GPO, 1994).

21. Boutros Boutros-Ghali, *An Agenda for Peace 1995* (New York: United Nations 1995), contains the original 1992 Report and a 1995 *Supplement*. For a discussion of these terms and their military content, see Bills, et al., *Options for U.S. Military Support to the United Nations* and British American Security Information Council, *NATO, Peacekeeping, and the United Nations* and British American Security Information Council, *NATO Peacekeeping, and the United Nations*.

22. Thomas G. Weiss and Kurt M. Campbell, "Military Humanitarianism," *Survival* 33, no. 5 (September/October 1991): 451–465, and Thomas G. Weiss, "Military-Civilian Humanitarianism: The 'Age of Innocence' Is Over," *International Peacekeeping* 2, no. 2 (summer 1995): 157–174. See also Chris Seiple, *The U.S. Military/NGO Relationship in Humanitarian Interventions* (Carlisle, Penn.: U.S. Army War College, 1996).

23. The best-known proponent is Allison, *Essence of Decision*; see also Wilson, *Bureaucracy*.

24. Posen, *The Sources of Military Doctrine*; Zisk, *Engaging the Enemy*; Rosen, *Winning the Next War*; Wilson, *Bureaucracy*.

25. The literature is immense, including Michael M. Boll, *National Security Planning: Roosevelt through Reagan* (Lexington, Ky.: University of Kentucky Press, 1988); Russell F. Weigley, *The American Way of War: A History of United States Military Strategy and Policy* (New York: Macmillan, 1973); John Lewis Gaddis, *Strategies of Containment* (New York: Oxford University Press, 1982); Maurice A. Mallin, *Tanks, Fighters & Ships: U.S. Conventional Force Planning Since World War II* (McLean, Va.: Brassey's, 1990); Allan R. Millet and Peter Maslowski, *For the Common Defense: A Military History of the United States*, Revised and Expanded (New York: Free Press, 1994); and Carl H. Builder, *The Masks of War: American Military Styles in Strategy and Analysis* (Baltimore, Md.: The Johns Hopkins University Press, 1989). For the nuclear dimension, Lawrence Freedman, *The Evolution of Nuclear Strategy*, second Edition (New York: St. Martin's Press, 1989), and David Alan Rosenberg, "The Origins of Overkill: Nuclear Weapons and American Strategy, 1945–1960," *International Security* 7, no. 4 (spring 1983): 3–71.

26. Aspin, *Annual Report*, xiii, emphasis added.

27. Wilson, *Bureaucracy*, 90–110.

28. See generally John Lewis Gaddis, *Strategies of Containment* (New York: Oxford University Press, 1982). On threat assessment, see Lawrence Freedman, *U.S. Intelligence and the Soviet Strategic Threat*, Revised Edition (Princeton, N.J.: Princeton University Press, 1986).

29. For a critical review of U.S. success, see John M. Collins, *U.S.-Soviet Military Balance* (New York: McGraw Hill, 1980) and *U.S. Defense Planning: A Critique* (Boulder, Colo.: Westview Press, 1982).

30. Congressman Ike Skelton, "Joint and Combined Operations in the Post-Cold War Era," *Military Review* 73, no. 9 (September 1993): 2–12.

31. See Samuel P. Huntington, *The Common Defense: Strategic Programs in National Politics* (New York: Columbia University Press, 1961); Alain C. Enthoven and K. Wayne Smith, *How Much Is Enough?: Shaping the Defense Program, 1961–1969* (New York: Harper Colophon Books, 1971); Michael M. Boll, *National Security Planning: Roosevelt through Reagan* (Lexington, Ky.: University of Kentucky Press, 1988); and Maurice A. Mallin, *Tanks, Fighters and Ships: U.S. Conventional Force Planning Since World War II* (Washington, D.C.: Brassey's, 1990).

32. See Huntington, *The Common Defense*; Millet and Maslowski, *For The Common Defense*; and Weigley, *The American Way of War*.

33. Robert F. Futrell, *Ideas, Concepts, Doctrine: a History of Basic Thinking in the United States Air Force 1907–1964* (Maxwell Air Force Base, Ala.: Arno Press Inc., 1980); Michael E. Brown, *Flying Blind: the Politics of the U.S. Strategic Bomber Program* (Ithaca, N.Y.: Cornell University Press, 1992); and Norman Polmar and Timothy M. Laur, eds., *Strategic Air Command: People, Aircraft, and Missiles*, second edition (Baltimore, Md.: Nautical and Aviation Publishing Company, 1990).

34. The most comprehensive review of post-World War II Navy history is James L. Lacy, *Within Bounds: The Navy In Postwar American Security Policy* (Alexandria, Va.: Center for Naval Analysis, July 28,1983): 83–1178. See also Michael T. Isenberg, *Shield of the Republic: The United States Navy in An Era of Cold War and Violent Peace, 1945–1962*, Volume 1 (New York: St. Martin's Press, 1993); and Clark G. Reynolds, *The Fast Carriers: the Forging of an Air Navy* (Huntington, N.Y.: Robert E. Krieger Publishing Company, 1978).

35. Lacy, *Within Bounds*; and Isenberg, *Shield of the Republic*.

36. Karl W. Eikenberry, "The Challenges of Peacekeeping," *Army* 43, no. 9 (September 1993): 15.

37. For a useful overview of this connection between threat, strategy, and weapons, see Mallin, *Tanks, Fighters, & Ships*.

38. David E. Albright, "Threats to United States Security in a Post-Containment World: Implications for United States Military Strategy and Force Structure," *In Depth* 2, no. 3 (fall 1992): 149–199.

39. U.S. Department of Defense, *Conduct of the Persian Gulf War: Final Report to Congress* (Washington, D.C.: GPO, January 1993): 390. The prompt response of the Clinton administration in October 1994 to the movement of Iraqi troops near the Kuwaiti border was an explicit recognition of the need to move quickly in order to forestall any future problem.

40. Francis Tusa, "Is the West Ready for the Wars of the Nineties?," *Armed Forces Journal International* (July 1993): 39–40.

41. Abizaid, "Lessons for Peacekeepers"; Allen, Johnson, and Nelsen, "Peacekeeping and Peace Enforcement Operations"; Thurman, "Shaping An Army for Peace, Crisis, and War."

42. Richard Halloran, "An Army for the 21st Century," in Robert L. Pfaltzgraff, Jr. and Richard H. Schultz Jr., eds., *The United States Army: Challenges and Missions for the 1990s* (Lexington, Mass.: Lexington Books, 1991): 250–251.

43. *USA Today*, June 7, 1995, p. 11.

44. The experiences of US forces in OOTW in Somalia and Florida (following Hurricane Hugo) suggest that at the lowest unit levels there is little need for specialized training. What is needed is expanded training at the upper levels of service staffs, as it is their orientation and outlook that will affect how their troops operate in these new environments. S. L. Arnold and David T. Stahl, "A Power Projection Army in Operations Other Than War," *Parameters* 23, no. 4 (winter 1993/1994): 22. Abazaid suggests that new training is needed at all levels, in "Lessons for Peacekeepers."

45. *Atlanta Constitution*, September 20, 1993, 5.

46. *Wall Street Journal*, September 8, 1994, p. 18.

47. Quoted in Kenneth Allard, *Somalia Operations: Lessons Learned* (Washington D.C.: National Defense University Press, 1995): 3.

48. Ted Greenwood, "Strategic Mobility in the 1990s" in Robert L. Pfaltzgraff, Jr. and Richard H. Schultz Jr., eds., *The United States Army: Challenges and Missions for the 1990s* (Lexington, Mass.: Lexington Books, 1991): 225–226.

49. The time to deploy U.S. forces to Kuwait in October 1994 in response to Saddam Hussein's feint towards Kuwait was considerably shorter than it had been in August 1990. During the October 1994 deployment, the U.S. moved as many troops to Kuwait in 24 hours as it had in three weeks in August 1990 because much of the equipment for the troops was already in Kuwait or on supply ships in the Indian Ocean. *Journal of Commerce* (October 20, 1994): 2–B. See also Greenwood, "Strategic Mobility in the 1990s," 229–233.

50. Greenwood, "Strategic Mobility in the 1990s," 228–229.

51. *US News and World Report,* November 15, 1993, 50.

52. Some have suggested that it would be unusual for brigade-sized units to remain intact, possibly splitting up into three different units. However, in order to support

deployments as small as this, with training prior to deployment and post-mission recovery, a whole division might be affected, thus limiting further deployments. Allen, Johnson, and Nelsen, "Peacekeeping and Peace Enforcement Operations," 59–60.

53. Baker, "Policy Challenges of UN Peace Operations," 21.

54. U.S. General Accounting Office, "Peace Operations: The Effect of Training, Equipment, and Other Factors on Unit Capability." October 1995, Document NSIAD–96–14, 3.

55. "A Few Good Men Are Being Stretched Too Thin," *Christian Science Monitor,* August 19, 1994, 1.

56. For details, See *Washington Post*, July 29, 1994, 29; *New York Times* July 31, 1994, 3, and *US News and World Report*, November 15, 1993, 50. Under current planning projections for FY 1999, the U.S. will face significant shortfalls, particularly of Army divisions and Air Force fighter wings, if it attempts to stick by its two medium-sized conflict scenarios and still have forces prepared for lesser contingencies and OOTW. See *Economist*, October 15, 1994, 26. The estimate is that the shortfall will be two active duty and three reserve Army divisions and one active duty and three reserve Air Force fighter wings.

57. Zisk, *Engaging the Enemy*, 26–27. Amos Perlmutter, *The Military and Politics in Modern Times: Of Professionals, Praetorians, and Revolutionary Soldiers* (New Haven: Yale University Press, 1977): 2–3.

58. Zisk, *Engaging the Enemy*, 13–14, and Perlmutter, *The Military and Politics in Modern Times*, 8.

59. This was clearly the case when Navy admirals put up unprecedented public resistance to a plan to cancel the *U.S.S. United States*, a new aircraft carrier design that had strong Navy support, in 1949. Paul R. Schratz, "The Admiral's Revolt," *Proceedings* 112, no. 2 (February 1986): 64–71.

60. Zisk, *Engaging the Enemy*, 27.

61. Wilson, *Bureaucracy*; Lucas and Dawson, *The Organizational Politics of Defense.*

62. See Futrell, *Ideas, Concepts, Doctrine*, especially 182–209. For an update to include Vietnam and beyond, see Earl H. Tilford, Jr. *Crosswinds: The Air Force's Setup in Vietnam* (College Station, Texas: Texas A&M University Press, 1993); Carl H. Builder, *The Army in the Strategic Planning Process: Who Shall Bell the Cat?* R-3513-A (Santa Monica, Cal.: RAND Corporation, April 1987): 55–62, and Polmar and Luar, *Strategic Air Command.*

63. See U.S. Department of Defense, *National Defense Budget Estimates for FY 1994* (Office of the Comptroller, March 1993). See also Kevin N. Lewis, *The U.S. Air Force Budget and Posture Over Time*, R-3807-AF (Santa Monica: RAND, February 1990): 14–15, 26–30; Donald C. F. Daniel, "Beyond the 600-Ship Navy," *Adelphi Papers*, No. 261 (London: International Institute for Strategic Studies, August 1991): 6–8, which provide budgetary data detailing the allocation of funds between and within the services.

Richard A. Stubbing and Ernest Mendel, *The Defense Game* (New York: Harper & Row, 1986): 112–116. Tilford provides an excellent discussion of this history. *Crosswinds*, 3–30.

64. Stubbing, *The Defense Game*, 116–123. Lacy, *Within Bounds*, and Isenberg, *Shield of the Republic* are sources on Navy history and identity. See also Rhodes, "Do Bureaucratic Politics Matter?" for a creative test of the power of these various Navy subgroups. For a useful interservice comparison of self image, see Builder, *The Army in the Strategic Planning Process*, 22–49. For a more detailed discussion of the Army's image, see John K. Satear, Carl H. Builder, M. D. Baccus, and Wayne Madewell, *The Army in a Changing World: The Role of Organizational Vision*, R-3822-A (Santa Monica, Cal.: RAND, June 1990); for the Navy, see Daniel, *Beyond the 600-Ship Navy*; and for the Air Force, Tilford, *Crosswinds*.

65. Mallin, *Tanks, Fighters, and Ships*, 28–29.

66. Halloran, "An Army for the 21st Century," 257; Russell F. Weigley, *History of the United States Army*, Revised Edition (Bloomington, Ind.: Indiana University Press, 1984).

67. These missions have the potential to engage the entire spectrum of U.S. military capabilities, while the peacemaking and peacekeeping missions engage substantially less, particularly with respect to the Air Force and Navy. Bills, et al., *Options for U.S. Military Support to the United Nations*, 13–14.

68. See Donald Burdick, "Army National Guard: An Essential Element of National Strategy" *Army* 40, no. 10 (October 1990): 116–121; and John R. D'Araujo, Jr., "National Guard: The Dual-Role Force," *Army* 43, no. 10 (October 1993): 120–124.

69. Arnold Kanter, *Defense Politics: A Budgetary Perspective* (Chicago, Ill.: University of Chicago Press, 1975): 18–20, 29.

70. The head of SAC, General John T. Chain, argued as late as early 1990 that there had been insufficient changes in the Soviet threat to justify cutting back on the planned purchase of 132 B-2 bombers or scaling back U.S. modernization plans for its strategic nuclear forces. *Los Angeles Times*, February 17,1990, 24; *Washington Post*, March 6, 1990, 8.

71. For an early discussion, see Robert E. Cushman, "The Marine Corps Today—Asset or Anachronism," *International Security* 1, no. 2 (fall 1976): 123–129. For a discussion of the questions raised following the Gulf War, see "No More Iwo Jimas?" *Baltimore Sun*, February 13, 1992, 17, and "Send in the Marines—But Where?" *Government Executive*, March 1992, 16.

72. Tilford, *Crosswinds*. Despite considerable evidence, including much from Air Force sources, that bombing did not have a decisive impact in World War II, the Air Force continued to use it in Korea and Vietnam. Perrow, *Complex Organizations*, 171.

73. Motley, *Beyond the Soviet Threat*, 30–31, 197–199.

74. For a general discussion, see Yoav Ben-Horin and Benjamin Schwarz, *Army 21 as the U.S. Army's Future Warfighting Concept: A Critical Review of Approach and Assumptions*,

R-3615-A (Santa Monica: RAND, July 1988), and Jennifer Morrison Taw and Robert C. Leicht, *The New World Order and Army Doctrine: The Doctrinal Renaissance of Operations Short of War?*, R-4201-A (Santa Monica, Cal.: RAND, 1992).

75. Massimo A. Annati, "Stand By, We Are Boarding," *Proceedings* 120, no. 3 (March 1994): 54–55.

76. Builder, *The Army in the Strategic Planning Process,* 37–38, 76. Builder argues that of the services, the Army is the most secure in its view of its relevance to national security and the Air Force the least so.

77. Kanter notes that when Army officials reach flag rank, they remove their branch insignia from their uniforms. Kanter, *Defense Politics*, no. 6, 127.

78. Builder, *The Army in the Strategic Planning Process,* 31.

79. See Andrew F. Krepinevich, *The Army and Vietnam* (Baltimore, Md.: Johns Hopkins): 4–7, and Wilson, *Bureaucracy*, 218–220, for two discussions of changes in the Army's approach to defending Europe.

80. An indication of the desperate lengths that Air Force supporters went to find post-Cold War roles for Cold War weapons can be seen in the suggestion by Col. John A. Warden III, Commandant of the Air Command and Staff College at Maxwell AFB, that the B-2, a billion-dollar aircraft, be used in famine areas to drop 1,000 calorie food pellets—"We could push starvation back by a couple of days." *Defense News*, 30 May–5 June 1994, 2.

81. William D. Smith, "Peacemaking From The Sea," *Proceedings* 119, no. 8 (August 1993): 25–28.

82. Mundy, "The US Marines Are Old Hands at Humanitarian Intervention," *Armed Forces Journal International* 130, no. 7 (February 1993): 42–43.

6

Somalia, Bosnia, and Haiti: What Went Right, What Went Wrong?

Andrew Bennett[1]

The post-Cold War world has proved to be a tough testing ground for collective conflict management, resulting in wide swings between optimism and pessimism on its prospects.[2] This is especially true of the problematic gray area between peacekeeping and peace enforcement, termed "selective enforcement" by the editors of this book, which is the focus of the present chapter.[3] From the summer to the fall of 1993, for example, the United States went from pursuing nation building in Somalia to announcing the withdrawal of all U.S. forces from that country. The ensuing pessimism on collective conflict management, dubbed the "Somalia syndrome," contributed to the international community's failure to prevent genocide in Rwanda in 1994. Subsequent peace operations have avoided excessive optimism or pessimism and have thus far proved largely successful, including the Multinational Force (MNF) in Haiti and the Implementation Force (IFOR) in the former Yugoslavia.

This chapter reviews the experiences and lessons of the three most prominent attempts at selective enforcement: the UN operation in Somalia in its critical phase from May to October of 1993 (UNOSOM II), the MNF in Haiti, and the UN Protection Force in the former Yugoslavia (UNPROFOR). The analysis highlights recurrent difficulties in four key areas in UNOSOM II and UNPROFOR: multilateral coordination and burden-sharing; operational and organizational procedures; definition of peace forces' missions and mandates; and management of the domestic politics of peace operations.

Problems in these areas have led some observers to advocate avoiding selective enforcement altogether, and to urge undertaking only more limited peacekeeping missions, which require the consent of all parties, a prior cease-fire, and strict UN impartiality.[4] These critics rightly argue that selective enforcement has inherent difficulties and should be attempted only when its risks are justified by the interests at stake.

Still, a close analysis of the flaws of UNOSOM II and UNPROFOR and the successes of the MNF in Haiti suggests that many of the problems with selective enforcement are preventable or at least manageable. Moreover, as events in the Balkans and Rwanda in 1994 demonstrated, restricting collective conflict management to only its most and least ambitious forms—peace enforcement and peacekeeping—would prevent the great powers from addressing large-scale humanitarian disasters or genocide. Such a policy also would inhibit early preventive actions that might remove the need for later and more costly interventions. A refusal to address conflicts that do not immediately threaten the vital interests of great powers could embolden political, ideological, religious, and ethnic extremists, causing conflicts to proliferate, spread geographically, and escalate in intensity.

Rather than rejecting selective enforcement or treating it as a panacea, theorists and policymakers should attempt to identify the circumstances and policies likely to lead to its success or failure. This chapter concludes that selective enforcement is most likely to succeed when the countries contributing forces agree on the mission, deploy forces where they have a comparative advantage, enforce impartially their mandate while empowering its local supporters and overpowering its local opponents, deploy sufficient forces to overwhelm potential opposition, agree upon a unified and decisive command structure, and integrate military actions with viable political strategies in the target country and at home. Although seemingly obvious, these admonitions often have been glossed over in attempts to reconcile the conflicting domestic politics, international pressures, and local realities of collective conflict management. The conclusions briefly suggest that IFOR can be usefully judged by these criteria, even though it fits the definition of peacekeeping better than that of selective enforcement.

The Definition and Dynamics of Selective Enforcement

Selective enforcement challenges the orthodoxy of both peace enforcement and peacekeeping in three ways. First, selective enforcement can involve internal as well as international conflicts, and it encompasses a variety of missions that fall between peacekeeping and peace enforcement, including "forcible" humanitarian aid, protection of "safe havens" for threatened groups, forcible disarmament of factions or maintenance of demilitarized zones, capture of internationally indicted war criminals, support of democratic processes, or assistance to weak and victimized groups to create a stable, local balance of power as a basis for negotiations or power sharing.[5]

Second, in contrast to peacekeeping, selective enforcement does not necessarily require the prior consent of all local combatants or a preexisting cease-fire. Such prerequisites would hold selective enforcement hostage to the most recalcitrant and best-armed local factions. Similarly, selective enforcement does not require impartiality toward all parties to a conflict, but only impartial enforcement of a given mandate, which may involve the use of force against factions that act to oppose that mandate. Often, this requires forces and rules of engagement that allow not only for self-defense, but for offensive operations. Yet unlike peace enforcement, selective enforcement does not imply forcible eviction of or an immediate offensive against any particular party or complete endorsement of a party's agenda. It requires taking action against those who use force to attempt to prevent peace forces from implementing their mandate. Thus, peace forces should retain one element of impartiality, "the idea that the UN represents a set of interests, values, and tasks that are distinct in some respects from those of any one belligerent."[8]

Third, because of these requirements, selective enforcement calls for a very different force structure from the light arms of peacekeeping or the heavy and concentrated conventional forces of peace enforcement. Selective enforcement may require small unit patrols in unpredictable and potentially hostile environments for delivery of humanitarian supplies or protection of "safe havens." This can make troops vulnerable to being ambushed, taken hostage, or overrun, all of which happened in UNPROFOR, if they are not adequately armed and present in sufficient numbers. It also requires small unit commanders trained to use force in ways that deter or compel adversaries but do not unduly escalate conflicts.

Lessons Learned in UNOSOM II and UNPROFOR

The inappropriate application of peace enforcement or peacekeeping concepts to selective enforcement missions has been the source of many mistakes, amply illustrated by UN efforts in Somalia and the former Yugoslavia. The lessons are discussed under four headings: coordination and burden-sharing; operational and organizational problems; missions and mandates; and domestic politics.

Coordination and Burden-Sharing

One key determinant of the success or failure of selective enforcement is the strength of shared interests and understandings among the permanent members of the UN Security Council and the states that contribute forces to an operation. Unresolved disagreements within either group, or between the two groups, can undermine the local, international, and domestic requirements of success. The most difficult tradeoff here is that between mobilizing a broad coalition, to share burdens and provide legitimacy, versus employing a narrower coalition that has a more coherent mandate.

In the case of UNPROFOR, a strong concert of interests proved elusive. Russia, driven in part by nationalistic domestic politics, was more sympathetic than the West to the Serbs. At times, this disagreement proved useful, as when Russia and the West in effect used a good-cop/bad-cop approach to get Serbian forces to honor safe-haven zones around Sarajevo, Gorazde, and other Bosnian cities in early 1994. For the most part, however, disagreements among the Permanent Five hampered the UN mission. In particular, recurrent disagreements arose between the United States, which favored air strikes and the lifting of the arms embargo against the Bosnian Muslims, and France, Britain, and Canada, which feared that lifting the embargo would lead to retaliatory strikes against their peacekeeping troops. As a result, in 1993 and 1994 there were no systematic and sustained air strikes, the arms embargo remained in place, and there was no substantial deployment of U.S. ground forces in UNPROFOR.[7]

The states carrying out the UN operation in Somalia also suffered from debilitating disagreements. By the summer of 1993, Washington wanted to disarm the Somali clans and capture Mohammed Farah Aideed. Italy, however, preferred to negotiate with Aideed, reportedly reaching an agreement with him, allowing Italian troops to return to a contested sector in Mogadishu as long as they did not conduct weapons searches in that area. This effectively provided a safe haven for Aideed's arms depots.[8] In another instance, the commander of the Italian contingent in Somalia, General Bruno Loi, undertook operations without informing the UN command, sending a force of 800 Italian soldiers on a weapons search. The first notice that the UN had of this operation came when the Italian forces were ambushed and their commander requested American support after two hours of heavy fighting.[9] At one point, Washington so distrusted the Italian forces that when U.S. Rangers observed a Somali leaving the Italian Embassy compound in Mogadishu, they mistook him for Aideed and arrested him a half-hour later, only to find that he was in fact Ahmed Jilao, an ally of the UN operation.[10]

Such disagreements exacerbate the inherent difficulties of achieving deterrence or coercive diplomacy *multilaterally* vis-à-vis highly motivated local forces that are willing to sustain heavy casualties to reach their goals. Because of the veto, local actors need to win only one vote among the permanent members. In Bosnia, U.S. threats to launch air strikes were repeatedly undermined, often within a matter of hours, by French, British, or Russian objections. Moreover, local opponents have an incentive to attack the forces of states whose casualties have the greatest symbolic and political effect. Often, this has meant that American forces are targeted. A spokesman for Aideed's clan, for example, confirmed that after the American attack on Aideed's forces on July 12, 1993, the Somalis "tried to kill anybody American . . . There was no more United Nations—only Americans. And if you could kill Americans, it would start problems in America directly."[11]

A third and related difficulty concerns other dimensions of the problem of collective action. Often, successful UN operations have required a major power to bear much of the burden, push others to contribute, and make credible threats against local actors. Until the Dayton Accords, no single state played this role in Bosnia, resulting in inadequate forces to achieve UN goals. In Somalia, the UN operation proceeded smoothly during the Unified Task Force (UNITAF) to which the U.S. contributed most of the 28,000 troops, but it bogged down in May 1993 when the United States turned the operation over to a more multinational UN force of 16,000 troops.

On the other hand, when one state is the clear leader in a selective enforcement mission, that mission will be vulnerable to changes in the lead state's policies. When Washington pulled its troops from Somalia in March 1994, for example, Italy, Germany, and others did the same, and within a year the UNOSOM II force withdrew completely from Somalia.[12]

A fourth problem has been coordinating the roles of the UN, regional states, regional arrangements, and ad-hoc "coalitions of the willing." Each has assets and liabilities that must be taken into account if the UN is to "subcontract" peace operations effectively to regional actors or ad-hoc coalitions, which is an increasingly common practice.[13] The world organization's strengths are its wide political legitimacy and embodiment of international norms, but the UN lacks its own forces, has no rapid deployment capability, and is incapable of making decisions without the unanimity of the Security Council's permanent members. This effectively limits the UN to peacekeeping and forces it to turn to others for more ambitious missions.

Regional states and arrangements can have superior knowledge of the dynamics of local conflicts and strong incentives to resolve them and, by definition, they have staying power. Except for the NATO alliance, however, few regional actors or organizations have appropriate forces and effective decision-making mechanisms, and many have strong political biases. This suggests that the United Nations might legitimize peace operations by regional actors if these actors agree to rules, norms, mandates, and observers that guard against political biases.

The most challenging missions may require highly capable military forces that only ad-hoc coalitions can provide. The potential difficulties with such coalitions, however, is that they may lack staying power in conflicts that do not threaten their vital interests, may have to devise decision mechanisms and chains of command from the ground up, and may have difficulty in taking over from or handing off to UN forces.

In the case of the former Yugoslavia, the world organization and regional actors did not coordinate their policies in ways that effectively used these comparative advantages. The United Nations took a back seat through the first half of 1992 as the Conference on Security and Cooperation in Europe (CSCE), the European Community (EC), and the Western European Union (WEU) attempted to address the conflict. The mediation efforts of these organizations failed, partly because they lacked the combination of decisive policy processes, substantial military forces, and the ability to impose broad economic sanctions. By the time that Western leaders realized that only the UN and NATO had the proper mandate and capabilities to address the conflict, it had acquired a deadly momentum. In Somalia, the UN made the opposite mistake of giving regional states a leading role in local negotiations only after the UN mission had run into stiff opposition.

A final burden-sharing dilemma has been that the states most willing to contribute troops to peace operations have often lacked the necessary equipment. More than 20,000 of the 70,000 UN peacekeepers deployed as of the fall of 1994 came from five Asian states that lack adequate peacekeeping equipment and air transport: Pakistan, India, Bangladesh, Nepal, and Malaysia. Malaysian forces in UNPROFOR, for example, arrived without winter gear or armored personnel carriers.[14] A little-noted U.S. Department of Defense program, proposed in 1996, would begin to address such problems by providing equipment to countries that have proven themselves to be willing contributors to peace operations.[15]

Operational and Organizational Problems

The patchwork nature of the coalitions undertaking multilateral peace operations and the unfamiliar demands of selective enforcement have resulted in recurrent operational problems, including insufficient joint training among participating forces, inappropriate equipment and tactics, inadequate intelligence, and convoluted chains of command. Many of these factors came together in a disastrous peace operation in Somalia on October 3, 1993, in which 18 American soldiers were killed and 84 were wounded. In this operation, U.S. Special Operations Forces set out to capture Aideed's top associates but came under heavy fire and lost their mobility when Somali forces shot down two helicopters. The larger force of American quick-reaction troops in Mogadishu, which had little advance notice of the raid, set out in a rescue convoy but encountered intense fire and had to return to its staging area because it lacked heavy armored vehicles. This force then turned for assistance to Malaysian and Pakistani troops, who had the only UN armored forces in Mogadishu. A relief column headed by these forces eventually did reach the pinned-down American units, but only after several hours of delays, which might have been prevented if the forces involved had trained more closely together. Confusion and language problems, for example, caused the leading Malaysian armored vehicles to take a wrong turn, after which they were destroyed by rocket-propelled grenades.[16] In the end, it took 10 hours for a relief convoy to reach the U.S. Special Operations Forces pinned down in Aideed's territory.

The October 3 tragedy arose not only from inadequate joint training among UN forces, but also from a lack of equipment and weapons suited to the tasks undertaken by U.S. troops. Selective enforcement missions require weapons that can defeat well-armed opponents, but this raises the risks of civilian casualties. The United States had difficulties with both ends of this dilemma in Somalia. In late September 1993, Secretary of Defense Les Aspin rejected a request from the U.S. commander in Somalia, Major General Thomas Montgomery, for 4 tanks and 14 Bradley armored vehicles to protect U.S. troops. Even if approved, these forces would not have arrived in time to rescue the American soldiers attacked on October 3, and even before this, U.S. forces had taken casualties from rocket-propelled grenades and mines.[17] Similarly, Major General Garrison, commander of the U.S. Special Operations Forces in Somalia, had requested deployment of AC-130 gunships as backup protection for his forces as they carried out commando raids. Although the AC-130s had been used in previous raids in Somalia, Garrison's request was denied.[18] Soon after the clash on October 3, the U.S. deployed both AC-130 aircraft and M-1A1 tanks to Somalia.

On the other hand, a UN report later argued that the U.S. had used helicopters in Somalia in ways that caused excessive civilian casualties.[19] In retrospect, and as generals Montgomery and Garrison may have intended at the time, the best approach would have been to deploy heavy forces but to use them only when U.S. or UN troops were in imminent danger.

A third general problem of selective enforcement is acquiring intelligence on potential adversaries and sharing it effectively between countries and between military and police forces. Although peace forces may at times have access to information from satellites and other high-technology sources, they almost inevitably have poorer information than local combatants, who are operating in their own neighborhoods, languages, and cultures. Washington compounded this imbalance in Somalia by reducing its intelligence gathering assets there as it cut back its forces in early 1993. This contributed to an underestimation of the numbers of Aideed's troops and rocket-propelled grenades, which were key factors in the October 3 battle. Intelligence problems also contributed to a mistaken U.S. raid on the office of the UN Development Programme (UNDP), and sophisticated electronic eavesdropping equipment proved ineffective against the low-technology communications used by clans.[20] Analogous problems hampered UNPROFOR. For example, a United Nations "Who's Who" of local leaders omitted or erred on key information, including individuals' alleged war crimes.[21]

A fourth operational problem with UNOSOM II and UNPROFOR concerns the chain of command. When contributing states differ on missions and mandates, some inevitably feel that UN officials or designated commanders are asking their troops to do too much, while others worry that their troops will be required to do too little. In Somalia, for example, UN military officials complained about the cumbersome chain of command and institutional reluctance of UN officials to approve military operations. In particular, officials suggested that Aideed escaped a June 17 attack by U.S. AC-130 gunships, because the UN command called off offensive operations and allowed Aideed to regroup and rearm. Moreover, each UN task in Somalia had to be approved in advance, and every country involved had a de facto veto. Italian, French and Pakistani forces declined at points to take part in offensive operations. In one instance, Pakistani forces refused to surround and arrest Aideed's followers at a house where they were known to be meeting on July 12, leading U.S. commanders to attack the house instead, thereby killing its occupants.[22]

Contrary to a widely shared view, however, the October 3 tragedy in Somalia was not the result of a flawed UN chain of command. The chain of command for the U.S. Special Operations Forces operations was exclusively American, going from Lt. Colonel Danny McKnight, commander of the Third Battalion of the 75th Rangers, to Major Gen. William Garrison, of the Joint Special Operations Command, to General Joseph Hoar, head of U.S. Central Command. Both the U.S. Special Operations Forces involved in the October 3 raid and the U.S. quick-reaction troops sent to rescue them were under an American chain of command. Only the 2,700 U.S. logistical troops in Somalia, who were not involved in the October 3 events, were under the UN chain of command.[23]

The chain of command problems in UNPROFOR were more pervasive and damaging than those in UNOSOM II. In the summer of 1993, UN and NATO agreed upon a "dual command" structure. A UNPROFOR unit under attack could send a request for close air support through the NATO forces that would actually supply the necessary aircraft. This request would then be relayed to the UN chain of command, and ultimately the UN secretary-general would have to approve the first air strikes by NATO aircraft in defense of a given ground unit.[24]

In January 1994, the outgoing commander in the Balkans, French Lt. General Jean Cot, criticized this ungainly chain of command and called for giving NATO the authority to order air strikes in defense of UN ground forces without prior approval from the secretary-general. Cot argued that air strikes needed to be prompt to protect ground forces, and he warned that in practice exercises the secretary-general's office had taken up to five hours to approve such requests.[25] Cot's concerns were validated in March 1994 when French peacekeeping troops came under fire and requested air strikes, but this request took more than three hours to pass up the UN chain of command. By this time, the Serbian forces who had been attacking the French troops had withdrawn, and air strikes were not launched. Even more troubling, the senior UN official in the region, Yasushi Akashi, reportedly tried to contact Serbian leaders during the three-hour delay to urge them to move their forces before they might be hit by air strikes.[26]

It is easy to criticize this convoluted chain of command, but procedures for multilateral military operations involve a difficult tradeoff between establishing a clear structure and creating a coalition of peace forces that is both politically broad and militarily sufficient. Even if there is full and detailed agreement among potential troop contributors on missions and rules of engagement, states may be wary of contributing forces unless they have a role in the chain of command. This became a central issue in the U.S. policy review on peace operations, some early drafts of which reportedly would have allowed U.S. officers to "disobey UN orders they judge illegal or militarily imprudent."[27] Clearly, if all contributors insisted on such rights, multilateral peace operations would be virtually impossible. The final version of Presidential Decision Directive 25 (PDD-25) endorsed a more reasonable rule of thumb: the more troops the United States contributes to a given operation, the greater the role in the chain of command. Although this principle was followed in Somalia and would not have prevented the problems that arose there, its application could have led to a more unified command process in UNPROFOR.

Defining Missions and Mandates for Selective Enforcement

Defining missions and mandates for selective enforcement requires confronting dilemmas that are far more complex and ambiguous than those of either peacekeeping or peace enforcement. First, selective enforcement requires an ability to treat warring factions as either friends or foes depending on their behavior. Those carrying out selective enforcement forces are more like diplomats who create a balance of power than conquerors who impose a solution or mediators who police one. The concept of unconditional impartiality toward contending factions, while essential to peacekeeping, has proven to be counterproductive in selective enforcement missions.[28] In many conflicts there are alleged atrocities on all sides, but when it is clear that one side is responsible for the vast majority of human rights abuses, as was true of the Serbs in Bosnia and the Hutus in Rwanda, multilateral intervention loses its legitimacy if it gives equal status to the victims and perpetrators of genocide. In addition, a commitment to impartiality removes any credible threat to use force, diminishes leverage over extremist parties, and reduces the ability to deter attacks on peace forces.

Even worse, impartiality prevents arms or other assistance (such as intelligence information) from reaching the victims of aggression, as they try to organize against stronger persecutors and exercise the most fundamental principle in the UN Charter, the right of self-defense. Ironically, rather then helping weak and exploited parties to help themselves, international coalitions have put their own troops at risk and undercut support from their own publics and parliaments. Moreover, local actors—whether motivated by outrage at injustice as were the Bosnian Muslims or seeking a balance of power like the anti-Aideed clans in Somalia—are fully committed to their homes and goals. With appropriate arms and training, such local forces might be a more credible, coercive, and deterrent force than multinational coalitions that are well-armed but more likely to withdraw if casualties mount. Ironically, UNPROFOR became the leading justification for not supplying the Bosnian Muslims with weapons for self-defense. There is of course a danger that victimized groups, once empowered, may abuse human rights themselves; but international coalitions can respond by threatening to cut off arms and other supplies.

On this issue, selective enforcement requires delicate balancing abroad and at home. If an operation is to involve impartial enforcement of a mandate rather than impartiality among parties, the publics and parliaments who contribute troops must be convinced that the risk of casualties is justified and potential adversaries must be convinced of the peace forces' capabilities, will, and staying power. Failure to fulfill either condition invites attacks on peace forces by those who hope to see them withdrawn. Yet if such troops become too aggressive and personalize their attacks on obstructionist parties or seek their destruction, as happened in the attacks on Aideed and his forces in the summer of 1993, there is no incentive for compromise.

A second set of dilemmas surrounds decisions on whether to negotiate with extremist leaders—perhaps offering them amnesty, policy concessions, or comfortable exile—or try to capture them, bring them before international tribunals, or use lethal military force against their headquarters and troops. The former course risks undermining the regional and international legitimacy of peace operations, while the latter encourages factional leaders to fight to the finish. Ideally, these options should be made contingent on local leaders' behavior and orchestrated in a carrot-and-stick fashion to entice them to pursue peace. In practice, however, these are political problems within the states contributing troops, and are difficult to implement. In Bosnia, for example, the international community negotiated with the Bosnian Serb leader Radovan Karadzic even as an international tribunal prepared to try him as a war criminal.[29]

The experience in Somalia is even more instructive. After 24 Pakistani peacekeepers were killed in Somalia on June 5, 1993, with strong evidence implicating Aideed's forces, the Security Council adopted a resolution calling for the arrest of those responsible and the disarmament of all armed parties in Somalia. One week later, U.S. forces undertook a series of attacks on Aideed's headquarters and arms depots. On June 17, Retired U.S. Admiral Jonathan Howe, commander of the UN mission, called for Aideed's arrest and offered a $25,000 reward. But this public pronouncement merely allowed Aideed time to go underground.[30] As hostilities escalated, Washington adopted an unwieldy "two track plan" in late September, seeking a political settlement that might include Aideed, but meanwhile continuing efforts to capture him.[31] The intent may have been to pressure Aideed into negotiations, but the result was a series of escalating clashes. After the climactic October 3 battle, Washington reversed course, rescinding its order for Aideed's arrest on November 16, and arranged for Aideed to meet with U.S. envoy Robert Oakley two days later. Within two weeks after that, Aideed was flown to negotiations outside of Somalia in an American military aircraft. Thus, within just two months, the U.S. went from putting a price on Aideed's head and seeking his capture to escorting him.[32]

A third dilemma exists between the principle of self-determination of peoples and that of the inviolability of borders. Favoring either of these principles to the exclusion of the other risks secessionist conflicts along the hundreds of international and domestic administrative borders that cut across nationality groups. This dilemma has been most evident in the conflict in the former Yugoslavia. In 1991, the United States refused to offer diplomatic recognition to Yugoslavia's secessionist republics. Croatia and Slovenia nonetheless declared independence in June 1991, sparking the first round of fighting, and they won diplomatic recognition from Germany in December. This initially pressured Serbia into a cease-fire with Croatia in January 1992, but when it became apparent that the West would not take any steps to ensure Croatia's sovereignty, fighting flared up again in Croatia and extended into Bosnia. By early April, the hostilities prompted Germany and the European Community to recognize Bosnia, after which the U.S. also recognized Bosnia, Croatia, and Slovenia.

The principle of inviolable borders was diluted further over the next two years by offering various plans for redrawing the borders of the newly independent republics. Ironically, whereas international recognition of the secessionist republics, linked to protections of minority rights, might have prevented conflict in early 1991, by 1993, the new-found international willingness to redraw borders extensively could not achieve peace because Serbian forces had taken Bosnian and Croatian territory and created a patchwork of battle lines and enclaves across and within previous borders.

Integrating military actions with viable political strategies for conflict resolution presents a fourth challenge in defining selective enforcement missions.[33] As noted above, selective enforcement forces must be ready to take offensive action against groups that forcibly oppose their mandate, but they must avoid making inalterable enemies out of any parties that they are unable or unwilling to defeat militarily. This requires limiting both the ends and the means of selective enforcement.

This problem was evident in Somalia, where the UN mission failed to temper and coordinate its ends and means. With the transition from the US-led

UNITAF to UNOSOM II in May 1993, UNOSOM's forces shifted the political strategy from negotiating with Somalia's most powerful clans to attempting to marginalize them.[34] By seeking to disarm the clans and trying to establish independent local and judicial authorities without consulting Aideed and other clan leaders, the United Nations set an increasingly confrontational course in the months before the June 5 attack by Aideed's forces on Pakistani peacekeepers.[35] After this attack, UN forces, in addition to announcing publicly a $25,000 reward for Aideed, escalated the military conflict with Aideed through attacks on his strongholds killing some of his clan's elders.[36] In the context of Somali politics and culture, these actions made it likely that Aideed would attack American and other peace forces despite the likelihood of incurring heavy casualties.

The disjuncture of military and political strategies worsened when President Bill Clinton decided to deemphasize the goal of capturing Aideed. Secretary of State Warren Christopher communicated this decision to UN Secretary-General Boutros Boutros-Ghali in a meeting on September 20, 1993.[37] However, it appears that the mission statement and rules of engagement of U.S. forces were not suitably updated to reflect this change in policy, as the U.S. attempted once again to capture Aideed just two weeks later. The resulting October 3 firefight and its aftermath revealed that Washington was unwilling to take the military risks that its political strategy required.

The mission in Somalia exhibited a disjuncture not only of the nature of the military means and political ends, but also of their scale. The transition from UNITAF to UNOSOM II did not involve a change in political strategy, but a decrease in the size of the force to 16,000 multinational troops—far less than the 28,000 troops authorized by the United Nations and deployed initially. During the UNITAF phase from December 1992 to May 1993, the United States had decided not to disarm Somali factions. Yet now UNOSOM II troops—a smaller, less well-trained, less heavily armed, and less integrated force—had the more ambitious mandate under Security Council Resolution 814 of disarming the Somali clans, establishing a police force, and building a viable state.[38] Not only was the force smaller and under new leadership, but also no one had been involved in previous negotiations with the Somali clans.[39]

A gap between ends and means was also a central cause of UNPROFOR's inability to help establish peace in the former Yugoslavia. Through much of the Balkan conflict, the West embraced the ambitious objective of maintaining the borders of the newly-independent republics. To achieve this goal against the wishes of the large and well-armed Serbian populations in Bosnia and Croatia, as well as the desires of Serbia's leaders, would have required by most estimates more than 100,000 ground troops with a strong mandate to take the offensive. The West, however, proved willing to provide fewer than 30,000 troops under restrictive rules of engagement. Caught between its unwillingness to ratify the consequences of Serbian ethnic cleansing and its reluctance to risk its forces, the

West muddled through with an irreconcilable chasm between its ends and means.[40] The "Vance-Owen" and "Contact Group" peace plans began to bridge this gap by accepting that borders would have to be redrawn, but without the backing of a credible threat to use force, these plans lacked adequate leverage to compel Serbian acceptance.

Managing the Domestic Politics of Collective Security

The domestic political challenges of selective enforcement are similar to those of other uses of force, which Alan Lamborn has detailed in chapter 2. Selective enforcement missions are among the most controversial due to their multilateral nature, inherent complexity, and focus on less-than-vital interests. These realities require that debates over war powers between legislative and executive bodies be handled carefully if they are not to undermine multilateral diplomacy.

The American example demonstrates how the use of force in collective conflict management has added a new dimension to debates over war powers in democracies.[41] Repeatedly, American presidents—including Harry Truman during the Korean War, George Bush in the months before he finally requested a congressional vote on using force against Iraq in 1991, and Bill Clinton in the weeks prior to the U.S. deployment to Haiti—have argued that they had the option of committing U.S. forces to peace operations without prior approval from the Congress. Many in the Congress have disagreed, and in recent years, the Congress has attempted to constrain presidential authority in this area, using nonbinding resolutions or proposing legislation to require prior congressional approval of the use or deployment of American forces in specific peace operations.

Members of Congress rightly complain that presidents have too readily used force without prior congressional approval. Presidents justifiably argue that the Congress avoid votes before using force and then to criticize the president if an operation goes badly or claim credit if it goes well. Although no simple legislative fix is likely, a close reading of the constitutional intent and political precedents on war powers suggests that the need for prior congressional approval increases to the extent that large numbers of U.S. forces might be involved, high casualties are likely, and the events leading to the possible use of U.S. forces allow time for an unhurried vote.

Within these broad guidelines, however, it is hard to ensure that legitimate debates over war powers and over specific missions do not encourage potential adversaries to challenge collective conflict management. Sometimes smaller and less dangerous operations are much more likely to succeed with limited casualties if they have explicit congressional approval, as this signals to potential adversaries that they cannot easily force an American withdrawal by inflicting casualties on American forces. In the weeks before the U.S. deployment to Haiti, for example, Haitian military leaders may have discounted military threats because of opposition in Congress to the use of force. Potential adversaries need to be reminded that open disagreements do not prevent democracies from taking forceful and united action once a decision has been legitimized through the democratic process.

Similarly, the U.S. experience in Somalia illustrates the importance of sending consistent signals at home and abroad. After early successes in attacks on Aideed's forces in June 1993, U.S. officials publicly suggested that Aideed had been severely weakened, but his forces soon proved more capable than anticipated. By the end of September, continuing clashes led Washington to announce that it was stepping back from the goal of capturing Aideed and focusing instead on the creation of Somali political institutions that would marginalize him.[42] Congress and the public were thus psychologically and politically unprepared for the final, disastrous attempt to capture Aideed, leading to a firestorm of public and congressional criticism. This suggests the importance of presidential or prime ministerial leadership in clarifying and articulating interests early and often to inoculate peace operations against sudden reversals at the first casualties. Zero-casualty foreign policy is hardly a realistic expectation if collective conflict management is to succeed.

A third problem is that bureaucratic as well as legislative disagreements can undercut deterrent and coercive threats. Robert Gosende, the U.S. State Department liaison officer in Mogadishu, argued strongly against negotiations with Aideed, and Howe pushed to capture him. However at the same time, General Joseph Hoar, chief of U.S. Central Command, opposed the hunt for Aideed and was increasingly skeptical of a military solution. The request for heavier armored forces in Somalia was also the subject of an active bureaucratic debate.[43] These debates were kept private from potential adversaries in Somalia and did not undermine deterrence there. But in the case of UNPROFOR, periodic leaks on some American officials' reluctance to use force weakened multilateral deterrence and diplomacy.[44]

Finally, the conflict in the former Yugoslavia indicates the necessity and the difficulty of mobilizing the public before a conflict has escalated. Early involvement can diffuse a conflict before boundaries are redrawn on the battlefield and growing casualties raise political stakes. But the same low stakes that make early intervention useful also make it harder to mobilize political support within contributing countries. As the editors of this book argue, the most propitious times for engaging in peace operations may be either early in conflicts, before they escalate, or late, when they have reached a stalemate and exhausted the military forces and strengthened the political wills to compromise the conflicting parties. Unfortunately, public and media attention and political pressure for intervention is often highest at the peak stages of conflicts, when the costs of intervention are highest. This underscores how important it is for national leaders to be ready to make the case for embarking on early intervention, and to resist pressures for ill-timed operations.

MNF in Haiti: Lessons Learned, Lessons Applied

The MNF in Haiti successfully applied many of the lessons learned painfully in Bosnia and Somalia, reversing a period of vacillation in U.S. policies on Haiti. American credibility in Haiti hit a low point in October 1993, when Washington's decision to withdraw from Somalia emboldened Haitian military leaders to renege on their acceptance of a force of U.S. and Canadian police and observers sent to Haiti on board the *U.S.S. Harlan County*. Reports of bureaucratic, congressional, and public reluctance to commit forces in Haiti further eroded American credibility, to the point that Haitian military leaders did not agree to go into exile until U.S. military forces were actually in the air and on their way to invade Haiti.

The deployment of the MNF reflected significant learning about the requirements of selective enforcement. Washington sidestepped any disagreements over the mission and the chain of command in the first five months by providing the vast majority of the 15,000 troops. Other countries deployed only about 300 soldiers in this first phase of the operation, which demonstrated the breadth of the political coalition supporting the U.S. but without creating interoperability problems. In fact, the invasion displayed remarkable operational flexibility in switching, literally overnight, from a force ready for insertion against active opposition, to one designed for a less confrontational but more complicated relationship with Haitian military, police, and paramilitary forces. The United States further demonstrated the legitimacy of the operation by winning support from the Organization of American States (OAS). In contrast to Somalia and Bosnia, foreign forces and regional organizations provided legitimacy without becoming a hindrance to action.

The one operational difficulty that the MNF shared with UNPROFOR and UNOSOM II was that of obtaining and disseminating usable operational intelligence, such as that on distinguishing potential friends from likely foes.[45] A more serious problem in Haiti was that of building up an effective and impartial local police force to take over once U.S. forces established control. If Washington had started many months earlier in building up such a force from Haitian exiles, it might have forestalled the problems that it later encountered in trying to create one quickly inside Haiti, where recruits often lacked training or loyalty to the Aristide government.[46] Also, the existence of such a force would have demonstrated American resolve and helped convince Haiti's junta to accept exile. Still, the handover from the predominantly American MNF to UN blue helmets (the UN Mission in Haiti, or UNMIH) was far smoother than that in Somalia, as the United States neither rushed this exchange nor allowed ends to expand as means contracted.

Apart from these difficulties, the military and political strategies of the MNF were closely coordinated. In a calibrated series of diplomatic and military moves, Washington signaled that it was willing to use force against the Haitian military regime if necessary, but that it was not seeking the complete destruction of that regime and its personnel. This was critical to getting Haitian military leaders to agree not to oppose the insertion of U.S. forces. The cooperation between Haitian military and police forces and the MNF was not trouble-free, and it broke down when Haitian forces attacked crowds of Haitian civilians. The MNF, however, responded appropriately. After first refraining from intervening in clashes between Haitian forces and civilians, the United States adopted more forceful rules of engagement and admonished the Haitian military and police forces to exercise restraint. The tougher stance was underscored in a firefight a few weeks after the invasion in which U.S. troops killed ten Haitian police. After this, Haitian police and military forces were far more cautious in using force against civilians. At the same time Washington did not overreach its success and refrained from forcible disarmament of the Haitian forces even though the UN secretary-general urged such a step.[47] The MNF succeeded by limiting its ends and employing sufficient means to achieve them. The U.S. ruled out engaging in "nation building," leaving that task to a restored democratic government, while it deployed more than enough troops to overwhelm Haiti's military and police forces, even if they had forcibly opposed the mission.[48]

The United States also successfully combined the credible threat of overwhelming force with financial incentives to forestall opposition to the MNF, win the return of President Jean Bertrand Aristide, and convince Haiti's de facto military leaders to go into exile. Even as President Clinton made a prime-time speech to justify the use of force in Haiti, news reports indicated that Washington was prepared to offer safe passage to a comfortable life in exile for the top three Haitian military leaders.[49] When they went into exile, the United States released their frozen assets, reportedly totaling in the tens of millions of dollars, and it even took responsibility for renting out property in Haiti owned by General Raoul Cédras.[50] The offer of exile succeeded in Haiti where it had failed in Somalia, because the threat of overwhelming force was credible and immediate, the timing of threats and inducements was coordinated, and the United States had not raised the stakes by attacking or capturing any of the Haitian regime's forces or leaders.

Although Haiti has yet to achieve political stability and sustainable economic growth, the United States has met its objectives of ending widespread human rights abuses and massive refugee flows. The most troubling aspect of the MNF was that the absence of a congressional vote authorizing this force made it politically fragile. A firestorm of political criticism, much like that in Somalia in October 1993, might have ensued if the first firefight in Haiti in the weeks after the invasion had resulted in the deaths of ten Americans rather than ten Haitians. Such political fragility raised the incentives for attacks on MNF forces, but their overwhelming military superiority successfully deterred such attacks (one combat fatality in the first phase of the mission). In future operations where the capabilities and operational unity of peace forces are weaker, domestic political support will be a more important component of successful deterrence.

Conclusions: Implications for Theory and Policy

The foregoing analysis has touched only briefly upon several theoretical questions that deserve more thorough attention. First, multilateral and multiparty deterrence and coercive diplomacy deserve greater attention. Most of the literature on deterrence, driven by Cold War policy concerns, focuses on a two-player game, but most peace operations have involved multinational groups that try to deter or coerce more than one actor at the same time. Second, the dynamics of ethnic conflicts, their escalation processes, and the potential for early intervention and preventive diplomacy require further research. What makes conflicts arise over identity, and what kind of interventions can ameliorate them and make full-scale selective enforcement unnecessary? Third, the domestic politics of multilateral peace operations and burden sharing in ad hoc coalitions require the same sustained attention as that given to superpower military interventions and established alliances during the Cold War.

For policymakers, the four operational lessons of early experiences at selective enforcement are clear. The first and most fundamental is that selective enforcement requires a clear consensus among the countries that hope to achieve it. If disagreements are papered over in the Security Council, they will reappear in a more intractable form in actual operations, where their consequences are immediate and deadly.

Second, states should deploy forces in which they have a comparative advantage. The United States, for example, should usually contribute the noncombat forces at which it excels: airlift and sealift, communications, logistics, and intelligence units. Combat units should be held in reserve for the most demanding missions, where U.S. interests are clearly engaged, where a large and unified force is necessary, and where a coalition leader is needed to get others to contribute. It is entirely appropriate that the United States has led peace operations in the Gulf War, Somalia, and Haiti, as well as more recent IFOR operations in Bosnia. At the same time, the United States has also rightly refrained from deploying small American forces in the many conflicts where they could become the easiest symbolic target. In the long run, the United States and others must work together to ensure that those able to contribute remain willing to do so, and those willing to contribute become more able to do so. This will require joint training, provision of appropriate equipment, and discussions on means of unifying chains of command and using common tactics and strategies. Proposals advanced by Washington in 1996 on a regional peacekeeping force for Africa, and on equipment transfers to leading contributors to peace operations, are steps in the right direction.

Third, several inevitable tensions have to be managed rather than solved. These include the dilemma of inviolable borders versus the self-determination of peoples, the trade off between coaxing human rights abusers into exile versus prosecuting them and risking their inalterable opposition, and the balancing act of impartially enforcing peace operation mandates, while empowering those who support those mandates and overcoming those who oppose them. When the community of states pursues selective enforcement, it must do so with a full awareness of these difficulties and with sufficient consensus, resolve, and resources.

Finally, successful selective enforcement requires integrated military and political strategies that are attuned to the realities of the conflict as well as the domestic politics of the states contributing troops. This will require reconciling the operational demands of selective enforcement, which could include use of force and assertive rules of engagement, with political realities at home, including limited tolerance for casualties when national interests are less than vital. When the gap between these competing imperatives is unbridgeable, selective enforcement should not be undertaken. This argues for presidential and prime ministerial leadership to motivate publics and legislatures for early intervention, when less force is necessary.

These criteria offer insight into the IFOR mission in Bosnia, even though this mission is rather more peacekeeping than selective enforcement. IFOR has succeeded in limiting conflicts and casualties because it has rigorously followed the limited ends of peacekeeping: enforcing a prior cease-fire and peace agreement (the Dayton Accords), policing agreed-upon demilitarized zones, employing impartial rules of engagement, and foregoing forcible disarmament or active attempts to capture factional leaders indicted for war crimes. Yet IFOR has pursued these goals with a highly capable and unified military force led by NATO that could, if necessary, engage in selective enforcement.

This has led some observers to call for using IFOR to pursue war criminals actively and take on nation building and policing functions more aggressively. However, this would run two risks. The first is that IFOR, by pursuing limited goals to keep casualties low, has predictably had to stay in Bosnia longer than originally promised. The second is that the political goal of a multiethnic and unified Bosnian state, enshrined in the Dayton Accords, is at odds with the de facto ethnic partition created by Bosnia's long civil conflict and perpetuated by the cease-fire lines policed by IFOR. Taken together, these create the following dilemma: IFOR cannot stay long if it pursues selective enforcement, because staying would entail casualties, but it cannot implement the political goals of Dayton without selective enforcement. Ultimately, IFOR may have to settle for a long-term transitional partition, however distasteful, rather than inviting the risks of the kind of selective enforcement that would be necessary to achieve a viable power-sharing arrangement in the near term.[51]

The requirements of selective enforcement operations are daunting, and it is better to forego these operations than to undertake them half-heartedly. Still, the successful experience of selective enforcement in Haiti demonstrates that such missions are possible and that Washington and others have already learned from setbacks in Somalia and Bosnia. As selective enforcement establishes a longer track record, all sides of the debate can work to identify more clearly the conditions under which it is possible and the practices most likely to make it succeed.

Notes

1. I would like to thank the editors and Alexander George for suggestions on this chapter as well as Ruth Wedgewood for the opportunity to participate in a Council on Foreign Relations study group on peacekeeping in 1995.

2. On the rapid evolution of the Clinton Administration's views on collective conflict management, see Ivo Daalder, "Knowing When to Say No: The Development of U.S. Peacekeeping Policy in the 1990s," in William Durch, ed., *U.N. Peacekeeping, American Policy, and the Uncivil Wars of the 1990s* (New York: St. Martin's Press, 1996).

3. See John Gerard Ruggie, "Wandering in the Void: Charting the U.N.'s New Strategic Role," *Foreign Affairs* 72, no. 5 (November/December 1993): 26.

4. A UN study of the mission in Somalia, for example, advocated a strategy of peacekeeping rather than peace enforcement, and emphasized the importance of neutrality, even though it also concluded that the Somali forces loyal to General Aideed were behind the killing of 24 Pakistani peacekeepers on June 5, 1993. See Julian Preston and Daniel Williams, "Report on Somali Clash Faults U.S., U.N., Aideed," *Washington Post*, March 31, 1994, A28.

5. See Adam Roberts, "The Crisis in UN Peacekeeping," *Survival* 6, no. 3 (autumn, 1994): 97.

6. Ibid., 115.

7. The U.S. has also had to make repeated foreign policy tradeoffs to prevent other Security Council members from exercising their veto. Examples include continuation of Most-Favored Nation status for China, U.S. approval for a Russian peacekeeping mission in Georgia in exchange for Russian approval of the use of "all necessary

means" in Haiti, and muted U.S. criticism of Soviet actions in the Baltics as the UN deadline for the GulfWar approached.

8. Donatella Lorch, "Italian Forces Come Under Fire in Tense Somalia," *New York Times*, July 17, 1993, 3.

9. Donatella Lorch, "Disunity Hampering U.N. Somalia Effort" *New York Times*, July 12, 1993, A8. Ironically, the U.S. did the same to Italian forces when, in the midst of the disastrous October 3 raid, U.S. General Garrison urgently requested several dozen tanks from an Italian base 30 miles away to help rescue American troops from a major operation that Italian forces had not been aware of in advance. The Italians agreed to send the tanks—after checking with Rome—but they were not necessary once Malaysian and Pakistani armored forces rescued the American soldiers. See Rick Atkinson, "Night of a Thousand Casualties," *Washington Post*, January 31, 1994, A11.

10. Rick Atkinson, "The Raid That Went Wrong" *Washington Post*, January 30, 1994, A27.

11. Keith Richburg, "In War on Aideed, U.N. Battled Itself," *Washington Post*, December 6, 1993, A18. Notably, Pakistani forces began their mission in Somalia earlier than those of the U.S., and they stayed almost a year beyond the U.S. withdrawal, even though more Pakistani than American troops were killed in Somalia.

12. Mats Berdal, "Fateful Encounter: The United States and UN Peacekeeping," *Survival* 36, no. 1 (spring 1994): 43. UN forces in Somalia after the U.S. withdrawal included about 5,700 Pakistanis, 5,000 Indians, 1,700 Egyptians, and 1,400 Moroccans.

13. See S. Neil MacFarlane and Thomas G. Weiss, "Regional Organizations and Regional Security" *Security Studies* 2, no. 1 (autumn 1992): 6–37; see also Roberts, "Crisis in UN Peacekeeping," 95.

14. John Pomfret, "U.N. General In Bosnia Says He is Hamstrung," *Washington Post*, January 22, 1994, A11.

15. Interview with DOD officials.

16. Rick Atkinson, "Night of a Thousand Casualties," A31.

17. Reportedly, Montgomery's request was approved by Chairman of the Joint Chiefs of Staff Colin Powell. Aspin's caution in rejecting it may have been due to possible opposition in the Congress, as the Senate had overwhelmingly voted in a non-binding resolution in early September to require President Clinton to obtain Congressional approval of the U.S. mission in Somalia by November 15. See Barton Gellman, "The Words Behind a Deadly Decision," *Washington Post*, October 31, 1993, A1.

18. The request for AC-130s was reportedly opposed by General Hoar, head of Central Command, and Frank Wisner, Undersecretary of Defense for Policy. See Michael R. Gordon, "U.S. Officers Were Divided on Somali Raid," *New York Times*, May 13, 1994, A8.

19. See Preston and Williams, "Report on Somali Clash," A28. In the October 3 clash, Somali casualties were an estimated 312 killed and 814 wounded. See Terrence

Lyons and Ahmed Samatar, *Somalia: State Collapse, Multilateral Intervention, and Strategies for Political Reconstruction* (Washington, D.C.: Brookings Occasional Paper, 1995): 59.

20. See R. Jeffrey Smith, "Tracking Aideed Hampered by Intelligence Failures," *Washington Post*, October 8, 1993, A19; and Atkinson, "The Raid That Went Wrong," A27.

21. Barton Gellman, *Washington Post*, September 22, 1993, "U.S. Considers Putting GIs Under U.N.," A1.

22. Keith Richburg, "In War on Aideed, U.N. Battled Itself," *Washington Post*, December 6, 1993, A18. Reportedly, Italian, Saudi, and Kuwaiti forces in Somalia also at times refused orders from UN commander, Turkish Lt. General Cevik Bir. September 22, WP: "U.S. Reconsiders Putting GIs Under U.N."

23. On these points, see Berdal, "Fateful Encounter," 40.

24. Confirmation hearings of Charles Freeman to be assistant secretary of defense for International Security Affairs, Senate Armed Services Committee, First Session, 103rd Congress (U.S. GPO, 1993), 940.

25. John Pomfret, "U.N. Balkan Commander Demands Airstrike Power," *Washington Post*, January 25, 1994, A15.

26. Michael R. Gordon, "With NATO Ready to Strike, U.N. Sought to Warn Serbs" *New York Times*, March 18, 1994, A8. Later, Akashi tried to call Bosnian Serb leader Radovan Karadzic to urge him to pull back the Serbian forces from around Bihac to forestall UN air strikes, and he also rejected a request in April 1994 from NATO Secretary-General Manfred Wörner for air strikes on Serbian forces that shelled the town of Gorazde despite a NATO ultimatum. Although in the latter case Akashi's diplomacy eventually helped convince the Serbs to end their shelling of Gorazde, NATO and UN credibility were compromised. Julia Preston, "Diplomat Holds Key to Bombing," *Washington Post*, April 26, 1994, A8.

27. Berdal, "Fateful Encounter," 41.

28. Ibid., 43–44. See also Richard Betts, "The Delusion of Impartial Intervention," *Foreign Affairs* 73 no. 6 (November–December 1994): 30–33, and Lori Fisler Damrosch, "Concluding Reflections" in Damrosch, ed., *Enforcing Restraint: Collective Intervention in Internal Conflicts* (New York, Council on Foreign Relations, 1993): 354–355. For a view that is more ambivalent on the dilemmas between impartiality and selective enforcement, see Roberts, "The Crisis in UN Peacekeeping," 100–103, 113.

29. Roger Cohen, "Tribunal to Cite Bosnia Serb Chief as War Criminal," *New York Times*, April 24, 1995, A1.

30. In a 1995 article Admiral Howe articulates very insightfully many of the same operational and organizational "lessons of Somalia" as those raised in the present chapter, but he defends the political strategy toward Aideed in the fall of 1993. See Jonathan Howe, "The United States and United Nations in Somalia: The Limits of Involvement," *The Washington Quarterly* 18, no. 3 (1995): 49–62.

31. Gwen Ifill, "U.S. Mixes Signals To Somali General on its Next Steps," *New York Times*, Oct. 9, 1994, A1.

32. Howe later stated that the U.S. had had "many opportunities" to kill Aideed but had not done so, preferring to arrest him and put him through legal proceedings. See Dana Priest, "Administration Aides Defensive on Foreign Policy Strategies," *Washington Post*, October 11, 1993, A28.

33. Chester A. Crocker and Fen Osler Hampson, "Making Peace Settlements Work," *Foreign Policy* 104 (fall 1996): 61.

34. Lyons and Samatar, *Somalia*, 54–55.

35. Patrick Sloyan, "How the Warlord Outwitted Clinton's Spooks," *Washington Post*, April 3, 1994, C3.

36. On the deaths of Somali clan elders, see Berdal, "Fateful Encounter," 42.

37. Elaine Sciolino, "The U.N.'s Glow is Gone," *New York Times*, October 9, 1993, A1,7.

38. On these issues, see Keith Richburg, "Aideed Exploited U.N.'s Failure to Prepare," *Washington Post*, December 5, 1993, A1.

39. Lyons and Samatar, *Somalia*, 32–54.

40. Mats Berdal, "Fateful Encounter," 36.

41. The argument draws on Jane Stromseth, "Rethinking War Powers: Congress, The President, and the United Nations," *Georgetown Law Journal* 81, no. 3 (March 1993): 597–673.

42. Elaine Sciolino, "Pentagon Alters Goals in Somalia, Signaling Failure," *New York Times*, Sept. 28, 1993, A1; Michael Gordon and John Cushman, "U.S. Supported Hunt for Aidid; Now Calls U.N. Policy Skewed," *New York Times*, October 18, 1993, A1; Barton Gellman, "U.S. Rhetoric Changed, but Hunt Persisted," *Washington Post*, October 7, 1993, A37.

43. Gellman, "The Words Behind a Deadly Decision," A1.

44. See, for example, Michael Gordon, "Pentagon is Wary of Role in Bosnia," *New York Times*, March 15, 1994, A6. Elaine Sciolino, "Top U.S. Officials Divided in Debate on Invading Haiti," *New York Times*, August 4, 1994, A1.

45. Bob Shacochis, "Our Two Armies in Haiti," *New York Times*, January 8, 1995, Section 4, 19.

46. Ann Devroy and Bradley Graham, "U.S. Readies Force For Policing Haiti Following Invasion," *Washington Post*, September 9, 1994, A34.

47. John Hirsch and Robert Oakley, *Somalia and Operation Restore Hope: Reflections on Peacemaking and Peacekeeping* (Washington, D.C.: U.S. Institute of Peace, 1995): 47.

48. Elaine Sciolino, "Invasion of Haiti Would Be Limited, Clinton Aides Say," *New York Times*, September 13, 1994, A13.

49. Douglas Jehl, "Clinton Addresses Nation on Threat to Invade Haiti: Tells Dictators to Get Out," *New York Times*, September 16, 1994, A1. According to Jehl's sources, President Clinton approved a $12 million covert program in September to encourage Haiti's top military leaders to leave peacefully, and much of this money was made available for direct payoffs to the top leaders.

50. Douglas Farah, "U.S. Assists Dictators' Luxury Exile," *Washington Post*, October 14, 1994, A1.

51. For a similar assessment, see Crocker and Hampson, "Making Peace Settlements Work," 60–66. On the conditions under which power-sharing arrangements are likely to be viable solutions to internal conflicts, see Timothy Sisk, *Power Sharing and International Mediation in Ethnic Conflicts* (Washington, D.C.: U.S. Institute of Peace Press, 1996). On the conditions in which partition may be more successful, see Chaim Kaufmann, "Possible and Impossible Solutions to Ethnic Wars," *International Security* 20, no. 4 (spring 1996): 136–175.

Part Three

Collective Conflict Management: The Humanitarian Impulse

7

Changing Norms of Sovereignty and Multilateral Intervention

❑

Bruce Cronin

Collective security traditionally has been understood as a mechanism for protecting the territorial integrity and national independence of all states. Scholarly debates have tended to revolve around issues of viability, practicality and desirability—that is, the conditions under which collective security regimes arise—leaving the identity and purpose of the regime itself unaddressed.[1] Absent from much of the literature is an examination of how international institutions determine the norms of behavior that states would be expected to follow, beyond nonaggression. Thus, while there is a growing literature on how a collective security system could work—or not, depending upon the perspective—little has been written about how the international community determines the range of issues that would fall within the jurisdiction of a collective security regime.[2]

In a generic sense, the primary goal of a collective security system is to oppose aggression and protect the territorial integrity of states. The three previous attempts to establish such a system—the Concert of Europe, the League of Nations, and the United Nations (UN)—were formed in the aftermath of a major war largely for this purpose. Yet in each case, the standards of behavior to which states were expected to adhere went well beyond "negative limits" of nonaggression. The systems created in Vienna, Versailles, and San Francisco included a body of international law and multilateral agreements that stipulated specific obligations to the international community. In this regard, history has demonstrated that collective security regimes typically involve a second goal beyond the security of states: the protection of specified populations, institutions, or political communities *within* states. For example, the Concert of

Europe pledged to protect monarchs and royal families throughout Europe, the League of Nations tried to protect national minorities, and the United Nations focused on individual citizens through the concept of human rights. In each case, the principle of nonintervention that is implied in the concept of sovereignty was conditioned on states adhering to specific standards of behavior.

In examining this second goal, we are led to ask how collective security regimes determine what international obligations states have and to whom these obligations are owed. Whereas the principle of sovereignty provides the international community with a standard from which it can evaluate territorial and political claims, as the norms of sovereignty change,[3] our understanding of what constitutes an international, as opposed to domestic, concern changes as well. Thus, it is difficult to discuss violation and sanction within the framework of collective security without identifying the range of issues that would fall within the jurisdiction of a collective security regime. The kind of blatant aggression exhibited by Iraq in its invasion of Kuwait would likely be considered a violation in any system of collective security. Many of the problems that have recently promoted collective action by the international community, however—ethnic cleansing in Bosnia, repression of the Kurds and Shiites in Iraq, genocide in Rwanda, repression and overthrow of an elected government in Haiti, and civil war in Somalia—traditionally have been considered domestic matters, which are beyond the jurisdiction of international organizations.

This chapter attempts to recast the collective security debate more broadly by demonstrating that international obligations are historically contingent—there can be no one-size-fits-all model. Collective security regimes are built around a "consensus agenda" for international society.[4] Through this agenda, member states make commitments to specific populations or political communities within states, and over time these commitments form the basis for obligations toward these communities. The commitments reflect a general consensus concerning where sovereignty ultimately resides, for example, within an ethnic or cultural community; among the citizens living within a territorially-bound political unit; within the political institutions of an internationally-recognized state; or within a community of religious faithful. This determines who has the legitimate "title" to the state, and in the broader sense, defines what constitutes a "legitimate" state. In other words, the norms of the international system are derived from the identities of participating states.

The first section offers a theoretical framework for examining the normative foundation for collective security. This section establishes a relationship between the international community's definition of legitimate sovereignty and the expectations of states' obligations to that community. The second section examines recent multilateral conventions and agreements to determine if a consensus agenda is evolving around the legitimate source of sovereignty. In doing so, it explores whether commitments toward specific political communities are developing into a set of international obligations. If so, this could have major implications for definitions of sovereign rights and obligations ranging from a "right" to democratic government to an obligation for states to respect human rights and claims of self-determination. Consequently, more domestic conflicts are likely to be reconceptualized as matters of concern for international diplomacy. In this way, the international community is likely to be more interventionist in matters that have been traditionally considered domestic questions.

The Conception of Sovereignty in the Creation of Collective Security Regimes

Sovereignty, territorial integrity, and the legal equality of states provide the foundation of international relations.[5] On its most fundamental level, collective security can be understood as a mechanism for protecting these principles. Traditionally, the literature on collective security has focused primarily on territorial integrity, as indicated by what scholars hold to be its basic principles: Peace is indivisible; no grievance warrants resorting to force to overturn the status quo; military force is legitimate only to resist attack; and all have a legal and moral obligation to consider an attack on any nation as an attack upon themselves.[6] Although this focus addresses an important component of collective security, it is limited in at least three ways.

First, it fails to provide any grounds for purposeful or meaningful action beyond the preservation of self and system.[7] Collective security systems defend particular orders. As Kenneth Thompson argues, for a collective security system to work, the members must enjoy a minimum of political solidarity and moral community, as well as agreed upon concepts of justice.[8] Charles and Clifford Kupchan add that the major powers must have fundamentally compatible views of what constitutes a stable and acceptable international order.[9] Anne-Marie Burley goes even further, arguing that the democratization of a majority of the major powers is an explicit prerequisite for any peacekeeping enterprise.[10]

Joseph Lepgold's and Thomas Weiss's typology in chapter one spells out how these ideal types go beyond what is necessary for the creation of a collective security system. But most students of collective security posit a system that reflects a particular set of values that goes beyond simple nonaggression. Thus, the principles of nonaggression and "one for all and all for one" can tell us about the form international relations could take within a collective security system, but say little about its content. By focusing solely on territorial integrity as the basis for a collective security regime, many scholars postulate the protection of state possession without discussing the nature of state responsibility.

Like all multilateral institutions, collective security systems are built upon political and normative frameworks that define just and unjust behavior. Its authority is based not only on power—the ability to create and enforce rules—but also on a legitimate social purpose.[11] All international institutions embody sets of political practices and rules that prescribe behavioral roles, constrain activity, and shape expectations.[12] These rules and practices are not generic entities, but concrete manifestations of purposeful goals. The goals vary during different periods of history. There can be no single "one size fits all" model of collective security system; it must be contextualized within the specifics of a particular historical period. Thus, by focusing on collective security only as a mechanism for maintaining territorial integrity, much of the current literature posits self-preservation as its sole raison d'être.

Second, the focus on territorial integrity privileges territoriality as the primary organizing principle of international relations. As the nation-state system is territorially-based, the organization of space is only one of several functions of the sovereign state. There are at least two others: legitimating political and social institutions; and acting as a vehicle for managing class, ethnic, economic, and religious conflicts within and between societies.[13] Borders may define the geographic limits of a state's authoritative control, but they do not define the basic nature of the state itself. Although the distribution of territory among various sovereign authorities is certainly an important question in international relations, the sources of authority itself are equally important.

Moreover, states often define their interests in terms of protecting values and institutions that extend beyond national borders. Woodrow Wilson sought to make the world safe for liberal democracy and capitalism; Austrian minister Clements von Metternich sought the same for monarchy. Leon Trotsky promoted class internationalism. And the theocratic leadership of Iran has advocated an Islamic "revolution without borders." In each case, the advocates were articulating a vision for a different type of state in which sovereignty resided in a different political community. Multilateral organizations and institutions were created to promote these forms and reflected these visions.

Third, the principle of territorial integrity does not tell us how members of a collective security regime would differentiate between an international and a domestic issue, nor the nature of states' obligations toward the international community. The concept of external sovereignty confers upon a state the exclusive right to control its own internal affairs, but it does not stipulate what is to be considered internal. The line between domestic and international is often arbitrary; it is dependent upon how the international community defines the extent and limits of sovereign authority.[14] For example, throughout history we have seen alternative claims about jurisdiction over religious persecution, dynastic succession, protection of ethnic minorities, and human rights.

Finally, the principle of territorial integrity does not tell us which authorities will be recognized as holding sovereign rights within a specified political space. This question is crucial, for example, in determining whether borders can be redrawn to accommodate nationalist claims of self-determination, or in deciding whether to intervene in a civil war between competing authorities.

The traditional analytical emphases have been on territorial integrity and to a lesser extent on the legal equality of states; but it is the principle of sovereignty that defines territory as political space and determines when a political community can be considered a state. If sovereignty were a constant, there would be little need to make it the focus of investigation. However, throughout modern history, changing definitions of populations, territories, and legitimate authority have altered the norms of sovereignty.

The state has been recognized as the legitimate actor in world politics since at least the eighteenth century, but the source of sovereign authority with the state has varied considerably across time and space. For example, since the seventeenth century, sovereign authority has been legitimized alternately through divine right, tradition, natural law, dynastic lineage, social contract, and the national principle. In each case, the legitimizing principle conferred a right to rule on specific authorities, which are recognized both internationally and domestically. The determination by the international community as to the legitimate source of authority has had important effects in such areas as defining international obligation, redrawing borders, deciding whether self-defined political communities can form their own state, and what constitutes a legitimate state. Thus, states are entitled to protection from aggression according to international law and multilateral treaties (such as the UN Charter), but this "right" is not absolute.

Sovereignty can be broadly defined as "the institutionalization of public authority within mutually exclusive domains."[15] While these "domains" are territorially-based, the key idea embedded in this definition is that of institutional authority. Virtually all states in the system have undergone territorial changes at some point in their history, often instigated or at least validated by diplomatic institutions. Moreover, definitions of "nationality" have not remained constant—for example, what it means to be "German." Boundaries and populations can change over time. However, as long as a particular authority is not seriously challenged by a competing one within the same domain at the same time, it remains sovereign.[16] Simultaneously, authority can take a wide variety of forms and these different forms can and have occupied the same territory during different periods of history, changing not only the identity of the state itself, but the definition of the populations within it.

The principle of territorial integrity can be understood as an international property right;[17] possession is exclusive and mutually recognized. In theory, this defends each state from encroachment by other states, but only insofar as the state is governed by a recognized authority. Although sovereignty connotes a set of exclusive rights over a specified territory and population, the principle of territoriality does not tell us *which* authorities will be recognized as holding legitimate sovereign rights within that political space. In any social system, possession is understood in terms of ownership, which is recognized either through law or a set of norms legitimizing possession.

Which authorities have the legitimate "title" to a territory and the populations within it has always been a systemic and domestic issue. The rights to sovereign dominion (territorial integrity, autonomy, and noninterference) only belong to the state as a participant in the international sovereignty game, rather than to the people who have delegated specific powers to the government.[18] Therefore, the legitimation of internal and external sovereignty has always been closely connected.

This point has been demonstrated continually. Over time states have been created, reorganized, and dissolved on the basis of changing definitions of legitimate sovereignty.[19] For example, until the post-war era, colonized populations and their local authorities had no territorial rights; international norms held these terrorists to be *terra nullius* and open to acquisition by soverign states.[20] At the same time, self-proclaimed nations such as the Kurds, the Palestinians, the Basques, and the Quebeçois have not been recognized by the international community as having the rights of sovereign statehood; their populations are considered to be "citizens" of the multiethnic states to which they are a part. During this same period, however, the international community either created or recognized such sovereign states as Taiwan, East Germany, and "North" and "South" Vietnam.

Territory has been only one of several factors in defining the political boundaries and identity of the state. As definitions of populations and legitimate authority change, the conditions under which the international community recognized "possession as ownership" change as well. Despite the longevity of many states, state identities have not remained stable over time; definitions of individual states often change with shifting locations of sovereign authority.

For example, following World War I, the Austro-Hungarian and Ottoman Empires were broken up, reorganized, and redefined as a series of "nations" by the international community that emerged from the war. The location of sovereignty was no longer the dynastic family or the monarchy, but its cultural and ethnic communities comprised the "nation." Following World War II, some of these same "nations"—for example Yugoslavia and Germany—were reorganized as juridical or populist states, with the location of sovereignty moving to either the citizens or the institutions of the state. More recently, the international community has recognized five states in what is now the former Yugoslavia, but there is once again a single German state.

The sovereign state has been recognized by the international community and international law as the legitimate actor in world politics. Yet, the source of sovereign authority within the state, and the identity of the state itself, has varied considerably across time and space. Since the institutionalization of sovereignty as the constitutive principle in European relations, sovereign authority has alternately resided within the person of the king, a recognized dynastic family, an ethnic or cultural community, the citizen, the body of the faithful, and the institutions of a recognized juridical state. In each case, a corresponding legitimizing principle conferred a right to rule on specific authorities. As Daniel Philpott points out, all particular historical uses of the term "sovereignty" have meant a particular form of supreme legitimate authority, reflecting a specific philosophy in a given era.[21] This has not only been important domestically, but also internationally. It has determined who the legitimate polities in international politics are and who is entitled to become one.

Sovereign Authority as an International Issue

Over the past several hundred years, the nation-state system has accommodated various forms of authority within the institution of sovereign statehood. There have been dynastic states, legitimized through family lineage, marriage ties, and legal titles to territory; national states, legitimized through the principle of ethnic and cultural autonomy; theocratic states, legitimized through divine law; citizens or populist states, legitimized through social contract; and juridical states, legitimized through the principle of civic nationalism and tradition. In each case, legitimate sovereignty has resided within a different political community within society, and had been legitimized by a corresponding principle.

At the same time that sovereignty has been residing within a particular polity inside a state, other domestic political communities continued to exist within such state, often making counter-claims to being the source of sovereignty. In many cases, they sought to redefine the territories and populations that comprised the state itself. This conflict, for example, was at the root of the English Civil War in the late seventeenth century, when king and Parliament clashed over whether English sovereignty resided within the monarchy or the aristocracy.[22] In more complex cases, for example, the conflict between the nation, the citizen, and the monarchy resulted in a reorganization of the state itself and a redistribution of territorial borders and populations.

Historically, the political and normative institutions of international orders have tended to favor a particular form of state, and international communities tend to recognize specific forms of authority as legitimate. The principles upon which states are organized have international as well as domestic implications. In a royal or dynastic state, the population has no independent existence. Populations could and were regularly "bartered about" and "reassigned" to other states, either as compensation to sovereigns or to facilitate the balance of power. In a theocratic state like the Ottoman Empire, sovereignty resides in the body of the faithful. The identity of the population is fixed, however, borders that divide those of the faith are not recognized; this in fact was the claim made by Iran, which has called for a "revolution without borders."[23]

In an ethnic/national state, sovereignty rests with a defined political community based on ethnocultural characteristics, while in a populist state it rests with citizens. In both cases, the population is more important than the territory, however, the populations are defined very differently. In a liberal or social democratic state, sovereignty resides with the body of citizens.[24] Citizenship is derived from individual autonomy rather than a community. "Nationality" in this context is a juridical, rather than a cultural concept, which can be traced to the French Revolution. As Eric Hobsbawm points out about the post-revolutionary state in France, "French nationality was French citizenship: ethnicity, history, the language or patois spoken at home, were irrelevant to the definition of the 'nation.'"[25] This has been referred to commonly as civic nationalism. In this case, neither the individual nor a group of individuals is recognized as having a right to secede from their political community. The theory of "government by consent of the governed" only requires a right to participate or be represented within the existing political unit, not to form a new unit.[26]

In a national state, on the other hand, the ethnic community is the basis for sovereignty. Citizenship is derived from membership in that community. The community exists apart from the individuals that comprise it, and its members inherit their identities.[27] Whereas *civic* nationalism is inclusionary within defined boundaries, *ethnic* nationalism is exclusionary and not limited by political borders. This distinction is crucial, for example, in determining whether borders can be redrawn to accommodate nationalist claims of self-determination. Consequently, by adopting the national principle as its standard for legitimate sovereign authority, the international community has at times broken-up and reorganized existing states. Recognition of this principle has also turned civil wars into international ones. A domestic dispute among ethnic or national groups can be reconceptualized as an international war.

History has shown that following major revolutionary periods and systemic wars, political actors attempt to build a new international consensus around a set of principles that would provide a political foundation for a new order. Some of the issues requiring such a consensus are immediate: borders often need to be redrawn and/or reconfirmed; new governments need to be installed within territories where authority has collapsed or is contested; and a new set of workable diplomatic arrangements needs to be created among states. Although the most powerful actors clearly have the greatest influence in this process, they usually seek to achieve a consensus among a broad group of states by legitimizing a particular set of political principles.[28]

These principles become codified in treaties and documents, institutionalized through multilateral institutions, and redefined and fixed through collective action. Through these mechanisms, certain kinds of states are legitimized and commitments are made to specific political communities that are viewed as the source of sovereignty within the state. Thus, the Concert of Europe was built on the legitimation of the monarchic state, and commitments were made to protect monarchs and royal families throughout Europe. The concert intervened in Spain, Portugal, Piedmont, and Naples in support of this principle. In accepting two new states, Greece and Belgium, into the European system, the concert required their establishment as monarchic states with ties to a recognized European royal family.

Following World War I, the international order created through the Versailles Treaty and the League of Nations system rested on the legitimation of the national state. Commitments were made to national minorities who were "trapped" within an otherwise homogenous ethnic or cultural community. After World War II, the term "national" was dropped from the concept of "self-determination," as the international community sought to legitimize "populist" states. Human rights replaced minority rights in political discourse, and commitments were made to citizens as individuals rather than as a national community. In each case, there was a link between the political communities that were cited for protection and the form of authority that the international community promoted as legitimate. The collective security systems that were envisioned—the Concert of Europe, the League of Nations, and the United Nations—were each based on a specific definition of sovereignty and obligation.

A New Legitimist Principle and the Future of Collective Security

The relationship between conceptions of sovereign authority and definitions of state obligations has important implications for the future, particularly as it pertains to issues that traditionally have been considered to be of domestic concern. Conflicts over the source of legitimate sovereign authority dominate current international politics. Among these are competing definitions of the "nation" in the Balkans, the former Soviet Union, the Middle East, Canada, and Ireland; competing authorities in Somalia and Rwanda; arbitrary rule and human rights abuses in Haiti and Nigeria; competing claims by sub-state, state, and suprastate authorities in the European Union.

Aside from questions of commitment and sacrifice, the political leadership of most states has appeared uncertain about their responsibilities and interests. The line that divides domestic from international issues appears to have shifted. The end of the Cold War changed the structure and alliance patterns of the international system as well as the frames of reference used by states to evaluate behavior. The old pattern of obligations and prerogatives has been altered. In this context, what would constitute a violation of the rules of coexistence, when the rules themselves may be changing?

The collective security debate needs to go beyond its focus on territorial integrity and non-aggression. We should examine the way that world leaders will likely understand the nature of sovereignty. The international community tends to make commitments to political communities and institutions within sovereign states during periods of rapid political change. In making these commitments, diplomats and national leaders may not intend to create general obligations toward these groups. However, over time they often become institutionalized in multilateral conventions, treaties, and associations. Many international actors interpret this as recognition for their political claims and an expectation of international support.

If this is in fact the case, we need to understand the types of international commitments made over the past few decades and their consequences to explain the dilemmas faced by world leaders. Admittedly, evidence will be sketchy; we are too close to draw definitive conclusions. Yet, it is possible to demonstrate a relatively consistent pattern of diplomatic discourse that clearly favors one particular understanding of sovereignty over others.

The demise of bipolarity has offered an opportunity to construct an international community based on a "consensus agenda"—not present since 1815. As Arnold Wolfers points out, collective security is difficult, if not impossible, in a balance-of-power system in which alliance membership prevents sanction against allies.[29] In the aftermath of the Cold War, states once again have an opportunity to put into practice the principles that were developed after the end of World War II. Since that time, the international community has indicated that it recognizes three primary forms of sovereign authority: of the state, which links authority to a historically-defined territory; of the nation, which links authority to a defined population that comprises a unique cultural and/or ethnic polity; and of the people, which links authority to a defined citizenship.

During the Cold War, the bifurcation of the international system made it impossible for the major powers to agree on a consensus agenda. The collective security system envisioned in San Francisco in 1946 was never developed. After the Cold War, it is helpful to examine the "seeds" that multilateral bodies and agencies have planted over the past 50 years. In this regard, the conventions, treaties, and institutions that were signed or created outside the Cold War framework clearly indicate a strong bias toward popular sovereignty. This bias can be seen in at least some areas: definition of a legitimate state, human rights agreements, and policies and new justifications for intervention.

Definition of a Legitimate State

The end of World War II brought forth a crisis of legitimacy for the nation-state, particularly in Europe.[30] In addition to reestablishing states that had been occupied by Germany, the internal organization of states was an important issue for the victors. The issue of legitimate authority arose almost immediately within the United Nations over the case of Spain. In 1946, the General Assembly adopted a resolution stating that the "Franco Fascist Government . . . does not represent the Spanish people," and recommended that it be barred from membership in international institutions. Moreover, it continued that the Security Council should take action:

> . . . if within a reasonable time, there is not established a government which derives its authority from the consent of the governed, committed to respect freedom of speech, religion and assembly and to the prompt holding of elections, in which the Spanish people, free from force and intimidation and regardless of party, may express their will . . .[31]

That same year, the General Assembly passed the Universal Declaration of Human Rights, in which Article 21(3) stated that "the will of the people shall be the basis of the authority of government."[32] This sentiment was largely lost, except rhetorically, during the Cold War, as the major powers favored the stability of absolute borders over the potential instability of competing sovereignties.[33] However, the end of the Cold War revitalized it when the Conference on Security and Cooperation in Europe (CSCE) issued a joint document with the then-Soviet Union in 1990, which stated in part that "the will of the people, freely and fairly expressed through periodic and genuine elections, is the basis of the authority and the legitimacy of all government."[34] Indeed, the first post-Cold War document to emerge out of Europe, the Charter of Paris, pledged to "build, consolidate and strengthen democracy as the only system of government of our nations," and affirmed that "democratic government is based on the will of the people." These principles, the document continues, "form the basis for our relations."[35]

These documents and statements of principle, all widely supported, suggest a normative consensus about popular sovereignty as the accepted source of authority for states. Such a consensus is only a first important step in the establishment of obligations. The Preambles to the United Nations Charter and the Covenant of the League of Nations, for example, never mentioned popular sovereignty, although they vaguely referred to self-determination (which was largely viewed as being confined to anti-colonialism).

It remains to be seen whether states will in fact institutionalize the implications suggested in such a consensus within domestic law, as the treaties theoretically do, and more importantly within their foreign policy institutions. If so, it would have profound implications for the understanding of states' obligations to the international community. Whereas the Concert of Europe saw an attack on any royal authority as an international violation, future collective security regimes may question the legitimacy of states that cannot credibly claim to represent the "will" of their people, however defined. Indicative of this, even the Organization of American States (OAS), a regional organization that has traditionally held sovereignty to be absolute and opposed foreign intervention, voted to take action when there is a "sudden or irregular interruption of the democratic political institutional process or of the legitimate exercise of power by the democratically elected government in any of the Organization's member states."[36]

Indications that the international community considers a legitimate state to be popularly, rather than nationally or juridically based, are also evident in the recent criteria for recognition of new states. For example, in recognizing the former Yugoslav republics, the European Community (EC) set as a condition that the new states demonstrate "respect for the . . . Charter of the United Nations . . . the Final Act of Helsinki . . . and the Charter of Paris, especially with regard to the rule of law, democracy and human rights."[37] Just as the Concert of Europe had conditioned the creation of Belgium and Greece by establishing a monarchic government headed by a recognized European royal family, recognition for new states in the current era could require establishing democratic institutions. In a document issued from Moscow in 1991, the Conference on Security and Cooperation in Europe (CSCE) pledged to condemn any overthrow or attempted overthrow of a democratically-elected government and "to support vigorously . . . the legitimate organs of that state upholding human rights, democracy and the rule of law."[38] If "royal rights" is substituted for "human rights," and "monarchy" for "democracy," this document could have been issued by the Holy Alliance a century and a half ago.

A consensus that sovereignty resides within the citizen rather than the state or ethnic community also has been indicated by commitments made by multilateral bodies to human rights. The UN Charter places a clear priority on the territorial integrity of states over commitments to individuals and political communities within states, but a large body of multilateral conventions and treaties has eroded this priority. Many of these agreements clearly reflect commitments to individual citizens through the protection of human rights. National rights, religious rights, and other forms of group rights largely have disappeared from diplomatic discourse. Rather, there appears to be an emerging consensus that the international community has an obligation to protect at least a minimal level of human rights within states. This obligation is taking on the force of international law, although enforcement mechanisms lag behind the articulation of principles.

Since the end of World War II, a majority of states have signed treaties and conventions acknowledging an international obligation toward maintaining a minimal level of protection for basic rights. These agreements include the Helsinki Accords, the Universal Declaration of Human Rights, and International Covenants on Civil and Political Rights, and on Economic and Social Rights. In addition, there are conventions such as those prohibiting forced labor and racial discrimination and providing equal rights for women.[39]

In all, nations have signed approximately 25 human rights conventions and protocols. For example, 99 countries have thus far signed the Convention on the Prevention and Punishment of the Crime of Genocide.[40] The United States took this convention seriously enough so that Washington consciously refused to characterize the 1994 Rwandan conflict as "genocide," lest they be required to intervene. The codification of this principle in treaty form indicates that a majority of states consider genocide to be an international, rather than a domestic issue.

Accused human rights violators, such as China, have faced trade and other economic sanctions.[41] The Bush and Clinton administrations both preferred to separate the issues of human rights from questions of trade and military cooperation; but they found it difficult to avoid their perceived obligation to uphold the principles that the U.S. had itself promoted. Moreover, China's position on sovereignty and obligation has changed. Peking traditionally held that the principle of sovereignty prohibited any interference in the internal affairs of independent nations (reflecting a state sovereignty perspective). But in the early 1990s, they agreed that human rights are a valid subject of international dialogue and with certain limits are a subject of international law.[42]

As Jack Donnelly points out, prior to World War II, states rarely claimed obligations to protect citizens from their own governments. Such issues were considered to be protected exercise of the sovereign prerogatives of states. Claims were generally limited to foreign nationals.[43] Reflective of the principle of sovereignty of the people, international discourse has shifted from obligations to protect "minority rights" (a legacy of the post-Versailles order) to the protection of "human rights."

Moreover, "national" self-determination has been superseded in most international forums by "self-determination." This reflects a shift from viewing the "nation" as the legitimate source of sovereign authority to the "people." Sovereignty of the nation is still very present as a competing principle, yet sovereignty of the people has tended to be stronger. For example, the UN resolution pronouncing colonialism to be illegitimate was based not on *national* self-determination (the right of a cultural community to form their own state) but rather *individual* self-determination (the right of a people to self-government). This reflects a change in legitimizing principles from the "nation" to the "people."[44] Thus, new states were created not on the basis of traditional ethnic or tribal populations, which would reflect obligations toward the nation, but rather from the people who inhabited what had been the old colonial administrative boundaries. The principle of self-determination was implemented by granting a set of sovereign rights to a geographically-bound population, rather than to a specific national community.

This normative concept is beginning to be applied to an area that has traditionally been focused solely on strategic calculations, namely military alliances.

In discussing the expansion of the North American Treaty Organization (NATO), U.S. Secretary of Defense William Perry stated that any new member must agree to uphold democracy, protect freedom and human rights within their borders, and respect sovereignty outside their borders.[45] If NATO is moving in this direction, it challenges the traditional thinking on the role of military alliance in the balance-of-power system.[46]

In addition to traditional definitions of human rights, new commitments have been made to populations rather than states: the development of "safe zones" to protect populations from their governments. This idea was used in Iraq (to protect the Kurds and Shiites) and Bosnia and has been proposed in Rwanda. The international position was based on the protection of populations from human rights abuses and genocide, and not on the particular claims to statehood or nationality. More significantly, protected populations were located within established states. The United Nations did not grant rights of statehood but justified interventions by citing violations by existing authorities and by noting their obligations to protect populations from gross and consistent human rights abuses.

Although there remains uncertainty about the international community's willingness to enforce such rights, a new concept of international responsibility toward populations is emerging that reflects new understandings of the limits and prerogatives of state sovereignty. Moreover, there has been a proliferation of international tribunals to punish gross human rights violators in the former Yugoslavia and Rwanda. These tribunals were set up by international institutions comprised of countries that are not parties to the conflict. Unlike tribunals for German and Japanese war criminals, they cannot be dismissed as simply "victor's justice."

A third indication that the international community recognizes sovereignty as residing within a body of citizens is the growing use of international monitoring of elections in such countries as Mexico, El Salvador, Nicaragua, Cambodia, South Africa, and Haiti. The way that a country chooses its political leadership has been traditionally among the most absolute of domestic prerogatives. Yet aside from a desire for regimes to legitimize themselves domestically, many countries now find it necessary to legitimize their rule internationally. For liberal democracies, this is done through periodic elections, and as Anne-Marie Burley argues, liberal states tend to hold other liberal states to a higher standard than they do non-liberal regimes.[47] Thus, for states to enter the "club," they have an obligation to choose their governments according to liberal rules. In short, domestic political processes are now routinely viewed as international issues.

Finally, there are new criteria for defining a legitimate basis for intervention by the international community. This question is covered extensively in both the international law and political science literature.[48] However, this literature tends to focus on the question of whether there is a right to intervention rather than the circumstances under which the international community is obligated to act, or how much target states are considered to be violating their international obligations through their domestic policies. Although the question of rights is certainly an important and controversial issue, this chapter is more concerned with the connection between the norms of sovereignty and the obligations of states.

Actions in the past decade suggest that the normative acceptance of popular sovereignty as the source of authority has produced two new types of international action: "humanitarian" intervention and intervention against "illegitimate" regimes.[49] Neither of these principles can be found in either the League's Covenant or the UN Charter.[50] To find a similar principle, we need to look back to the Concert of Europe, which promoted collective intervention when the sanctity of royal institutions was threatened, or interventions on behalf of "minority" rights during the late nineteenth and early twentieth centuries. Although intervention to topple foreign governments was common during the Cold War, they were almost always unilateral actions aimed at promoting the self-defined interest of the intervening state, not collective actions based on a commonly accepted normative principle.[51] In this context, interventions in Haiti, Somalia, and Rwanda could be viewed as conceptually different. They appear to reflect a new understanding of sovereignty and obligation on the part of both the target states and the international community.

Most conflicts since World War II have been internal to states, and most actions taken through the United Nations and NATO have been in response to domestic crises. These actions and recent UN activities suggest that the definitions of "domestic" and "international" have changed. Thus, we can expect collective security to be as much concerned with what goes on *within* established states as without.

Conclusion

Collective security deals with standards of behavior and accepted practices. These standards cannot be deduced through general theory, but they are derived from the norms of sovereignty which change over time. As these norms change, so does the nature of international responsibility. These responsibilities are reflected by the international commitments toward specific populations and institutions. Throughout history, international institutions have sought to legitimize a particular type of state defined by the location of sovereign authority. From the perspective of the international community, these norms assume different obligations both to their domestic populations and to the community as a whole. Different conceptions of sovereign authority lead to qualitatively different definitions of state obligations. This in turn determines how much a government's behavior is classified as domestic or international.

Understanding international relations in terms of sovereign rights versus sovereign responsibilities can help scholars and public officials better understand future problems and issues. Conceptions of sovereignty influence the direction of academic scholarship and affect the thinking of policymakers and journalists, who have defined the range of legitimate perspectives, set normative guidelines, and guided strategic thought.

Over the past few decades, there has been a growing consensus that governments have specific responsibilities to their populations that cannot be averted under the cover of so-called domestic prerogatives. These responsibilities have tended to be legal and moral rather than political. There is as yet no agreement on international mechanisms for enforcing these responsibilities on revisionist states, but they have been codified in both international law and diplomatic practice. This can have profound implications for the future of multilateral security management. Gidon Gottlieb argues, for example, that if sovereignty of the people rather than sovereignty of the state becomes the accepted norm, autocratic rulers may no longer be insulated from international intervention, since the rights of sovereignty would not be theirs to evoke.[52] If the international community views the source of legitimate sovereign authority as emanating from the people rather than the state, then "gross and consistent" human rights abuses, arbitrary rule, and a denial of national self-determination could be viewed by the international community as violations of international obligations. Issues traditionally considered as domestic will likely be reconceptualized as international.

The international community, for example, through the United Nations, could credibly claim the right to take action against the offending state or government. Gottlieb refers to this as collective intervention rather than collective security,[53] but in practice this distinction has always been somewhat arbitrary. As Gottlieb argues, when the Security Council is intent on acting, it invokes Chapter VII of the Charter.[54] This distinction is arbitrary in theory as well. Violations of a state's obligations to the international community are international, not domestic, issues, regardless of the nature of these violations.

Variation in how the norms of sovereignty are implemented by the international community are to be expected. There are still states that either fail to acknowledge the legitimacy of popular sovereignty or a larger number that do so in name only. Sovereignty of the people is becoming the primary accepted form, but the international community is unlikely to require all nonconformists to adopt such principles as a condition of diplomatic recognition.

Nor should it be expected to enforce uniformly these norms because there is both a supply and a demand problem. Since sovereignty norms create a far higher standard for state behavior than simple principles of nonaggression, the instances of noncompliance should be expected to be higher. Thus, enforcement will have to be selective. Also, power considerations and domestic politics will constrain how much states may collectively enforce these norms, even if the political will exists. Military intervention is less likely in cases where the target state is strong or where a long conflict could result. In these cases, international institutions may rely on other, less direct, means for enforcement such as diplomatic and economic sanctions.

At the same time, so long as the international obligations toward human rights and humanitarian treatment of populations are accepted in principle, the community can accept a moderate level of violations in practice. Anne-Marie Burley offers a helpful model for balancing the values of coexistence and peace with those of human rights. She argues that liberal states make distinction between a "zone of politics" and a "zone of law" in the contemporary international system. A zone of politics is comprised of both democratic and authoritarian states and is characterized by a lack of consensus about the norms of sovereignty and coexistence. Within this zone, political considerations dominate diplomatic and dispute resolution processes. A zone of law consists of liberal (and social) democratic states that agree to a specific set of norms, rules, and principles concerning the limits and prerogatives of sovereignty.[55] In the zone of politics, collective action will be likely reserved for the more egregious cases, and will often be balanced against other values such as peaceful coexistence. In addition, international institutions and diplomatic practice still recognize "historic states," and other forms of legitimation of authority continue to compete with the will of the people—for example, nationalism and divine law.

In conclusion, the argument here leads to normative questions about how states should understand the consequences of their commitments toward populations and how these commitments could have important policy implications. For a number of years, the international community has made commitments to protect human rights, implicitly recognizing citizens as the legitimate holders of sovereignty within established states. These commitments have been institutionalized through multilateral organizations and treaties. If the international community promotes the populist state as the legitimate form, collective security regimes are obligated to protect individuals by labeling human rights abuses as international violations. Thus, the debate during the Haiti crisis over whether the U.S. had a "vital interest" in that country was misplaced. In an international order that seeks in part to protect populations from gross and consistent human rights abuses, it is in the interest of all states to uphold the principles that help to maintain a democratic international order.

Notes

1. The two articles that have defined the current debate from opposing perspectives are Charles A. Kupchan and Clifford A. Kupchan, "Concerts, Collective Security, and the Future of Europe," *International Security* 16, no. 1 (summer 1991): 114–161; and Richard K. Betts, "Systems of Peace or Causes of War?," *International Security* 17, no. 1

(summer 1992): 5–43. Other recent articles include: John Mueller, "A New Concert of Europe?," *Foreign Policy* 77 (winter 1988–90): 3–16; James E. Goodby, "A New European Concert," *Arms Control Today* 21, 1 (January/February 1991): 77–101; and Gregory Flynn and David Scheffer, "Limited Collective Security," *Foreign Policy* 80 (fall 1990): 77–100. The more classic works include Arnold Wolfers, *Discord and Collaboration, Essays on International Politics* (Baltimore, Md.: The Johns Hopkins University Press, 1988), chapters 11 and 12; Hans Morganthau, *Politics Among Nations: The Struggle for Power and Peace* (New York: McGraw-Hill, 1993), chapter 19; Kenneth Thompson, "Collective Security Reexamined, *American Political Science Review* 47, no. 3 (September 1953): 753–756; and Inis Claude, *Swords into Plowshares* (New York: Random House, 1971), chapter 12.

2. "International community" refers to the collectivity of recognized political authorities who maintain formal, ongoing relationships with each other in international affairs during a particular historical period. Such authorities include national leaders, diplomats, and officials from international organizations and institutions. Robert Jackson argues that an international community of sovereign states (represented by diplomats) can be identified by generally-accepted procedural norms and standards of conduct that are specified in the charters of international organizations and in customary international law. See Robert Jackson, "International Community Beyond the Cold War," in Gene M. Lyons and Michael Mastanduno, eds., *Beyond Westphalia: State Sovereignty and International Intervention* (Baltimore, Md.: The Johns Hopkins University Press, 1995): 62, 69.

3. The norms of sovereignty prescribe the following: who are the legitimate polities in international politics, who is entitled to become one, and what are the essential prerogatives in making and enforcing decisions that the legitimate polities enjoy? See Daniel Philpott, "Sovereignty: An Introduction and Brief History." *Journal of International Affairs* 48, no. 2 (winter 1995): 353–368.

4. The term "consensus agenda" is drawn from Andreas Osiander, *The States System of Europe, 1640–1990: Peacemaking and the Conditions of International Stability* (Oxford, U.K.: Clarendon Press, 1994): 8–9. He defines such an agenda as a set of principles regarding the identity of the actors, their relative status vis-à-vis each other, and the distribution of territories and populations between them.

5. See Kal Holsti, *International Politics: A Framework for Analysis* (Englewood Cliffs, N.J.: Prentice-Hall, 1967): 83.

6. These principles can be found in Betts, "Systems of Peace or Causes of War?"; Thompson, "Collective Security Reexamined"; Morganthau, *Politics Among Nations*; Kupchan and Kupchan, "Concerts, Collective Security, and the Future of Europe"; and Wolfers, *Discord and Collaboration*, 183.

7. E. H. Carr argues that this is a limitation of realism in general. See his *The Twenty Years Crisis, 1919–1939* (New York: Harper and Row, 1939): 92.

8. Kenneth Thompson, "Collective Security Reexamined," 768. I am referring here to the more extensive Wilsonian type of collective security regime.

9. Kupchan and Kupchan, "Concerts, Collective Security and the Future of Europe," 161.

10. Anne-Marie Burley, "Toward an Age of Liberal Nations," *Harvard International Law Journal* 33, no. 2 (spring 1992): 399.

11. John Ruggie defines political authority as a fusion of power with legitimate social purpose. See "International Regimes, Transactions, and Change: Embedded Liberalism in the Postwar Economic Order," in Stephen D. Krasner, ed., *International Regimes* (Ithaca, N.Y.: Cornell University Press, 1983): 198.

12. See Robert Keohane, "Multilateralism: An Agenda for Research," *International Journal* 45 (autumn 1990): 732.

13. See Joseph A. Camilleri and Jim Falk, *The End of Sovereignty? The Politics of a Shrinking and Fragmenting World* (Aldirshot, U.K.: Edward Elgar Publishers, 1992): 24–28.

14. A realist may argue that the line is determined by the ability of a state to back up its claims by military force. However, this avoids the question of rights and obligations. Even in a hierarchical (as opposed to anarchic) system, norms and rules are routinely violated. This does not negate the existence of the rule. See Helen Milner, "The Assumption of Anarchy in International Relations Theory: A Critique," *Review of International Studies* 17 (1991): 67–85.

15. John Ruggie, "Continuity and Transformation in the World Polity: Toward a Neorealist Synthesis," in Robert Keohane, ed., *Neorealism and its Critics* (New York: Columbia University Press, 1986): 143.

16. This is generally referred to as "internal" sovereignty.

17. John Ruggie, "Continuity and Transformation in the World Polity," 143–148. See also, Friedrich Kratochwil, "Sovereignty as Dominion: Is There a Right to Humanitarian Intervention?," in Lyons and Mastanduno, eds., *Beyond Westphalia?*, 21–42.

18. Kratochwil, "Sovereignty as Dominion," 34.

19. For one study examining this process, see J. Samuel Barkin and Bruce Cronin, "The State and the Nation: Changing Norms and the Rules of Sovereignty in International Relations," *International Organization* 48, no. 1 (winter 1994): 107–130.

20. *Terra nullius* refers to territory not heretofore allocated on an exclusive basis. See Oscar Schachter, "Sovereignty and Threats to Peace," in Thomas Weiss, ed., *Collective Security in a Changing World* (Boulder, Colo.: Lynne Rienner Publishers, 1993): 24.

21. Daniel Philpott, "Sovereignty: An Introduction and Brief History," *Journal of International Affairs* 48, no. 2 (winter 1995): 357.

22. For an account of this period of English history, see Lawrence Stone, *The Causes of the English Revolution, 1549–1642* (London: Routledge and K. Paul, 1972).

23. See David Armstrong, *Revolution and World Order: The Revolutionary State in International Society* (Oxford, U.K.: Clarendon Press, 1993).

24. See, for example, Julian H. Franklin, *John Locke and the Theory of Sovereignty: Mixed Monarchy and the Right of Resistance in the Political Thought of the English Revolution* (Cambridge, U.K.: Cambridge University Press, 1981).

25. Eric J. Hobsbawm, *Nations and Nationalism Since 1780: Programme, Myth, Reality* (Cambridge, U.K.: Cambridge University Press, 1992): 88.

26. See Lea Brilmayer, "Secession and Self-Determination: A Territorial Interpretation," *Yale Journal of International Law* 16, no. 1 (1991): 185.

27. This idea can be traced to the political theories of Rousseau and Hegel, although there has since been a large literature discussing nationalism as a legitimate source of sovereignty. See, for example, Walker Connor, *Ethnonationalism: The Quest for Understanding* (Princeton, N.J.: Princeton University Press, 1994); Ernest Gellner, *Nations and Nationalism* (Ithaca, N.Y.: Cornell University Press, 1983); and Hobsbawm, *Nations and Nationalism Since 1780.*

28. See Andreas Osiander, *The States System of Europe;* Henry Kissinger, *A World Restored: Metternich, Castlereagh and the Problems of Peace, 1812–1822* (Boston, Mass.: Houghton Mifflin Company, 1959); and David Armstrong, *Revolution and World Order: The Revolutionary State in International Society* (Oxford, U.K.: Clarendon Press, 1993).

29. Wolfers, *Discord and Collaboration.*

30. See Alan S. Milward, *The European Rescue of the Nation-State* (Berkeley, Cal.: University of California Press, 1992).

31. *General Assembly Journal,* no. 75, 825–26.

32. United Nations General Assembly Resolution 217 (III 1948).

33. See Barkin and Cronin, "The State and the Nation."

34. *Document of the Copenhagen Meeting of the Conference of the Human Dimension of the CSCE,* June 1990, number 1630 (Agence Internationale D'Information Pour La Presse), 1.

35. *The Charter of Paris for a New Europe,* Europe/Documents no. 1672, 14 December 1990 (Brussels: Agence Europe).

36. See OAS General Assembly Resolution 1080, Twenty-first Regular Session, June 3, 1991, Santiago, Chile.

37. Marc Weller, "Current Developments," *The American Journal of International Law,* 86 (1992): 587.

38. Conference on Security and Cooperation in Europe, "Document of the Moscow Meeting of the Conference on the Human Dimension of the CSCE," October 3, 1991, number 1630 (Agence Internationale D'Information Pour La Presse).

39. See Jack Donnelly, "State Sovereignty and International Intervention: The Case of Human Rights," in Lyons and Mastanduno, eds., *Beyond Westphalia: State Sovereignty and International Intrvention* (Baltimore, Md.: Johns Hopkins, 1995), table 1, 217.

40. See *Basic Documents in International Law*, 1993. It should be noted that 34 of the signatories signed "with qualification."

41. See Thomas M. Franck, "Intervention Against Illegitimate Regimes," in Lori Fisler Damrosch and David J. Scheffer, eds., *Law and Force in the New International Order* (Boulder, Colo.: Westview Press, 1991): 164.

42. See Andrew J. Nathan, "Human Rights in Chinese Foreign Policy," *The China Quarterly* (September 1994): 633, 641.

43. Donnelly, "State Sovereignty and International," 122.

44. General Assembly Resolution 1514 (XV), December 14, 1960, in part, labels colonialism as "a denial of fundamental human rights."

45. "Expand NATO? Yes, Say Most Experts, but What Does the Public Think?," *New York Times*, February 10, 1995, A6.

46. According to Edward Gulick, for example, the international coalition or alliance, is the prominent means of putting the balance of power to work. See his *Europe's Classical Balance of Power: A Case History of the Theory and Practice of One of the Great Concepts of European Statecraft* (Westport, Conn: Greenwood Press, 1982). Similarly, Stephen Walt argues that states form alliances in order to prevent stronger powers from dominating them. See his *The Origins of Alliances* (Ithaca, N.Y.: Cornell University Press, 1987).

47. Anne-Marie Burley, "Law Among Liberal States," 1913.

48. See, for example, Lori Fisler Damrosch, ed., *Enforcing Restraint: Collective Intervention in Internal Conflicts* (New York: Council on Foreign Relations, 1993); Lyons and Mastanduno, eds., *Beyond Westphalia*; Jack Donnelly, "Human Rights, Humanitarian Crisis, and Humanitarian Intervention," *International Journal*, vol. 49 (autumn 1993): 607–640; Laura Reed and Carl Kaysen, eds., *Emerging Norms of Justified Intervention* (Cambridge: American Academy of Arts and Sciences, 1993).

49. Both of these areas have been discussed by international law scholars in Damrosch and Scheffer, eds., *Law and Force*.

50. It should be noted that article 15, paragraph 7 of the Covenant does allow individual members to take action "as they shall consider necessary of the maintenance of right and justice." This section is so vague as to be meaningless.

51. The U.S. invasions of the Dominican Republic, Panama, and Granada fall into this category, as do the Soviet attacks into Hungary, Czechoslovakia, and Afghanistan. In these cases, the international community overwhelmingly opposed the unilateral actions. See Igor I. Lukashuk, "The United Nations and Illegitimate Regimes: When to Intervene to Protect Human Rights," in Damrosch and Scheffer, eds., *Law and Force*, 145.

52. Gidon Gottlieb, *Nation Against State: A New Approach to Ethnic Conflicts and the Decline of Sovereignty* (New York: Council on Foreign Relations, 1993): 22.

53. Ibid., 92–98.

54. Ibid., 95.

55. Anne-Marie Burley, "Law Among Liberal States: Liberal Internationalism and the Act of State Doctrine," in *Columbia Law Review* 92, no. 8 (December 1992): 1907–96.

8

Military Intervention and the Organization of International Politics[1]

Martha Finnemore

In surveying the global pattern of military intervention since the end of the Cold War, two features stand out. First, most of it is multilateral. At a minimum, states have sought multilateral authorization for their interventions (for example, the UN authorization for Russian "peacekeeping" in Georgia). More commonly the interventions have been multilateral in execution as well as authorization (for example, in Somalia, Cambodia, Bosnia, Haiti, Rwanda). Second, in many cases the geostrategic or economic interests of the intervening states in the target state are negligible. Certainly the U.S. has some interest in Haiti, and one can make a case for European and U.S. interests in stability in the Balkans. Why these states should care about Somalia, Cambodia, or Rwanda is less clear.

This chapter offers an argument that goes toward explaining this recent rash of multilateral interventions in strategically insignificant states. Understanding these interventions is important for both theoretical and practical reasons. If all of these actions were as small-scale as the Rwanda operation, we could dismiss them as trivial. But the interventions in Somalia and Cambodia, which are examined in some detail here, were large and costly for intervening states. The United Nations Transitional Authority in Cambodia (UNTAC) involved over 22,000 troops and cost approximately $1.7 billion; the intervention in Somalia involved over 30,000 military and logistic personnel for the second UN Operation in Somalia (UNOSOM II), which cost $1.64 billion in addition to the costs for the 17,700 U.S. troops sent as the United States Task Force in Somalia.[2] We need to be able to explain why when states make commitments of this size.

The first section discusses the limitations that realism and related theoretical frameworks face in explaining these interventions. As conventional theoretical approaches to international politics cannot explain this behavior, the second and third sections propose an alternative for analyzing them, one that focuses on changes in the organization of international politics and normative shifts associated with the increasingly dense set of multilateral institutions. The fourth and fifth sections establish the plausibility of this alternative focus with investigations into two of the largest post-Cold War interventions.

Somalia and Cambodia are useful illustrations that meet two criteria. First, they are large and costly for the intervenors; they cannot be dismissed as trivial. Second, they pose anomalies for conventional theories because of the lack of geostrategic interests involved. The other two large multilateral interventions, in Bosnia and the Persian Gulf, both involved conventional geostrategic interests for major intervenors—proximity to Europe in the case of Bosnia and oil in the Gulf. Then, it would be difficult to separate the effects of these conventional interests from the normative and organizational factors that concern me here. Only by choosing cases where conventional interests are negligible can we see the effects of these other forces promoting military intervention. In each case I examine the geostrategic interests of the principal intervenors and find them thin or nonexistent. By contrast, organizational connections and normative claims appear to have significant impact in both the decision to intervene and in the structure of the operation itself. The chapter concludes with limitations of the claims made.

For purposes of this article, "intervention" is *military action by a foreign power or powers whose goal is to redistribute political authority in the target state.*[3] Several features of this definition deserve comment. First, intervention here aims at redistributing political authority—at fundamentally reconstituting the target state. This is distinct from other more pedestrian kinds of state interaction that seek to change target states' policies, but not their leadership or underlying structure. Both the Somalia and Cambodia action clearly fit this criteria.

Second, consent by some parties to foreign military activity does not make it less of an intervention. Some critics might object that UN intervention cannot be counted as intervention because standard UN procedures for peacekeeping normally require consent of the target before UN forces enter the country. If the target consents, it is not intervention. This point is particularly relevant to the Cambodia operation where there was overt agreement among the factions about a UN presence. Consent and who gives it are not sturdy analytic characteristics on which to classify an operation. Often in unilateral interventions intervenors claim to have been "invited" into the country as, for example, the Soviet Union was "invited" into Czechoslovakia and Hungary. These invitations made their action no less an intervention.

The fact that large numbers of military personnel are required for an operation is evidence that consent has not been universal and that armed opposition is expected. In the Cambodia case, armed opposition from Khmer Rouge forces, on a sufficient scale to thwart one of the chief aims of the intervention, that is, disarmament, began very soon after UN troops arrived. If consent were not in question, multilateral institutions would not have to be military in character. In many states, multilateral action is not military at all; humanitarian or other types of international organizations (IOs) can act alone. In neither Cambodia nor Somalia were nonmilitary IOs sufficient for the goals laid out by the intervenors.

Military Intervention and the Limits of Realism

The rash of military interventions since 1989 presents two anomalies for conventional realist understandings: all have been authorized and/or executed by an international organization; and most have been in strategically insignificant states. Realism can account for some multilateral intervention but not much recent multilateralism; and it has no good explanation for costly action without geostrategic interests.

Action by international organizations can only be accommodated under realism if it is understood as the action of a state or states that control that organization. Thus, UN interventions must be understood as interventions of the most powerful members, particularly the United States. The UN is only a tool of these states (and not a particularly good one) through which they pursue their national interests in the realist view.[4]

This interpretation raises the question, why would a powerful state choose to pursue its interests through such a cumbersome forum and risk dilution of its goals by other members? The rational answer usually concerns burdensharing—intervention through an IO is believed to spread the cost of an intervention among more parties, thus making intervention cheaper for big powers, which may give up some control, but save in blood and treasure by intervening through an IO.[5] Empirically, however, this interpretation is weak. The U.S. may have made money on the Gulf war, but Somalia and Haiti involved minimal sharing of costs.[6] Further, in many of these operations (most notably Somalia), the Pentagon made it clear that multilateral "burdensharing" was a "burden"—that the logistics of dealing with other troops, often with incompatible equipment and different or inadequate training, was more trouble than it was worth. Foreign troops were chosen for political rather than practical reasons. However, the troops were nationals of politically relevant or neutral states in ways that legitimated the operation in line with UN principles.[7]

A more compelling response to the question of why states use IOs to intervene involves legitimacy. IOs make intervention easier, not for material or logistical reasons, but for political and normative reasons. Inis Claude wrote about this legitimization function of the UN thirty years ago, but his insights were neglected in the subsequent wave of rationalist theorizing that ignored legitimacy and other normative forces in international politics. As attention to social and normative components of international politics becomes respectable once again, Claude's argument deserves another reading.[8]

The second anomaly should be even more troubling to realists. Intervention is occurring in places where there are no conventional geostrategic interests at stake for the United States or most of the other permanent members of the Security Council. Under bipolarity, realists could make a plausible argument that virtually everywhere was in somebody's interests. With the world divided into only two hostile camps, a geopolitical gain for one side was a loss for the other. Even small, resource-poor states, far from either Washington or Moscow, became strategically important in the context of a global and ideological conflict. In this way, policymakers justified and scholars theoretically explained interventions in Vietnam and Afghanistan.[9]

With the end of bipolarity, realist logic suggests that these places should revert from being strategic outposts of a global ideological struggle to being simply small, remote states. With the end of the ideological struggle, great powers should stop caring and intervening. But intervention has continued, occurring on a very large scale in such places as Somalia and Cambodia and on a smaller scale in Mozambique, the Western Sahara, and other parts of Asia and Africa, where the security interests of large states do not seem even vaguely threatened.

If they were all small-scale UN peacekeeping missions as during the Cold War, realists could dismiss them as trivial. But as the Somalia and Cambodia operations make clear, these are some of the largest military interventions of recent decades. Both the size and the ambition of these UN interventions has increased dramatically since 1989. Realists are thus faced with the puzzle of why UN military intervention in small states has increased in size and scope at precisely the time when these states should become less, not more, consequential to the powerful states running the UN.

As the following sections show, the two anomalies—intervention by IOs (as opposed to states) and intervention where no conventional security interests exist—are related. A proliferation of international organizations has provided states with tools of action not previously available to them and, at the same time, has enmeshed states in webs of multilateral activity that make certain kinds of inaction and withdrawal increasingly difficult. Concurrently, there has been a shift in the kinds of interests used to justify intervention. What used to be a legitimate interest in justifying intervention may no longer be so and new interests have appeared. These new understandings of state interest are both a product of and a producer of the expanding web of international organization in world politics.

Changes in the Organizational Structure of World Politics

One of the striking changes in world politics over the past century has been the rapid proliferation of international organizations. In 1860, there were five international governmental organizations (IGOs) and only one international nongovernmental organization (INGO). By 1940, those numbers had grown to 61 IGOs and 477 INGOs. By 1996, there were 260 IGOs and 5,472 INGOs.[10] Whether this development is consequential has been a long-standing argument between realists and liberal institutionalists. Realists have consistently claimed that these organizations are of very limited importance. At best, they facilitate states pursuing their interests by helping them to overcome collective action problems or solve prisoners' dilemmas. At worst, they are window dressing for the pursuit of power and interest that has always driven international politics. Liberal institutions have argued conversely that IGOs are important actors in their own right with goals, interests, and powers independent of states.

Rather than address this debate directly as others have done already, I prefer to focus on the influence, not of formal international organizations in the plural but on the consequences of increased international organization in the singular—because international politics has become increasingly organized, structured, and bureaucratized over the past century. The increased number and diversity of IGOs is a direct reflection of this broader phenomenon. The consequences of increased international organization can be categorized broadly under three headings: strategic consequences, political and normative consequences, and social consequences.

Strategic consequences of increased international organization result because the proliferation of IGOs and formalized, bureaucratized procedures for action (in the form of international law, treaties, and agreements) offer states alternative strategies for dealing with problems and change the costs and benefits of following particular courses of action. For example, the fact that the UN exists as a tool of action influences U.S. policymakers' choices. They may choose not to use it in an intervention, but because the UN and other IGOs are out there changes policy calculus. Ignoring the UN may result in domestic opposition and criticism from allies. Probably more important, however, is that the UN creates policy opportunities that would otherwise not exist. Without a UN, U.S. options in Somalia or Cambodia would have been either unilateral action or *ad hoc* coalition-building, which is diplomatically costly, time consuming, and difficult.[11] With only these two options, Washington might have sat out these crises. The existence of a UN, however, presented a third option.

Political consequences of increased international organization flow from the fact that organization is never neutral in value. All organizations, bureaucracies, and rules of behavior embody certain normative principles. Prominent among the organizing principles undergirding contemporary IGOs have been the equation of self-determination with statehood and the principle of sovereign equality of states.

One remarkable feature of the way in which politics has been organized in the second half of this century is the elevation of the state as the legitimate political form. Previous periods offered a variety of legitimate forms of political organization—states, empires, colonies, city-states, fiefdoms. In the current world, "self-determination" means statehood. If an entity is not a state, it is nonexistent in international politics. National liberation movements understand this very well, but they are reacting significantly to the value that states themselves place on statehood. Places that are not organized into states are considered threatening and problematic in contemporary politics, and states or IGOs go out of their way to organize these communities into states so that they can recognize and deal with them. The decolonization experience illustrates this impulse.[12] More to the point, the failure of communities to sustain state organizations in places like Somalia and Cambodia does not lead to experimentation with alternative, nonstate forms of political organization. In both of these cases, trusteeships were proposed and rejected on normative grounds (they were "patronizing" and "smacked of colonialism.")[13] Instead, failure results in large-scale, state-building efforts even when there is no geostrategic reason to care about these places and no particular reason to think that state-building will be successful.

The organizing principle of sovereign equality also has normative corollaries and practical political effects. Chief among these has been the relative empowerment of small, weak states beyond what one would expect, given the actual distribution of capabilities in the system. One-state/one-vote is the norm in most international bodies, including the United Nations General Assembly. Certainly, the strong states have managed to organize some powerful and consequential IGOs (the Security Council, the IMF, and the World Bank) along principles other than that of sovereign equality, but the norm prevails frequently enough to give platforms to small states to push their agendas. It also gives them voting majorities in IGOs to pass resolutions concordant with their views. They usually focus on "rights and duties" of states in relation to one another. They include the right to self-determination and continued protection of stateness, even if sovereignty has to be shored up or completely rebuilt by others. The organizing principles of self-determination and sovereign equality combine to make it politically difficult to let states dissolve.[14]

Finally, social consequences of international organization occur as states get accustomed to multilateral action, specifically working through IGOs. States become socialized to this kind of behavior in two ways. First, multilateral action becomes institutionalized within the state bureaucratic apparatus. Consultation with other states, often through an international organization, is written increasingly into the standard operating procedures (SOPs) of state bureaucracies. The force of SOPs in state policymaking has been amply documented elsewhere.[15] Second, individual policymakers come to view multilateral action and the use of IGOs as increasingly necessary and appropriate. As the web of international organization grows denser, new generations of policymakers, who know of no other kind of international politics, increasingly view this kind of multilateral consultation and action through IOs as the only appropriate way to conduct policy.[16]

Changes in The Normative Structure of World Politics

As the foregoing discussion makes clear, normative changes and organizational changes are not easily separable. Implicitly or explicitly organizations embody some principles or values at the expense of others. Major changes in organization thus entail a reorientation of normative perspective. This may not be openly acknowledged, but it is always present.[17]

Conversely, normative changes in the organizational environment may have implications for international organizations and for the organization of international politics generally. They may circumscribe or delegitimate some kinds of action or open opportunities for new kinds of action. This section focuses briefly (other chapters in this book contain more details) on one normative change that has been particularly prominent in debates over intervention: the rise of humanitarian claims as a basis for intervention.

Justifications offered for intervention have changed markedly since World War I.[18] National interest and national prestige were the commonly offered and accepted rationales prior to the twentieth century, although these appeals were often combined with other more idealistic arguments. Further, national interests were often commercial and not linked to territorial or political security. In justifying his initial intervention in Cuba, President McKinley first referred to the need to put an end to barbarities, bloodshed, and starvation. But he went on to stress that "the right to intervene may be justified by the very serious injury to the commerce, trade and business of our people."[19]

Commercial concerns might be important reasons to intervene in contemporary politics, but they would not be paraded as primary justifications. Indeed, explicit economic justifications for intervention have largely disappeared.[20] Even national interest justifications are likely to be framed in multilateral terms as the pursuit of some common good, most often international peace and stability. Self-defense is still an acceptable justification for military action, but it is the only self-regarding claim that remains legitimate. Pursuit of purely national geostrategic or commercial interests is no longer a sufficient justification; at a minimum it must be heavily supported with collective-goods or other-regarding claims.

Accompanying the decline of justifications based on national interests for intervention in this century has been a rise in humanitarian justifications.[21] Humanitarian intervention was not unknown in the nineteenth century, but it tended to focus on protection of one's own citizens—an interpretation of "humanitarian" closely allied with the justification of dominant national interest. More generalized claims for legitimate intervention on behalf of non-citizens appeared in the nineteenth and early twentieth centuries, but were only made for groups who were ethnically and religiously similar to European intervenors, for example, Christian subjects under threat from Ottoman Turks. It was not until after World War II that more universal claims about who was human, and therefore deserving of protection, began to influence behavior.[22]

The concurrent expansion of humanitarian justifications for intervention and increased density of international organization during this period did two things. First, the two trends reinforced each other. Codification of human rights and humanitarian guarantees in multilateral agreements and as founding principles of international organizations gave new power to these claims as justifications for international action. Arguments that genocide and mass starvation were someone else's problems became harder to sustain in international discourse when states had signed international agreements that banned such practices and proclaimed certain minimum guarantees of life as "universal rights," for example, in the UN Charter, the Universal Declaration of Human Rights, and the Covenant on Economic, Social, and Cultural Rights.

Moreover, the proliferation of organizations provided a new set of legitimate tools with which the new set of humanitarian concerns could be addressed. As multilateral bodies, IGOs could rise above narrow state interests and serve broader humanitarian causes in ways that would not be tainted by the suspect national interests. Individual states might be self-serving and subvert humanitarian action to serve their own ends. The multilateral membership of international organizations would temper these self-serving and parochial interests of individual states. The organizations, not states, became the appropriate and legitimate means by which transnational, humanitarian goals could be pursued.

This combination of expanding human rights and humanitarian claims, together with the availability of instruments that can legitimately address these claims, has led states to attempt interventions in places, using means and for reasons that previously would not have been compelling, inviting, or even conceivable. When humanitarian disasters are coupled with state failure, as is true in both Cambodia and Somalia, normative justifications for intervention become even stronger. Norms against violating sovereignty are strong, but intervention to restore sovereignty takes on a very positive normative character. Instead of violating sovereignty, intervenors can claim to be promoting and protecting the powerful norm of self-determination. If they can do this through an

IO, their normative justifications and the political legitimacy of the operation will be that much stronger.

The presence of these normative claims and IGOs certainly does not compel or guarantee intervention, as citizens of Burundi and Sudan well know. Neither do they guarantee that these interventions will succeed. These norms and institutions do, however, create permissive conditions that enable intervention by new means for new ends. They allow the emergence of a new kind of intervention—intervention by an international institution for largely humanitarian, rather than geostrategic, ends.

The following sections examine two of the largest post-Cold War interventions by United Nations forces to illustrate this new pattern of intervention. In both cases, the array of interests at stake for each of the principal intervenors is inadequate to explain the robust action taken. Also in both cases, the material and strategic interests for intervening states were weak and the influence of international organizations and international norms relatively strong.

Cambodia and the UNTAC Intervention[23]

Proposals for United Nations involvement in Cambodia originated with former New York Democratic Representative Stephen Solarz who had urged that a UN trusteeship of Cambodia be instituted. Because of its neocolonial overtones, the proposal was not widely supported. UN involvement, however, received a different and more acceptable normative frame in November 1989 when the Australian Foreign Minister Gareth Evans proposed that procedures used by the UN to move Namibia to independence be applied to the problem of ending civil war and reconstituting a state in Cambodia. The fact that the Namibia case was one of decolonization (whereas instituting a trusteeship would smack of recolonization) made the proposal normatively palatable. Also, because the Namibia case was widely viewed as a UN success, furthered the cause.[24]

The Evans proposal broke a logjam in negotiations and completely recast the then-stalled debate over possible powersharing arrangements among factions. Previous regional negotiations had focused on reaching agreement on some kind of powersharing arrangement among the Cambodian factions. The possibility of UN involvement offered a new strategic policy option both to states involved in the negotiations over Cambodia's future and to the Cambodian factions themselves. Specifically, UN involvement reconfigured the situation in several ways. First, it turned what had been a regional set of negotiations into global ones. Before the Evans proposal, negotiations on Cambodia had been held through what had been termed the Jakarta Informal Meetings (or JIM conferences), which were organized and largely attended by neighboring states with clear geopolitical interests in Cambodia. The Evans proposal shifted the forum to a global one, specifically to the UN Security Council. The Permanent Five assumed the dominant role in organizing negotiations and brokering a solution.

Further, the Evans strategy was no longer simply one of persuading the four factions to agree on some powersharing arrangement among themselves. Operating on the Namibia model, the UN would step in and impose a solution or the democratic procedures by which power would be allocated among the factions and according to which those factions would exercise power. The proposal was more than simple peacekeeping. The UN was to be given de facto sovereignty in Cambodia. Among the tasks explicitly delegated to UNTAC were:

- Disarm combatants. Seventy percent of combatants were to be demobilized before the 1993 elections, their weapons given over to UNTAC; the remainder were to be demobilized after the elections. Foreign military assistance was to be halted.
- Organize free elections in early 1993. They were to educate voters, guarantee free and fair balloting.
- Develop a human rights program and investigate abuses.
- Run state ministries including defense, foreign affairs, finance, and communications.
- Repatriate refugees.[25]

The United Nations was given control over many core functions of a state, over violence and those wishing to wield it, over the day-to-day running of the state, and over political structures (i.e., election procedures) in which the political authority is allocated within the state.

This kind of control in Cambodia was costly. At the time of UN commitment to these actions, UNTAC forces were expected to number about 20,000 and cost over one billion dollars. It was by far the largest such operation ever undertaken by the UN and certainly the most sweeping in mandate. Why would a global organization whose most powerful members were not threatened by Cambodia put forth such an effort? This question breaks down into two parts: Why would the major UN member states (particularly the Permanent Five) invest resources in this task? To the extent that other states and not the Permanent Five shouldered the burden of supplying UNTAC, what were their motivations?

Favorable U.S. and Soviet attitudes toward UN involvement can be understood partially within the larger context of superpower rapprochement and the end of the Cold War. Indochina had been an important arena of conflict between the two by proxy; ending conflict there would help cement the more important decrease in tensions between the principals. However, credible disengagement might have accomplished this goal just as well. In fact, the Soviets ended support for their Vietnamese and Cambodian clients but contributed little to UN efforts toward a positive solution.

The more interesting behavior was on the U.S. side. Not only did the Americans halt support for the noncommunist resistance factions, they also funded nearly one-third of the bill for UNTAC.[26] With the strategic importance of Cambodia in doubt, the dominant motivation for an active U.S. role in promoting a UN-sponsored settlement in Cambodia appears to have been domestic opposition, particularly Congressional opposition, on moral grounds, to the return of the Khmer Rouge. The Senate Intelligence Committee had just voted against continued funding for covert operations and was pressuring the Bush administration to do something to prevent the growing military and political strength of the Khmer Rouge just before Secretary of State James Baker's announcement of support for the Evans plan. Solarz, probably the key Congressional player, was clear in stating that the U.S. interest in Cambodia was "primarily moral and humanitarian."[27]

China was the one permanent member of the Security Council that arguably had a geopolitical interest in Indochina. France and Britain certainly did not. France's interests were understood by all concerned to be "historical"—a formulation of interests that makes sense in a cultural and normative framework but not in a realist or geostrategic one. Britain's interest was probably the most attenuated of the five because London was never involved in the conflict. Support for UN activity was linked to a more general policy of diplomatic support for Washington and perhaps to a commitment to the UN as a multilateral institution that accorded Britain a status and powers exceeding its capabilities.

Japan's decision to provide substantial financial backing for UNTAC and to break with previous interpretations of Tokyo's "peace constitution" to deploy troops probably can be explained by stretching conventional realist formulations of interest. Cambodia certainly posed no political or strategic threat to Japan, but the situation offered Japan an opportunity to further some larger goals.

One of these was commercial; obtaining raw materials was a perennial concern for Japan. Unlike Australia, Japan had vigorously pursued trade and investment strategies in Indochina. It had cultivated trade with Vietnam even while the West was pushing a policy of ostracization. Imports from Hanoi rose from under $100 million in 1986 to nearly $600 million in 1990, much of it in crude oil and other raw materials.[28]

The other goal was political. During the Gulf War, Japan's weak participation came under heavy criticism from the West. The Cambodia operation presented an opportunity to offset Western criticism and shoulder some of the military and political burden of collective action. Because the opportunity came in an area in which Tokyo had commercial interests made the decision to become involved that much easier. As a result, Japan contributed almost a third of UNTAC's estimated $1.9 billion cost and 600–700 personnel, among them the head of UNTAC, Yasushi Akashi.[29]

Australia, the country that devised and pushed the proposal for UN involvement, also appeared to have less than compelling motives for its actions. Politically, Australia wanted to be supportive of its Southeast Asian neighbors but had no particular reason to shoulder a leadership burden when payoffs and chances of success were minimal. Australia proposed the use of a previously untried formula in the face of intractable opposition among the factions, and for what? A politically stable Cambodia might offer some trade and investment opportunities but nothing substantial, because militarily, Cambodia posed no conceivable threat.

Evans himself listed three reasons for involvement. One was regionalism and solidarity with Southeast Asian neighbors, but, as already mentioned, this did not explain leadership. A second reason was moral: "All the countries of the world owe the Cambodian people peace."[30] As noted in Washington's case, this reason looked odd from a realist or rationalist perspective. The third motive was personal, because Evans had traveled all over Cambodia in 1968 and had fond memories. Again, this reason is not easily accommodated within a realist or rationalist paradigm.

Beyond these most conspicuous players in the United Nations intervention, Table 8.1 lists other states that contributed troops to UNTAC. For some countries such as Indonesia, Thailand, and Malaysia, geopolitics may explain their action. For other poor Third World countries such as India, Bangladesh, and Ghana, there may be financial reasons to contribute peacekeepers; the UN pays countries about $1,000 per month for each soldier deployed. Most have costs that are substantially less, and the UN's reimbursement is in convertible currency. But that leaves unexplained the contributions of countries such as France, Uruguay, Bulgaria, and the Netherlands. France has historical ties to Cambodia, but they do not fall within the concerns of *Realpolitik*. The others have no ties or interests at all.

In sum, the only powerful states that had reasons for involvement in Cambodia, which fit clearly within a realist framework, were China and Japan. Japan, however, was not centrally involved in the decision to have the UN intervene, and China bore little of the burden of intervention. The powerful states that played central roles in the decision and provided troops and personnel were motivated by a combination of moral concerns, "historical" interests, and a commitment to global multilateralism as a means of solving problems. None of these motivations fits well within a *Realpolitik* or conventional geostrategic understanding of military intervention because all are either normative, principled, or based on culture and identity.

The structure of the intervention, including the composition of the force, was similarly disconnected from geopolitical logic. It was largely dictated by the

Table 8.1
Cambodia—Composition of Intervening forces

Number of military personnel at peak strength, June 1993
(excludes civilian police)

Country	*troop contribution*
Algeria	16
Argentina	2
Australia	685
Austria	17
Bangladesh	942
Belgium	5
Brunei Darussalam	3
Bulgaria	748
Cameroon	14
Canada	218
Chile	52
China	444
France	1,350
Germany	137
Ghana	912
India	1,336
Indonesia	1,779
Ireland	11
Japan	605
Malaysia	1,090
Namibia	43
Netherlands	809
New Zealand	67
Pakistan	1,106
Philippines	127
Poland	666
Russian Federation	52
Senegal	2
Singapore	35
Thailand	716
Tunisia	883
United Kingdom	130
United States	49
Uruguay	940
TOTAL	15,991

Source: United Nations, *The United Nations and Cambodia 1991–1995* (New York: United Nations, 1995), p. 23. The same source provides a breakdown of numbers and composition of civilian police forces contributed. The total is 3,359 with India, Bangladesh, Ghana, Indonesia, Malaysia, and Philippines the largest contributors (each over 200 people.)

standard operating procedures of the IGO that organized it. The existence of the United Nations offered parties a policy option that would not otherwise have been available. Once chosen, however, UN involvement had political and normative implications for the kinds of settlements that could be reached. As noted earlier, such organizations are never value-neutral. UN intervention could only occur if the Cambodia "solution" involved democratic elections on a liberal model; other possible principles for arbitering power would have been unacceptable and even inconceivable within the world organization. Similarly, UN involvement meant that the intervening military force would conform to certain long-standing UN criteria of political neutrality. It often recruits troops from precisely those states that have no interest in a conflict. The UN is able to recruit troops, not because contributors have an interest in the conflict but because they have an interest in the viability and success of the UN. They contribute in support of multilateralism. But as the editors argue in the introduction to this book, this "interest" in a multilateral institution is not the one expected by realists or consonant with their notion of state interests.

Somalia and the UNOSOM Intervention[31]

With the fall of the Said Barre government in January 1991, UN and most foreign government personnel and aid organizations retreated from Mogadishu. Unlike many private relief organizations, however, the UN did not return quickly to Somalia. Whereas groups like the International Committee of the Red Cross (ICRC) and Save the Children returned soon after the warlords had seized control, UN groups such as UNICEF stayed away, arguing that the country was not safe for their workers.[32] The two senior UN officials, James O. C. Jonah and Osman Hashim, spent most of their time in Nairobi, Addis Ababa, and New York rather than in Mogadishu. Furthermore, the UN twice failed in 1991 to pursue openings towards peace in Somalia. They declined to participate in a July meeting of clan leaders in Djibouti, and in October, Jonah actively dissuaded Ali Mahdi's faction from requesting a special session of the Security Council on Somalia.[33] Not until December 1991 did the UN announce it would return to Somalia, with the intention of organizing a large multinational relief effort.[34]

With the beginning of Boutros Boutros-Ghali's term as secretary-general in January 1992, the United Nations began to focus on Somalia. That month, Boutros-Ghali sent Jonah back to Somalia to mediate the conflict.[35] In April, Boutros-Ghali appointed a special representative to Somalia for the first time, former Algerian ambassador Mohammed Sahnoun. The same month the Security Council began to take action, approving 50 cease-fire monitors and 500 Pakistani peacekeepers. The secretary-general began to criticize publicly the slight consideration Somalia was receiving and argued that the "rich man's war" in Bosnia was siphoning UN resources away from Somalia.[36] Three thousand more peacekeepers were approved in August but could not be deployed because of resistance from local warlords. In November, Boutros-Ghali sent a letter to the Security Council stating that, "The cycle of extortion and blackmail . . . must be broken and security conditions established that will permit the distribution of relief supplies."[37] A day later, President George Bush offered the use of U.S. troops for this purpose.

Thirty-seven thousand troops from 29 countries were deployed in Somalia, beginning in December 1992, with the stated mission of establishing a secure environment for the delivery of humanitarian assistance. The contributions to this enterprise were more concentrated than was the case in UNTAC. In Cambodia, no state provided more than about 15 percent of the personnel. In Somalia, Washington provided roughly half of the troops—17,700 troops under U.S. command in the Unified Task Force (UNITAF) and 3,000 under UN command as part of UNOSOM I (see Table 8.2). Further, without U.S. diplomatic backing, many other states would have been less eager to commit troops. Washington's motivations for intervention are central to any explanation of the intervention.

The United States bore the lion's share of the burden of the Somalia intervention, but it is difficult, if not impossible, to find any compelling geopolitical motivation. Washington had just voluntarily abandoned its facility at Berbera, and the U.S. military establishment was never fully convinced about its utility, particularly in light of the political instability in the country. Further, if bases and military advantage were reasons for intervention, U.S. troops should have pursued military objectives when they landed. They did not. They occupied the northern section of the country in which Berbera is located. However, the U.S. government did not pursue a diplomatic strategy to secure the base, namely recognizing the breakaway northern "Republic of Somaliland" and cutting a deal for access to the Berbera facility.

Finally, Washington resisted UN pressures to "pacify" the country as part of the mission. If the U.S. truly had designs on Somalia, it would have welcomed the role of disarming the clans, but it did not.[38] In fact, U.S. officials were clearly and consistently interested, not in controlling any part of Somalia, but in getting out of the country as soon as possible—sooner, indeed, than the United Nations would have liked. Further, some administration officials and many top military leaders opposed the mission on precisely the grounds that no vital U.S. interest was involved.[39]

President Bush was clear about the humanitarian nature of the U.S. mission: "I can state with confidence we come [to Somalia] for one reason only, to enable the starving to be fed."[40] As with Cambodia, there was strong domestic pressure from both the public and from Congress to "do something" for the

Table 8.2
Somalia—Composition of Intervening Forces

United States (UNITAF) in Somalia:
17,700 troops under U.S. command

Composition of UNOSOM II as of 13 November 1993:

Country	*troop contribution*
Australia	48
Bangladesh	945
Belgium	948
Botswana	326
Canada	4
Egypt	1,100
France	1,107
Germany	726
Greece	102
India	4,937
Ireland	79
Italy	2,576
Kuwait	156
Malaysia	871
Morocco	1,424
Nepal	311
New Zealand	43
Nigeria	614
Norway	130
Pakistan	5,005
Rep. of Korea	252
Romania	236
Saudi Arabia	757
Sweden	148
Tunisia	142
Turkey	320
United Arab Emirates	662
United States	3,017*
Zimbabwe	958
Military Police Company (composite force)	100
Headquarters staff	240
TOTAL	29,284

Source: "Report of the Secretary-General to the Security Council on UNOSOM II, 13 November 1993", para. 47. The composition of the UNOSOM II changed somewhat during the course of the operation, but the UN does not compile total troop contributions over the entire course of its operations by country. November 1993 was near the peak of the operation's strength.

*Combined with the U.S. Task Force, this brings the total U.S. contribution to 20,717 troops.

starving people that were featured every night on the news.[41] Humanitarian relief agencies added to this pressure by providing extensive information to both the public and the administration about the scale of suffering in Somalia.[42] In addition, there was widespread optimism about the simplicity and brevity of the mission being undertaken. As one senior administration official noted, "[by] its nature, [the Somalia mission is] not too significant a military operation."[43] The U.S. was willing to undertake humanitarian action where it looked feasible, even if it was not cheap.[44]

Of course, the humanitarian fancy dress may have covered some baser set of motives but, again, it is not clear what these were. The usual electoral motives did not apply here. Bush already had lost the presidential election when he decided to commit troops and could have ignored public pressure if he had thought it was prudent. Perhaps he had more diffuse personal interest in mounting the operation. After all, the Somalia operation allowed him to leave office as "a decisive leader, not as a vanquished politician."[45] He was also interested in supporting the UN—in improving its credibility and demonstrating U.S. support for it—since the UN was a key means of securing his "new world order."[46] However, neither securing a place in history, nor interest in supporting the world organization is a geostrategic interest of the sort that realists would expect to matter. There simply was no geostrategic interest.

As in Cambodia, the most compelling explanation for intervention in Somalia is humanitarian. Again, the structure of the intervention action was strongly influenced by the IGO that authorized it and gave it political legitimacy. While it may have been militarily possible for the U.S. to mount this operation alone, it was not politically possible to do so without a multilateral, preferably a UN, blessing.[47] UN principles demanded substantial multilateral composition from disinterested parties. Consequently, Washington recruited additional contributors, not for reasons of burdensharing but for reasons of political legitimacy. Indeed, central command was explicit in its view that the reason to include other troops was political, rather than logistical, and chose African and Arab rather than NATO troops with whom its forces would have been more logistically compatible.[48]

Multilateral conflict management is no different than other kinds of political tools and policy options. There are risks as well as opportunities in using the option offered by the UN for intervention. Organization of the Somalia operation through the UN contributed to some of the most dramatic disasters of the operation—notably, the June 1993 attack by Somali faction fighters that left 25 Pakistani soldiers dead and 54 wounded, the subsequent unsuccessful (and politically disastrous) hunt for Mohammed Aideed, and the ignominious deaths of 18 U.S. marines in October.[49] The mixed record of this policy does not mean it will not or should not be used in the future.

The argument presented here is limited. It seeks to explain why one sees multilateral military intervention where the principal intervening states have no clear geostrategic or economic interests. The phenomenon is new and is a product of two factors, both associated with the increasing organization of international politics. First, it has provided new tools of collective intervention. IGOs offer states new policy options that had not existed previously. In this case, the UN offers states a framework through which they can exercise military force with different advantages and disadvantages than unilateral action. Specifically, acting through a UN framework can lower the political risks and costs of intervention by legitimating the operation and giving decisionmakers political cover. This legitimacy, coupled with the preexisting organizational structures and communications channels provided by the UN, can facilitate coalition-building. The disadvantages are that action through the world organization dilutes state control over the operation, and decisionmaking "by committee" can be dangerously slow and yield policy paralysis if the intervenors disagree.

The second factor producing this new pattern of intervention involves the principles around which international politics is organized and the ways that they have changed the normative fabric of international politics. Norms of self-determination and human rights in particular have become more powerful because of their organizational entrenchment. States now consider intervening in small remote states for largely humanitarian reasons because the organization and normative structures of international politics have created the means and justification to do so. This is not to say that states will always or even often choose to intervene. However, the combination of legitimate opportunity provided by the UN to intervene and often moral or humanitarian domestic political pressures will insure that the option is considered and sometimes chosen when it would not have been considered 100 or even 50 years ago.

The argument does not claim that this new kind of intervention has in any way displaced the old-fashioned unilateral intervention that realists are used to seeing. The two can exist side by side. The argument also does not explain non-intervention. The changes in norms and organization of intervention create conditions that permit and perhaps even encourage multilateral interventions in inconsequential places, which geostrategic logic says that states should ignore. It does not tell us why there has been no intervention in Sudan, Myanmar, and Burundi. From the two case studies presented here, it appears that unique events play a role in the determination of which of the many objects of international concern become objects of international military action. In Cambodia and Somalia, personalities (Gareth Evans, Boutros-Ghali) and CNN tipped the scales, but these are idiosyncratic and not generalized phenomena.

Finally, policy can be learned in this type of collective intervention just as is in unilateral intervention. The Americans and the Soviets both learned powerful lessons about the limits of unilateral intervention in Vietnam and Afghanistan, lessons that shaped subsequent policy choices and made both states more wary of intervention. Somalia provided a similar lesson about the limits of multilateral intervention. In neither case, however, has the unexpected costly or difficult intervention experience eliminated the intervention option from states' menu of policy choices. The U.S. experience in Somalia did not eliminate the option of collective intervention in Haiti and Bosnia; Russian efforts in Chechnya indicate that even unpopular unilateral intervention is possible.

The normative and organizational changes that created the multilateral option have not disappeared. Humanitarian disasters will continue to occur, creating domestic pressures in powerful states to act. The UN and such multilateral instruments as the North Atlantic Treaty Organization (NATO) are likely to intervene again. Experience in Somalia and Bosnia may make states more cautious in choosing to act in the near future, but they do not eliminate the policy option.

Notes

1. An earlier version of this paper was presented at the second SSRC/MacArthur conference on Norms, Identity and National Security organized by Peter Katzenstein at the University of Minnesota, January 13–16, 1994. I am grateful to the participants in that conference and to Jim Goldgeier, Joe Lepgold, and Henry Nau for comments. Darel Paul provided invaluable research assistance and discussion during the initial drafting of this paper. The SSRC/MacArthur Program on International Peace and Security in a Changing World and the United States Institute of Peace provided material support for this research.

2. United Nations, *United Nations Peacekeeping* (New York: United Nations, 1993): 30–35. United Nations, Department of Public Information, "The United Nations and the Situation in Somalia," (United Nations, New York, April 1995, reference paper).

3. For an extended discussion of definitions of intervention, see J. H. Leurdijk, *Intervention in International Politics* (Leeuwarden, the Netherlands: Eisma B.V. Publishers, 1986). The definition I use here draws on this chapter as well as definitions offered by Jim Rosenau and Oran Young. See James N. Rosenau, "Intervention as a Scientific Concept, and a Postscript," in Richard A. Falk, ed., *The Vietnam War and International Law* 2 (Princeton: Princeton University Press, 1964): 979–1015; and Oran R. Young, "Systemic Bases of Intervention," in John Norton Moore, ed., *Law and Civil War in the Modern World* (Baltimore, Md.: Johns Hopkins University Press, 1974): 111–126.

4. See John J. Mearsheimer, "The False Promise of International Institutions," *International Security* 19, no. 3 (winter 1994/95): 5–49.

5. Publics may prefer multilateral intervention for this reason. See Steven Kull, "What the Public Knows that Washington Doesn't," *Foreign Policy*, no. 101 (winter 1995): 102–115.

6. Andrew Bennett, Joseph Lepgold, and Danny Unger, "Burdensharing in the Persian Gulf War," *International Organization* 48 (winter 1995): 39–75.

7. See John G. Sommer, *Hope Restored? Humanitarian Aid in Somalia* (Washington D.C.: Refugee Policy Group, November 1994): 32–33, for a discussion of this process in the Somalia case.

8. Inis L. Claude, Jr., "Collective Legitimization as a Political Function of the United Nations," *International Organization* 20 (summer 1966): 367–379.

9. Aside from the purely structural and bipolar explanation for the strategic importance of virtually all points on the globe, there is another, second explanation to which realists of a more classical variety have appealed at times. The argument here is that, although these small states clearly had little to do with protecting the territorial integrity of the superpowers, their roles were crucial to the political integrity of these two states, which were ideological rather than ethnic in their national identity. The connection was sufficiently close that a defeat for one ideology was interpreted by that ideology's superpower champion as a defeat to itself. The fact that both communism and liberal-democratic capitalism are expansive and universalistic ideologies fueled this tension by ensuring that clashes between the two would be frequent at various points around the world. However, it did nothing to ensure that those clashes would occur at locations with any other territorial or geopolitical significance.

10. Werner J. Feld and Robert S. Jordan with Leon Hurwitz, *International Organizations: A Comparative Approach*, 2nd ed. (New York: Praeger, 1988): 14–15; Union of International Associations, ed., *Yearbook of International Organizations, 1996/97*, 33rd ed., vol. 1 (Munich: K. G. Saur, 1996): 1684.

11. Even within the Security Council, coalitions must be built to support intervention. However, coalition-building is easier to carry out in the UN context than outside it both for organizational reasons and normative reasons. Organizationally, having existing channels of communication and standard operating procedures in place lowers transaction costs in these negotiations. Normatively, the UN imprimatur on an operation gives it political legitimacy that, in turn, makes it much easier to attract support. George Bush's experience during the Gulf War illustrates the normative argument. Both potential allies and Congress demanded UN authorization for the operation before they would support the Bush administration's effort. The best explication of the UN's political legitimization function is still Claude's, "Collective Legitimization as a Political Function of the United Nations."

12. For an extended presentation of this argument, see Robert H. Jackson, *Quasi-states: Sovereignty, International Relations, and the Third World* (Cambridge, U.K.: Cambridge University Press, 1990).

13. For an example of this debate, see Paul Johnson, "Colonialism's Back—and Not a Moment Too Soon," *New York Times Magazine*, April 18, 1993, 22; and the letters in response to this piece on May 9 (8–10), May 16 (12) and June 6 (12).

14. Again, Robert Jackson's arguments about quasi-states and the power of what he calls "negative sovereignty"—juridical sovereignty accorded to Third World states that

have little real empirical authority—illustrate this point. Most Third World states cannot be understood as lean, mean competitors emerging from some state-building process of the kind Tilly documents in sixteenth and seventeenth century Europe. They are creatures of external forces—of international society and especially often of the UN, which promoted and presided over much of the decolonization process. They continue to exist because the contemporary sovereignty regime, unlike past sovereignty regimes, provides "an insurance policy for marginal states." Intervention by international-level actors to prop up these states is precisely what Jackson would expect. See Jackson, *Quasi-states*, 24, and Charles Tilly, *The Formation of National States in Western Europe* (Princeton, N.J.: Princeton University Press, 1975). See also Mohammed Ayoob, *The Third World Security Predicament: State Making, Regional Security, and the International System* (Boulder, Colo.: Lynne Rienner, 1995).

15. Graham Allison's work was one of the early applications of this kind of organization theory to foreign policymaking in *Essence of Decision* (Boston, Mass.: Little, Brown, 1971). More recently Scott Sagan has used organization theory to examine the safety of nuclear weapons systems in *The Limits of Safety* (Princeton, N.J.: Princeton University Press, 1993). Keohane and Nye's argument about multiple channels connecting states and other actors under complex interdependence focuses on a similar phenomenon but may have different microfoundations. Organization theory arguments about SOPs grow out of a social psychological literature on bounded rationality and the use of scripts, schemas, and rules of thumb in human cognition. Keohane and Nye do not address bounded rationality issues in this argument. They imply that multiple channels are used by international actors, not because they have become standard procedures, but because they are well-considered means to known ends. Robert O. Keohane and Joseph Nye, *Power and Interdependence*, 2nd ed. (New York: Harper Collins, 1989).

16. For a fuller discussion of what they call the "logic of appropriateness" and the ways it shapes political action, see James March and John Olsen *Rediscovering Institutions: The Organizational Basis of Politics* (New York: Free Press, 1989): especially pages 23–24, and Martha Finnemore, *National Interests in International Society* (Ithaca, N.Y.: Cornell University Press, 1996): 28–31.

17. For an extended discussion of the relationship between the organizational and normative dimensions of multilateralism see John Ruggie, ed., *Multilateralism Matters* (New York: Columbia University Press, 1993): 3–48.

18. The following section draws on Marc Trachtenberg, "Intervention in Historical Perspective," in Laura W. Reed and Carl Kaysen, eds., *Emerging Norms of Justified Intervention: A Collection of Essays from a Project of the American Academy of Arts and Sciences* (Cambridge, Mass.: Committee on International Security Studies, American Academy of Arts and Sciences, 1993): 15–36; and Fernando Tesón, *Humanitarian Intervention* (Dobbs Ferry, N.Y.: Transnational Publishers, 1988).

19. As quoted in Trachtenberg, "Intervention in Historical Perspective," 25.

20. The declining legitimacy of intervention for economic reasons is linked with the declining legitimacy of colonialism. When Britain and Iran came into conflict over ownership of Iranian oil reserves, the U.S. squelched British plans to intervene on these

grounds. International rejection, especially Washington's, of British and French action to protect their perceived economic interests in the Suez Canal in 1956 is well-documented.

21. Arguably, humanitarian intervention as a concept and a claim in international politics has a longer history going back to medieval Christian theology and politics. One historian traces it back to 1250, when Louis IX promised the Maronite Christians in the Levant "protection as though they had been French subjects." But the notion did not gain wide currency until the post-World War II period. See, R. W. Seton-Watson, *Britain in Europe, 1789–1914* (Cambridge, U.K.: Cambridge University Press, 1938): 419–420.

22. I have examined evolving norms of humanitarian intervention elsewhere. See Martha Finnemore, "Constructing Norms of Humanitarian Intervention," in Peter J. Katzenstein, ed., *The Culture of National Security: Norms and Identity in World Politics* (New York: Columbia University Press, 1996): 153–185.

23. See Michael W. Doyle, *UN Peacekeeping in Cambodia: UNTAC's Civil Mandate* (Boulder, Colo.: Lynne Rienner, 1995).

24. Michael Haas, *Genocide by Proxy: Cambodian Pawn on a Superpower Chessboard* (New York: Praeger, 1991): 217. For more on Evans' proposals and their origins see his "Introductory Address" to the Informal Meeting on Cambodia in Jakarta, February 26, 1990, reprinted in the *Monthly Record of Australian Foreign Affairs and Trade* 61, no. 2 (February 1990): 70–73; Evans' address to the Sydney Institute of March 13 entitled "Australia, Indo-China and the Cambodian Peace Plan," is reprinted in *The Monthly Record of Australian Foreign Affairs and Trade* 61, no. 3 (March 1990): 142–148; and his statement on "Cambodia: Major Progress by the UN Permanent Five," is reprinted in *The Monthly Record of Australian Foreign Affairs and Trade* 61, no. 3 (March 1990): 169–171. For more on the UN role in Namibia, see Virginia Page Fortna, "United Nations Transition Assistance Group in Namibia," in William J. Durch, ed., *The Evolution of UN Peacekeeping: Case Studies and Comparative Analysis* (New York: St. Martin's Press, 1993): 355–57.

25. "The Peace Agreement in Brief," *Washington Post*, October 24, 1991, A42; "Cambodian Factions Sign Peace Pact," *New York Times*, October 24, 1991, 16.

26. Trisha Thomas, "Into the Unknown: Can the United Nations Bring Peace to Cambodia?," *Journal of International Affairs* 44, no. 4 (winter 1991): 512. For political reasons, neither the U.S. nor the Soviet Union was expected to be a significant contributor of troops.

27. Al Kamen, "Domestic Politics a Factor in US Shift," *Washington Post*, July 19, 1990, 28; Stephen J. Solarz, "Cambodia and the International Community," *Foreign Affairs* 69, no. 2 (spring 1990): 99–115, quotation on p. 100. The role of domestic opinion in inserting morality into American foreign policymaking is by no means unique to this case and poses serious theoretical questions for realists. See Robert McElroy, *Morality and American Foreign Policy* (Princeton, N.J.: Princeton University Press, 1992).

28. David Sanger, "On Trade Ties to Hanoi, Japanese Jump the Gun," *New York Times*, November 6, 1992, 6; Murray Hiebert and Louise do Rosario, "Waiting in the Wings," *Far Eastern Economic Review* (May 30, 1991): 68–9.

29. Anthony Rowley, "Affluence with Influence," *Far Eastern Economic Review* (June 20, 1991): 41–44; Susumu Awanohara, "Apology Signals a Break with the Past," *Far Eastern Economic Review* (June 20, 1991): 44–7; Robert Delfs, "Looking for a Role," *Far Eastern Economic Review* (June 18, 1992): 41–4; "Japan Is Told to Support UN in Cambodia," *New York Times*, March 12, 1992, 8; Paul Lewis, "UN Votes to Send 22,000 to Back Peace in Cambodia," *New York Times*, February 29, 1992, 4.

30. Gareth Evans, "Informal Meeting on Cambodia," address to the Informal Meeting on Cambodia in Jakarta, February 26, 1990, reprinted in *The Monthly Record of Australian Foreign Affairs and Trade* 61, 2 (February 1990): 71.

31. This account draws on the following general sources: John L. Hirsch and Robert B. Oakley, *Somalia and Operation Restore Hope* (Washington D.C.: U.S. Institute of Peace, 1995); Mohamed Sahnoun, *Somalia: The Missed Opportunities* (Washington, D.C.: U.S. Institute of Peace, 1994); Ken Menkhaus with Louis Ortmayer, "Key Decisions in the Somalia Intervention" (Washington, D.C.: The Institute for the Study of Diplomacy, 1995); and Sommer, *Hope Restored?*

32. Safety concerns however did not keep UNICEF from operating in Bosnia. It had also been in Iraq during the Gulf War.

33. These accusations are leveled by Ray Bonner in "Why We Went: How the United Nations Turned its Back on Somalia and Subverted the Best Chance for Peace," *Mother Jones* (March/April 1993): 56.

34. "UN relief for Somalia," *New York Times*, December 29, 1991, 7.

35. See Jeffrey Clark, "Debacle in Somalia," *Foreign Affairs* 72, no. 1 ("America and the World 1992/93"): 119; and Ray Bonner, "Why We Went."

36. Patrick E. Tyler, "U.N. Chief's Dispute With Council Boils Over," *New York Times*, August 3, 1992, 1, 9; *New York Times*, July 6, 1992, 2.

37. Cited in "UN is Outraged," *New York Times*, November 26, 1992, 10; also Paul Lewis, "UN Chief to ask Use of Force to Back Somali Aid," *New York Times*, November 27, 1992, 14.

38. I am indebted to Darel Paul for pointing out these alternative courses of action. See also, Paul Lewis, "UN Says Somalis Must Disarm before Peace," *New York Times*, December 6, 1992, 15; Paul Lewis, "UN Chief Says Letter to Bush Outlines US Commitment to Disarm Somali Gangs," *New York Times*, December 13, 1993, 14; Paul Lewis, "UN Chief Faults US again on Disarming Somali Clans," *New York Times*, December 22, 1992, 15.

39. Menkhaus, "Key Decisions in the Somalia Intervention," 9; Sommer, *Hope Restored?*, 30. The U.S. ambassador to Kenya was another public opponent. See, Michael R. Gordon, "Envoy Asserts Intervention in Somalia is Risky and not in Interests of U.S.," *New York Times*, December 6, 1992, 14.

40. "Transcript of the President's Address on Somalia," *New York Times*, December 5, 1992, 4. Bush told Andrew Natsios of USAID and General Johnston that, "if the U.S.

can make a difference in saving lives, we should do it . . . No one should have to starve at Christmastime." Quoted in Sommer, *Hope Restored?*, 31.

41. For a discussion of media effects on these interventions see Edward Girardet, "Public Opinion, the Media, and Humanitarianism," in Thomas Weiss and Larry Minear, eds., *Humanitarianism Across Borders* (Boulder, Colo.: Lynne Rienner, 1993). The UN Special Representative, Mohamed Sahnoun, believed the role of the media to be crucial in prompting political action and thanks them explicitly in the preface to *Somalia: The Missed Opportunities*. Even those who are skeptical about the susceptibility of policymakers to TV images concede that media images do have some impact, if not directly on decisionmakers then indirectly, by creating public outrage and changing the public opinion climate in which decisions are made. See Nik Gowing, "Behind the CNN Factor: Lights! Camera! Atrocities! But Policy Makers Swear They're not Swayed by TV Images," *Washington Post*, July 31, 1994, C1. See also, Stephen Hess, "Crisis, TV, and Public Pressure," *The Brookings Review* 12 (winter 1994): 48. Paul Simon (D-Ill.) and Nancy Kassebaum (R-Kans.) led the Congressional push for action. For more on Congressional involvement see Menkhaus, "Key Decisions in the Somalia Intervention," 464, and Hirsch and Oakley, *Somalia and Operation Restore Hope*, chapter 3.

42. Hirsch and Oakley, *Somalia and Operation Restore Hope*, chapter 3.

43. Quoted in Eric Schmitt, "US Assesses Risks of Sending Troops to Somalia," *New York Timess*, December 1, 1992, 10.

44. Menkhaus, "Key Decisions in the Somalia Intervention," 464. For a more detailed account of the U.S. decision to intervene see Hirsch and Oakley, chapter 3 and Menkhaus, "Key Decisions in the Somalia Intervention."

45. Michael Wines, "Bush Declares Goal in Somalia is to 'Save Thousands,'" *New York Times*, December 5, 1992, 1,4.

46. Menkhaus, "Key Decisions in the Somalia Intervention," 5.

47. Elsewhere I have made a more extended argument that, while unilateral humanitarian intervention was acceptable in the nineteenth century, the unilateral option for humanitarian intervention has disappeared in the twentieth century. If intervention is to be justified on humanitarian grounds it must be multilateral. See Finnemore, "Constructing Norms of Humanitarian Intervention."

48. Sommer, *Hope Restored?*, 32–33.

49. The convoluted chain of command structure in Somalia certainly contributed to the incident on October 3, 1993 that left 18 Rangers dead and 75 wounded; however, most of the critical command errors there were within the U.S. force structure. For an assessment of military lessons learned from the Somalia operation by the U.S., see Kenneth Allard, *Somalia Operations: Lessons Learned* (Washington, D.C.: National Defense University Press, 1995).

9

Collective Humanitarian Conflict Management: More or Less than the Millennium?

❑

Thomas G. Weiss

Today, the hopefulness of 1989 already seems like ancient history. The almost giddy euphoria surrounding the end of the Cold War was remarkably short-lived; it is as if the policy and scholarly communities have awakened with a hangover and more sober appreciations of the state of international peace and security. This book is, in fact, a reflection of the crucial need to better understand the *volte-face* and the precise problems and prospects for multilateral conflict management as the twenty-first century dawns.

Collective security in the classical, Wilsonian sense[1] has never really been a serious option,[2] even though the first few years of the post-Cold War era reinvigorated the UN Security Council and heralded enhanced prospects for multilateral conflict management, especially within the humanitarian arena. Experimentation with various modes of humanitarian action—for both of the two main components, delivery and protection—has characterized the period since the Allied Coalition's response to the Kurdish crisis in northern Iraq in the aftermath of the Gulf War.[3] Most strikingly, the humanitarian impulse has been unleashed with the military in the forefront of the charge. Whether or not we actually have entered into Raimo Vayrenen's "age of humanitarian emergencies,"[4] ensuring access to victims clearly has become a priority for policymakers, pundits, parliamentarians, and the public, with a record number of war victims worldwide.

As mentioned in the introduction to this book and as argued in several of the preceding chapters, the positive atmosphere and the bullishness of successful international efforts to thwart interstate aggression and head-off humanitarian disaster in the Gulf have changed rather dramatically to pessimism and skittishness following a series of what were perceived as UN flops or quasi-failures. Observers usually point to the "Somalia syndrome" as the turning point, but former Assistant Secretary of State Richard Holbrooke suggests that "The damage that Bosnia did to the U.N. was incalculable."[5]

Where exactly are we following celebrations of the fiftieth anniversary of the world organization? Over the last five years, there have been numerous attempts at collective humanitarian conflict management, the main justification for operations under the auspices of the United Nations in this period. This essay takes stock of the UN's strengths and weaknesses and suggests a few ways to remedy the latter. It surveys recent literature about peace operations and argues that under certain circumstances collective humanitarian conflict management can work. It concludes by describing some new elements of an effective system.

Dominant Trends

Three trends have merged to dominate the UN's handling of post-Cold War crises.[6] The most significant feature of international responses in the last five years has been the growing willingness of the international community to address, rather than ignore, emergencies within the borders of war-torn states that are emerging as the dominant security challenges of our times.[7] Although lawyers continue to point out that the language of absolute state sovereignty in UN Charter Article 2(7) remains intact, humanitarian imperatives have led governmental, intergovernmental (IGOs), and nongovernmental organizations (NGOs) to redefine when it is possible "to intervene in matters which are essentially within the domestic jurisdiction of any state. . . ." Sometimes there is no effective sovereign (the case of collapsed states like Somalia), and sometimes sovereignty is overridden in the name of higher norms (the case of assisting the Kurds in northern Iraq). Civil wars do not fit neatly within the charter regime's foundation on interstate conflicts, but they do coincide with the more circumscribed and plausible definition of multilateral conflict management that is the point of departure for this volume.

The second trend relates to an ever-burgeoning demand for helping hands from UN soldiers. Secretary-General Boutros Boutros-Ghali wrote in 1995 that: "This increased volume of activity would have strained the Organization even if the nature of the activity had remained unchanged."[8] But neither the volume nor the nature of the tasks remained stable. After stable levels of about 10,000 troops in the early post-Cold War period, their numbers jumped rapidly. In 1994–1995, 70,000 to 80,000 blue-helmeted soldiers were authorized by the UN's annualized "military" (peacekeeping) budget that approached $4 billion in 1993–1995, while arrears approached $3.5 billion. The roller coaster ride continued in 1996 as the numbers of troops and the budget declined by two-thirds, but the arrears remained unchanged. These figures only hint at the magnitude of related problems because they represent just the additional costs of deployment and not the real costs to troop-contributing countries. In recent years, peacekeeping debts and arrears along with those for the regular budget have often been about three times the annual regular budget of the world organization, clearly an unsustainable situation.

The third trend in some ways grows from the first two, namely subcontracting for military services to both regional organizations or major states, on the one hand, and for humanitarian delivery services to NGOs, on the other.[9] The pursuit of the Gulf War and the creation of safe havens for Kurds are perhaps the best illustrations of military subcontracting, a subject that is in fact taken up elsewhere in this volume. Moreover, three Security Council decisions between late June and late July 1994 indicated the growing relevance of military intervention by major powers in regions of their traditional interests: a Russian scheme to deploy its troops in Georgia to end the three-year-old civil war; the French intervention in Rwanda to help stave genocidal conflict; and the U.S. plan to spearhead a military invasion to reverse the military coup in Haiti.

One analyst commented that "the increasing sense that peacekeeping is so ineffective a tool for resolving crises like Somalia or Bosnia that it might well be better to scrap it altogether and leave the policing of the world's trouble-spots to great powers or regional hegemons."[10] The secretary-general agreed in his first press conference of 1995, stating "that the United Nations does not have the capacity to carry out huge peace endorsement operations, and that when the Security Council decides on a peace enforcement operation, our advice is that the Security Council mandate a group of Member States, (those which) have the capability."[11] The decision in Budapest in December 1994 by the Conference (now Organization) on Security and Cooperation in Europe (OSCE) to authorize 3,000 troops after an official cease-fire in Nagorno-Karabakh is another illustration of the willingness to look to regional subcontracting. These experiments indicate that the evident gap between international capacities and increasing demands for help could be filled by regional powers or even hegemons operating under the scrutiny of a wider community of states that would try to hold the interveners accountable for their actions.[12]

The second part of the subcontracting phenomenon relates to the growing contribution of NGOs to mitigate suffering in internal conflicts.[13] This is part of a larger development, namely the burgeoning of nongovernmental organizations in all sectors that have injected new and unexpected voices into international discourse on every continent.[14] Over the last two decades, but especially since the end of the Cold War, human rights advocates, gender activists, developmentalists, and groups of indigenous peoples have become more vocal and operational in many contexts that were once thought to be the exclusive preserve of governments.[15] As the role of the state is reappraised and alternatives sought to solve problems, NGOs emerge as a critical actors—private in form but public in purpose.[16] Although the preamble of the UN Charter begins with the urgent exhortation, "We the peoples of the United Nations," the complex interactions among states, nonstates, and the United Nations are poorly understood. What is clear, however, is that "[n]ongovernmental organizations are now full participants in international life" and that the "fall of the Berlin Wall shattered the ideological screen that had concealed the reality of international relations." This evaluation comes not from the pen of an NGO-apologist but rather from the UN secretary-general.[17]

Operational NGOs are central to comprehensive international responses to internal conflicts in the post-Cold War world. Delivery of services is the mainstay of most of their budgets and the basis for enthusiastic support from a wide range of donors. Many NGOs operate development programs, but they have become increasingly active in migration and disaster relief, which may now be in total financial terms their most important operational or advisory activities. In the mid-1990s, at least 13 percent of total public development aid (over $10 billion) was disbursed by NGOs, and about half of this total, an ever-growing share, was accounted for by emergency relief.[18] Collectively they disburse more overseas development assistance (ODA) than the UN system (excluding the Bretton Woods institutions).

Is There an Agenda for Peace?

In January 1992, the Security Council requested that the then newly-elected secretary-general assess the promise of the United Nations in a changed world. No other recent international public policy document has generated so much discussion—by practitioners and scholars—as *An Agenda for Peace* since its June 1992 publication. Boutros-Ghali's report has framed debate and contains many intriguing suggestions, but it is at its most ambitious in defining the UN's potential for multilateral conflict management.[19]

The deployment of outside military personnel under UN command could be expanded usefully, as the secretary-general proposes, in several areas similar to those in which they have been used effectively in the past. With the consent of the parties and using force only as a last resort and in self-defense, such deployments include supervising confidence-building measures related to military downsizing, fact-finding, staffing early warning centers, and acting as buffers in either interstate or intrastate conflicts when belligerents agree. Regarding these activities, the secretary-general makes concrete recommendations for improving personnel, logistics, information, and above all, financing.

For many other activities, there is no UN track record. If there is, it is lackluster or worse. The protection of UN civilian and humanitarian personnel is perhaps the most obvious illustration. The experience of the UN Guards Contingent in Iraq—the secretary-general's principal illustration—provides a poor guide to thinking about the future. They were helpful for a time, but not because of their pistols and blue baseball caps. They were based in a country whose population and military had been defeated and temporarily subjugated; Iraq found them initially less odious than Western troops; and NATO air power was in nearby Turkey. The use of more numerous, but not significantly more effective, UN soldiers in Bosnia was an extension of wishful thinking.

An Agenda for Peace explores significant departures from past practice, including coercive economic and military sanctions under Chapter VII. The most significant was the proposal to create peace-enforcement units. Cease-fires would be guaranteed by UN soldiers when warring parties no longer agreed to respect a negotiated halt to carnage. The secretary-general underscored that these soldiers would be required to be more heavily armed than yesterday's peacekeepers. The experience in several situations—with at least 30 cease-fires for Bosnia and various agreements for Somalia and Rwanda before, during, and after carnage in them—suggests how much these departures exceeded the expectations of governments and the abilities of the United Nations.

In a progress report issued in January 1995 to mark the UN's fiftieth anniversary, *Supplement to An Agenda for Peace*, the secretary-general came to the same conclusion and trimmed his sails. He retreated and recommended caution because of phenomena that had been partially or totally unforeseen in 1992. Among them are precisely the two trends that were discussed in the previous section—the intensity and ugliness of internal conflicts and the quantitative and qualitative changes in the UN system's efforts to deploy multifaceted operations. The new document is mainly a call for reduced expectations and UN activities; and this new reticence vis-à-vis military efforts, which has been reinforced by a bipartisan set of proposals on the eve of the 1996 elections,[20] has a direct bearing on the possibilities for collective humanitarian conflict management in a changing world.

The Post-Cold War Literature

The dramatic acceleration in the number and variety of UN military missions has been widely noted—the Security Council approved over twice as many operations in the last eight years as in the previous forty. There also has been a proliferation of analyses about multilateral military operations. Space here does not permit an exhaustive literature review, the details of which are available in a *Review of the Peacekeeping Literature, 1990–1996.*[21] But it would be useful to summarize impressions about the recent literature as a prelude to exploring further conceptual problems in it with specific reference to humanitarian action.

There has been an avalanche of peace operations literature produced from a variety of perspectives since 1990, mostly in journal rather than book form. Judith Stiehm, currently an adjunct professor at the U.S. Army Peacekeeping Institute, remarked in an interview that this trend is reminiscent of the early 1960s when the women-in-politics literature exploded, and for many of the same reasons. A new field meant new opportunities for scholars and other interested parties to capture what amounted to an open market for the publication of ideas, analyses, and reflections about gender. Similarly for peacekeeping, generous government and philanthropic funding has provided an additional incentive to quickly establish oneself as an "expert" or perhaps to be "recycled" from such areas of inquiry as disarmament and East-West security studies that suddenly were in the wings rather than the center of the international security stage. The demand for analyses of peace operations partially explains the supply in the literature. This is not a judgment about the quality of analyses; it is simply an explanation for the quantity produced in a relatively short time.

The sheer volume of publications since 1990 is unsettling—our preliminary in-house database currently holds 1,600 entries, which is surely incomplete even for the English-language works on which we have concentrated. It has become increasingly arduous for newcomers to discern publications that are grounded equally in logic and hard data and provide the necessary description, analysis, and assessment to understand past and present peace operations and their potential future role in international conflict management. The literature overflows with claims to knowledge about the nature of changing world politics, theories and recommendations for institutional reform and conflict resolution, and first-hand accounts from the field. The volume and accelerated pace of literature production has equaled that of peace operations. As Shashi Tharoor remarked, it is similar to trying to repair a moving car, for we "too often find ourselves steering a rattling vehicle that is moving at breakneck speed, without an up-to-date road map, while trying to fix the engine at the same time."[22]

We are now at the point in the evolution of the literature to take stock of the insights gained by the community of writers, institutions, policymakers, and practitioners, as well as what lessons have been learned—keeping in mind, however, a clear distinction between the two activities of gaining insights and actual lessons learned.[23] If indeed lessons have been learned in policymaking and planning, those who profess such knowledge should address directly who has learned the lessons and which procedural and institutional changes actually have been implemented. Otherwise, one is vaguely speaking only of insights about patterns of behavior that either support or undermine the effectiveness of collective security. "The art of learning from experience begins with understanding linkages and the conditions under which events took place" and requires the institutional integrity to expose rather than paper-over mistakes.[24]

Categorization of the literature produced since 1990 is an important first step in identifying the problems of peace operations, the recommendations to resolve them, and the actual procedural and institutional changes that have occurred along the way of this six-year journey that might suggest lessons learned. Already a gap in the literature is revealed by the absence of investigation into the mechanisms of institutional memory that would support concrete claims to lessons learned.[25]

Our review of the peace operations literature of the post-Cold War era begins with sorting the literature and tracing the evolution of problems and recommendations. Categorization of the literature is quite similar to the military's understanding of the trickle-down from policy formation to planning to implementation. It is exceptional that those who write case studies attempt to capture the interplay of various levels of analysis—be they across multiple cases,[26] for a single case like Cambodia,[27] or for a single major issue like disarmament across cases.[28] The majority of authors tend to concentrate on a single level: the strategic, the operational, or the tactical, which is the most useful way to categorize recent publications.

Strategic-level literature describes and attempts to explain the source of peace operation policies within states, among states, and within the UN Security Council. This literature addresses structures and cultures of decisionmaking that determine whether peace operations will be mandated by the Security Council and, if so, who will contribute, who will not, and why.[29] Topics also include international law, ethics, and the guidelines for collective security activities outlined in the UN Charter—all of which constitute elements that expand or contract the discernible boundaries on the range of imaginable policy.[30] Although it is obvious that policymaking determines the *who, what, when, where,* and *why* of participation in peace operations, many writers by-pass this top level of analysis by using such phrases as "political will" or "national interest." Use of these amorphous terms means that the author assumes everyone knows to what he or she is referring; in reality, these terms say everything by saying nothing. Unpacking the terms "political will" or "national interest" is the most essential step in understanding the evolution of peace operations, although it is clear that the success of peace operations also has a feedback effect on subsequent decisionmaking about new commitments to new crises. And as a number of authors argue, the success of peace operations, once troops are contributed, is determined by institutions and behavior at the operational level.[31]

Literature at the operational level, in contrast, focuses on the institutional actors, actions, and interactions of those who receive broad policy mandates from strategic-level actors and then "operationalize" them. This literature speaks to questions of military doctrine and its determination of force structure, command and control, and decisionmaking processes; training and deployment preparation; management structures, procurement and financial processes; interpretation of unclear mandates; and the how-to manuals for field behavior, including how to cooperate with nonstate actors.[32] Literature that focuses on standardizing codes of conduct for humanitarian actors falls into this category—so too does literature that addresses the mandates of various UN agencies and the actions of the secretary-general, who is responsible to the Security Council for the organization, conduct, and direction of peacekeeping operations, as well as for providing the council with ongoing information about the nature and effectiveness of missions.

Underrepresented in the literature is the tactical level, where conflicting military doctrine and rules of engagement, poor procurement procedures and communications systems, and a myriad of other problems generated or ignored at the operational level play themselves out. The literature from the field primarily comes in the form of military after-action reviews, mission assessments by various UN agencies, cables, letters, transcribed oral interviews, diaries, and memoirs. Tactical-level literature consists of the hard data and narratives about the impact of certain strategic-level policies or operational-level guidelines on the effectiveness of a particular mission. This literature consists largely of politically unfiltered and uninterpreted accounts by actors in the field who are without scholarly methods or pretensions. They put forward views about performances as best they can with the decisions about movement and resources that were dictated from above, frequently made without the input of those who must execute them.

The series of case studies by the Humanitarianism and War Project at Brown University's Watson Institute, for instance, emphasize obtaining and organizing overviews of tactical-level information.[33] Although there is certainly an abundance of documentation by practitioners, incorporation of the observations compiled at this level into lessons learned at the strategic and operational levels is currently undetermined. Moreover, it is uncertain how certain bits of this tactical-level literature are absorbed and responded to at the operational level. In the Rwandan case, for example, the special-representative to the secretary-general and the UNAMIR commander each sent a cable to New York prior to the Rwandan genocide but described different levels of tension. Understanding the primacy of certain tactical information over others on UN decisionmaking at the operational level is not available to date in the peace operations literature, and thus another gap is revealed.

So who is learning lessons according to the literature? Since 1990, changes in U.S. military manuals reflect lessons learned at the tactical level. According to a 1995 U.S. General Accounting Office report, some unit commanders are choosing to incorporate peace operations training into their standard combat training programs.[34] There is now an international association of peacekeeping training centers, and two new journals called *International Peacekeeping*. Military manuals and related texts about how to relate to NGOs and UN personnel during multifunctional operations are becoming more standard reading material.[35]

There is, however, little operational-level literature to suggest that the United Nations system or NGOs have gone beyond simply acknowledging tactical problems and asserting that lessons have been learned as they rush off to the next crisis. Nor has there been intensive primary source research conducted about state-level decisionmaking to advance an understanding of governmental lessons learned. An unwillingness or inability to devote scarce resources or, more seriously still, to assign scarce senior personnel to assist in analyzing, learning, and institutionalizing lessons plagues both the UN and NGO communities. For the military who actually spend a majority of their time preparing and training rather than executing, such activities as creating an institutional memory are standard operating procedures; for others, they are a luxury.[36]

Conceptual Problems

The dramatic increase in UN operations and analyses of them contains fundamental conceptual problems. Discussions in UN circles are still characterized by confusion about traditional peacekeeping and coercion, and especially the gray areas in between, or what has been called "selective enforcement" in this book but goes by other names such as "second generation," "wider peacekeeping," and "peace operations."[37]

The literal position of UN troops is dangerous and awkward. Many analysts, diplomats, and UN staff stumble more figuratively when they fail to distinguish clearly old-style "peacekeeping"—the interposition of neutral forces when warring parties have agreed to a cease-fire, or at least to putting one in place. They employ the same term—even if qualified by such adjectives as "wider" peacekeeping by Whitehall or "aggravated" peacekeeping by the Pentagon—for a variety of situations where consent is absent or problematic and where military capacity outranks moral authority. The confusion is even greater when an operation shifts from Chapter VI to VII (Somalia and Rwanda) or combines the two (the former Yugoslavia).

The United Nations has demonstrated for several decades that it can manage Chapter VI military operations. Peacekeeping is often called "Chapter six-and-a-half," former Secretary-General Dag Hammarskjöld's clever indication that this UN invention was not foreseen by the Charter's framers. But peacekeeping is really an extension of Chapter VI rather than a would-be Chapter VII. If governments so wished, management and financial reforms undoubtedly could improve peacekeeping because each operation is still put together from scratch in an ad hoc manner, based on best-case scenarios with inadequate resources.

At the same time, the United Nations also has demonstrated its inability to handle Chapter VII, which the secretary-general has now recognized in his *Supplement*: "[N]either the Security Council nor the Secretary-General at present has the capacity to deploy, direct, command and control operations for this purpose."[38] The inability to manage full-scale or even selective enforcement cannot be wished away; nor can it be overcome by tinkering. The world organization's diplomatic and bureaucratic structures are inimical to initiating and overseeing military efforts when serious fighting rages and where coercion rather than consent is the norm.

Part of the problem is that the United Nations has relied too heavily on the experience of past operations when coping with post-Cold War crises instead of delineating distinct new characteristics. Peacekeeping should be reserved for consensual missions, which is where the UN secretariat has a comparative advantage. Otherwise, peacekeeping becomes an infinitely elastic concept without operational significance. It is not a cure-all for the chaos of ethno-nationalism, but rather a discrete tool for conflict management when consent is present and political rather than military expertise is required.

In his first press conference of 1995, the secretary-general straightforwardly recognized "that the United Nations does not have the capacity to carry out huge peace endorsement operations, and that when the Security Council decides on a peace enforcement operation, our advice is that the Security Council mandate a group of Member States, (those which) have the capability."[39] In his *Supplement,* he notes that peacekeeping and enforcement "should be seen as alternative techniques and not as adjacent points on a continuum."[40]

Conceptual clarity is also absent from many considerations of "intervention."[41] This term covers the spectrum of possible actions—from making telephone calls to dispatching military forces—which are intended to alter internal affairs in another country. As such, it is almost synonymous with the state practice of international relations, which in the post-Cold War period has witnessed more significant outside intrusions into domestic affairs than previously.

Our specific concerns here, however, are Chapter VII decisions by the Security Council to enforce international decisions either through economic (or nonforcible) and military (or forcible) sanctions. Both have consequences for victims and humanitarians, although the focus in this volume is upon the latter, or armed intervention. Talk-show hosts, attendees of academic conferences, politicians, and the proverbial woman in the street are preoccupied with what the editor of *Foreign Affairs* described, prematurely, as the "springtime for interventionism."[42] They are hesitating at a fork in the road about using military force in support of humanitarian objectives. One route leads back toward traditional peacekeeping and the other toward the measured application of superior military force in support of more ambitious international decisions, including the enforcement of human rights.[43]

The balance of opinion at present definitely favors the former, and Somalia and Bosnia are critical in this weighting. Reticence from the armed forces about humanitarian intervention is widespread although it has been most publicized in the United States. In an era of no-risk and no-casualty foreign policy ironically joins the objections of critics who see U.S. dominance in multilateral military efforts as a continuation of American hegemony.[44]

Two unlikely apologists for outside military forces, Alex de Waal and Rakiya Omaar, have observed: "Humanitarian intervention demands a different set of military skills. It is akin to counterinsurgency."[45] This realization will not be comforting to those still recovering from the "Vietnam syndrome."[46] Yet lessons from the United Kingdom's efforts in Malaysia undoubtedly are more relevant for failed states than those from Operation Desert Storm. In Malaysia, relatively small numbers of well-disciplined soldiers, in this case from Britain, developed close links to local populations and had sufficient political support at home to stay the course.

Dissenters from humanitarianism intervention include many developing countries, which cling to the notion that state sovereignty does not permit outside intervention, and which serves to protect them against bullying by major powers.[47] They also argue, and perhaps rightfully, that intervention is messy and it is easier to get in than get out. The Security Council's definition of what constitutes "threats" to international peace and security is expanding to cover virtually any subject as well as remaining selective in application.

These countries essentially are trying to put on blinders in order to avoid an emerging reality of the post-Cold War era. Sovereignty should be exercised within the limits of human rights norms or be voided. "Use it responsibly or risk losing it" summarizes the framework beginning to characterize world politics in the last half decade.[48] As all the papers in this book make clear, state sovereignty remains the basis for everyday international relations, and it is likely to do so in the future. At the same time, several contributions also point to the fact that it can be overruled when mass suffering or genocide occurs and the international community is prepared to act. The acceptable degree of outside interference in the domestic affairs of rogue states and of insurgents is considerably more intrusive than in the past.[49]

As such, there is a distinction between international lawyers—for whom there normally are not degrees of sovereignty, it either exists or it does not—and political scientists. For the latter, sovereignty is not incompatible with human rights standards, and it is possible to be more or less sovereign. Third World countries are understandably concerned about where lines are drawn so that even greater infringements on their feeble sovereignty do not occur. However, mass civilian suffering in northern Iraq, Somalia, Rwanda, and Bosnia clearly qualify as locations where sovereignty was not sacrosanct, as was the case in the aftermath of a military coup against a democratically elected country in Haiti. In fact, the vast majority of developing countries have supported interventions in these countries.

Other critics of vigorous intervention are civilian humanitarians in the trenches. For them, "humanitarian war" and "military humanitarianism" are oxymorons.[50] Pacifists like the Quakers and Mennonites are not the only dissenters from more robust action. A fair number of other practitioners argue that humanitarian initiatives are strictly consensual and are premised on impartiality and neutrality. Protected by the international law of armed conflicts, of which the International Committee of the Red Cross (ICRC) is the custodian, political authorities in armed conflicts should be persuaded, according to this argument, to meet their commitments for access to and respect of civilians.

Reluctant developing countries and some humanitarians are joined in disputing the wisdom of armed humanitarian intervention by those whose reasoning is less ideological or philosophical, but based on a static interpretation of international law. In an anarchical world, according to this argument, states require reciprocal rules to mitigate inevitable competition; and thus state sovereignty is essential to the ground rules of balance-of-power politics to ensure some stability in international relations. A further refinement is that outside military forces encumber the task of the affected country's own civilian authorities and may undermine local coping capacities. Intervention not only raises the levels of violence and complicates the lives of civilian humanitarians in the short run, but it also makes reconciliation more difficult in the longer run. Any assistance that is not based on consent is unlikely to enhance human rights and may even exacerbate violence.[51] The logic of the argument is that intervention by foreign military forces leads to further instability and weakens democratic tendencies and institutions that must be locally sustainable to be meaningful.

A thornier position for which historical interpretations are controversial regards the futility of intervention because the failure of some states represents a natural process that should be allowed to run its course.[52] The vast majority of state formation attempts in Europe, for example, failed or involved considerable bloodshed over several centuries. There is no reason to believe that states created in the wake of colonization and decolonization will do better. Somalia may be a particularly obvious case to leave a failed state alone because it is such an obviously artificial construction.[53] A different spin has been given to this argument in the former Yugoslavia in that securing peace may have become more possible after ethnic groups occupied demographically separate territories.[54]

Yet with one in every 115 people on earth forced into flight from war, humanitarian intervention may sometimes be the only way to halt massive abuses of human rights, starvation, and genocide.[55] Thus, partisans of the other route at the fork in the road, including this author, are open to the option of outside military forces to assist civilians trapped in wars. When consent cannot be extracted, economic and military coercion can be justified in operational and ethical terms. When there is sufficient leadership and political will, effective humanitarian conflict management may include military backup that goes far beyond the minimalist use of force in self-defense by traditional UN peacekeepers. Rather than suspending relief and withdrawing, the international community can use enough force to guarantee access to civilians, protect aid workers, and keep thugs at bay.

Humanitarian intervention is not an end in itself, but a last-ditch effort to create breathing room for the reemergence of a modicum of local stability and order, which ultimately are prerequisites for the conduct of negotiations that can lead to consent about humanitarian space and eventually about lasting peace. The Commission on Global Governance has proposed "an appropriate charter amendment, permitting such intervention but restricting it to cases that constitute a violation of the security of people so gross and extreme that it requires an international response on humanitarian grounds."[56]

On its fiftieth anniversary, it is worth recalling that the United Nations was supposed to be different from its defunct predecessor, the League of Nations. The provisions for coercion in the UN Charter—as well as the experience with full-scale and selective enforcement in the post-Cold War era—were designed to stop atrocities in such places as Somalia, Bosnia, Rwanda, northern Iraq, and Haiti.

Problems in UN Operations

There is a fundamental ambiguity of trying to qualify any of these cases as a "success" or a "failure." Attaching a value to human life poses obvious and uncomfortable philosophical and moral challenges. Even if we finesse this problem and move to country cases, there are inescapable value judgments and differing time-frames and objectives used by various actors along with the hidden agendas that are the essence of UN politics and deliberations. Were military efforts in northern Iraq a success because 1.5 million Kurds were saved, or a failure because there is still no political solution with Saddam Hussein ensconced in Baghdad? Were military operations in Somalia successful because death rates dropped in 1993, or a long-term failure because billions of dollars were spent to stop the clock temporarily? Were military efforts in Bosnia successful because they saved lives and avoided a wider conflict in Europe, or a failure because the international community has not stood up to aggression, war crimes, and the forced movement of peoples? Were military and police operations to restore President Aristide in Haiti a success because a precedent against a seizure of power by a junta was set and peaceful elections for his successor held, or a failure because fundamentally skewed economic structures remain in place to exploit the vast majority of the population ? Were military efforts in Rwanda a success because the carnage was stopped and lives saved, or a failure because the genocide took place?

Whatever the criteria for success and failure, however, three major operational shortcomings have been manifest in the last five years. First, the United Nations has been unable to address what has entered the social science vocabulary as "failed" or "collapsed" states.[57] The disintegration of public authority entails the evaporation of state sovereignty, which has created a vacuum in local authority and public order. Recent civil wars have witnessed the massive looting and destruction of infrastructure and the killing or flight of many trained persons from the public and private sectors. There has been no meaningful attempt, external or internal, to get these failed societies back on their feet.[58] In fact, we are only at the beginning of even understanding how different and difficult mediation and negotiations in such conflicts are.[59]

Of course, the difficulties of nation-building should not be ignored. The hubris symbolized by American efforts in Vietnam or Soviet ones in Afghanistan should give pause. The citizens of post-conflict countries ultimately must take responsibility for the reconstitution of viable civil societies. But they require buffers and breathing space after protracted civil war, or even after a short but particularly brutal one.

Second, traditional deficiencies in United Nations command and control have worsened. On the purely technical side, communications are notoriously difficult because of multiple languages, procedures, and equipment, which are exacerbated by the lack of common training for individual contingents. Operations also suffer from multiple chains of command within a theater, and between the military and the civilian sides of the UN secretariat. The normal tendency for contingents to seek guidance from their own capitals is intensified with complexity and danger. The confused spring 1995 spectacle in Bosnia—NATO's bombing of the arms depot in Pale followed by the Serbian response of taking UN soldiers as hostages and human shields while shelling civilians in safe areas—illustrates these larger UN deficiencies. It is useful to note that NATO surmounted its own command and control problems only by building an integrated structure over decades; and the United Nations does not, and will not have any time soon, the permanent forces that are needed for such integration.

The one recent development of interest in this respect comes from a Canadian and Dutch initiative, joined by 22 other countries as "the friends of rapid reaction." They have proposed a mobile military headquarters capable of fielding command teams within hours of a Security Council decision. Although the existence of such a capability would perhaps be helpful in exercising a restraining effect on combatants, the real problem is the reluctance of states to move quickly and to authorize forces large enough to do the job.

The dearth of professionalism is serious and unlikely to improve. The United Nations has not kept pace with the dramatically increased demand for peacekeepers, nor do member states wish significant improvement because this feebleness enhances governmental leverage over the secretariat. The means to plan, support, and command peacekeeping, let alone enforcement, is scarcely greater now than during the Cold War. Or in one analyst's view: "The U.N. itself can no more conduct military operations on a large-scale on its own than a trade association of hospitals can conduct heart surgery."[60]

States have made some modest improvements—for example, a round-the-clock situation room and satellite telephones—to augment the UN secretariat's anemic military expertise and intelligence capacities, but these are hardly sufficient to make the militaries of major or middle powers feel at ease about placing the United Nations in charge of combat missions.[61] The assertive multilateralism trumpeted especially by U.S. Permanent Representative Madeleine K. Albright at the outset of the first Clinton administration became untenable as a result of Somalia. Alain Destexhe, the former secretary-general of Médecins Sans Frontières (Doctors Without Borders), linked this development with the international community's unwillingness to react to genocide in Rwanda: "[T]he intervention fiasco in Somalia and the deaths of more than 30 professional soldiers so shocked the American public that the Clinton administration had to rethink its foreign policies."[62] With the United Nations and its member states bogged down in civil wars—scarcely imagined by the founders and certainly not where successes have been common—there are increasing political, economic, and military pressures in Western capitals to avoid engagement.

Third, the comprehensiveness of recent UN operations creates new problems.[63] The side-by-side deployment of international personnel within multifunctional operations requires professional knowledge within each unit as well as the institutional means to ensure coordination. This routinely involves military, civil administration (including election and human rights monitoring, and police support), and humanitarian expertise with an overlay of political negotiations and mediation.

For example, a lesson from the former Yugoslavia is that when the humanitarian and military aspects of a UN operation cannot be separated—because they are both linked to Security Council decisions—they should be integrated. Greater efforts are required to spell out these relationships in advance to avoid the kind of ill-defined relationships into which drifted the main humanitarian organization, the Office of the UN High Commissioner for Refugees (UNHCR), and the UN Protection Force in the former Yugoslavia (UNPROFOR).

When UN forces provide humanitarian support directly, the major humanitarian organizations of the United Nations system must develop a better understanding of precisely how military structures operate and what priorities motivate military decisions at both the micro and macro levels to help guide the military. If these organizations intend to work with military forces in the future—which is likely to be the norm—they must also take steps to orient, train, and exchange information with military personnel. The recruitment of ex-military officers might go a long way toward determining how individual organizations could influence the military and better use the capabilities potentially at the disposal of humanitarian organizations.

No word is used more frequently in international organizations and governments than "coordination." But no other word connotes more things to more people. Everyone is for it, but no one wishes to be coordinated. The two existing "models" for coordination—the lead agency that UNHCR played in the former Yugoslavia[64] and the more system-wide orchestration provided by the Department of Humanitarian Affairs (DHA) in such hot spots as Rwanda.[65] Each has supporters and detractors.

The authority and responsibilities associated with the lead agency role have never been fully or formally defined. UN humanitarian organizations operate the way that the rest of the system does, as a loose association. Each organization has its own set of priorities, governing boards, and fundraising strategy. The absence of a system-wide response and the accompanying lack of guidance for NGOs is lamentable in most circumstances, and all the more so when so many lives are at stake.

The structural problems of DHA are well-known to all observers of the humanitarian arena—an extremely limited budget, little field presence, inexperience, and no leverage over the various moving parts of the UN system. DHA's creation was supposed to rectify the numerous operational problems criticized by donors during the international response to the crises in the Persian Gulf.[66] But to date, it has made little difference to leadership or performance, although information-sharing has improved. The structural weaknesses are obvious for a coordinator of a central coordinating unit that is without any real budgetary authority and who does not outrank the heads of subordinate units. Erskine Childers and Brian Urquhart have argued that the inability to establish a division of labor within the UN system and between it and nongovernmental organizations "remains seriously neglected in the continued jockeying and jostling of UN-system organizations vis-à-vis each other and the intrinsically weak new DHA 'coordinator.'"[67] There is no more urgent priority for humanitarian conflict management than the establishment of a better international division of labor and a more coherent structure to exploit the resources and energies of all humanitarians.

Three Policy Suggestions

This section cannot present the entire gamut of reforms to address the UN's ills as it pursues the primary task of maintaining international peace and security and addresses humanitarian conflict management at the turn of the next century.

Proposals for comprehensive reforms have been put forward recently by such groups as the Commission on Global Governance, Yale University's Commission on the Future of the United Nations, and the South Center.[68] They range from altering the composition of the Security Council to revitalizing the professional staff to overcoming the dismal financial picture of the world organization.

The purpose here is not to pick and choose among such a host of proposals but rather to embroider three ideas that address the three key shortcomings discussed in the previous section. The first concerns: failed states. In spite of the preoccupation with civil wars, the state is hardly obsolete. The appearance of imploded states, and others so obviously on the brink, suggest that "inadequate stateness" may be the overriding weakness in many areas where civil war rages. There is no need to be nostalgic about the repressive national security state to argue that a minimal ability to guarantee law and order and a functioning economy is a necessary, if insufficient, condition for civil society without civil war.

In spite of the past experience of the United Nations, in Palestine for over four decades and more recently in Cambodia,[69] there is little evidence that the world organization could, or would be permitted routinely to, be involved in substituting itself for state authority. The UN is reluctant to assume such an assignment, but the need is painfully obvious. In the new breed of internal conflicts, the functions of government—including social services, the police, and the judiciary—are suspended. The assets of the state also are looted systematically, while officials routinely are killed or forced to flee.

A modified system of trusteeship is required. Since 1994, when the last trust territory (Palau in the South Pacific) became independent, the Trusteeship Council, one of the six primary organs of the United Nations, has been without a portfolio. Could this organ not be transformed to temporarily handle the problems of states that have ceased to function and to provide a modicum of breathing space to permit the reconstitution of civil society?

Proposals calling for recolonizing countries unable to govern themselves are implausible, to say the least.[70] Local populations would not tolerate the imposition of external paternalism, and former colonial powers are hardly in line to resume the white man's burden. But proposals continue to surface in policy literature and debate,[71] and the United Nations could be called upon selectively to assume temporary control or governorship over certain functions.

There is, of course, no quick fix, and the record of the various types of international administration is mixed. As Adam Roberts noted: "Iraq and Rwanda, both of which were under trusteeship for substantial periods in the first half of this century, serve as reminders that trusteeship is no simple cure-all."[72] As the sensibilities of states that have been independent for only three decades or less are bound to be offended by the suggestion, such functions are more likely to be added piecemeal to UN mandates than through a new overall system of trusteeship. If the city of Boston, however, can turn over the administration of its public schools to a private university, then perhaps it is not out of the question that failed states could follow a similar logic in calling temporarily upon the United Nations.

The second suggestion seeks to address the military inadequacies of the world organization. Experience suggests that UN decisions should trigger interventions to be subcontracted to coalitions of major states. Regional powers (for instance, Nigeria within West Africa and Russia within the erstwhile Soviet republics) could be expected to take the lead combined with larger regional (that is, the Economic Community of West African States and the Commonwealth of Independent States) or global coalitions. Perhaps only when regional powers cannot or will not take such a lead should more global powers (for example, France in Rwanda or the U.S. in Somalia) be expected to do so. However, blocking humanitarian intervention, which some powers are willing to conduct when others are reluctant to get involved (for example, the U.S. vis-à-vis Rwanda between early April and late June 1994), should be ruled out.

The pursuit of the Gulf War and the creation of safe havens for Kurds were the first successful illustrations of this procedure and the US-led effort in Haiti and NATO's Implementation Force (IFOR) are more recent ones. In light of the "strategic overstretch" that Paul Kennedy attributes to empires,[73] alternatives to UN command and control of serious military operations must be found. As mentioned earlier, three Security Council decisions within a single month of the summer of 1994—for Russia in Georgia, for France in Rwanda, and for the United States in Haiti—indicated the growing relevance of military intervention by major powers in regions of their traditional interests. Along with the pending OSCE operation for Nagorno-Karabakh, these experiments suggest that the international capacity for humanitarian conflict management will no doubt depend upon ad hoc coalitions, regional powers, or even hegemons—hopefully held accountable for their actions by the wider community of states authorizing outside interventions.

Bill Maynes's "benign *Realpolitik*" straightforwardly recognizes this reality, which amounts to a revival of spheres of influence with UN oversight.[74] The Security Council is experimenting with a type of great power politics that the United Nations originally had been founded to end but that is increasingly pertinent for a feasible doctrine of humanitarian conflict management in light of the inherent difficulties of multilateral mobilization and management of military force.[75] As Boutros-Ghali has written: "[T]hey may herald a new division of labour between the United Nations and regional organizations, under which the regional organization carries the main burden but a small United Nations operation supports it and verifies that it is functioning in a manner consistent with positions adopted by the Security Council."[76]

The third suggestion relates directly to the efficacy of humanitarian action by civilians in war zones.[77] Military forces have an important logistic capacity in the most dire of circumstances; but the vast majority of relief should continue to be the responsibility of civilians. Governments resist the creation of new administrative entities, particularly for what is perceived as a bloated international bureaucracy, but one should be created to deliver emergency aid in active war zones with Chapter VII economic or military sanctions. This specialized cadre would be a truly "international" ICRC.[78] The volunteers should not be part of the common UN staff system because they would have to be appropriately insured and compensated. In many ways, these persons could be more in harm's way than soldiers.

In December 1994, the General Assembly recognized the vulnerability of soldiers and civilians in humanitarian operations, and approved the text of a treaty for ratification by states. It requires signatories to protect UN staff and to arrest those responsible for crimes against them.

The effective protection of the new category of humanitarian workers would be enhanced by the implementation of an international decision to treat attacks against all humanitarian personnel as international crimes. This would build upon the logic of earlier precedents in that the effective prosecution of terrorists and airplane-hijackers is now less subject than in the past to the vagaries of national legislation or the extraditional whims of host countries.

Resources and capable relief specialists could also be siphoned from existing humanitarian agencies with distinguished records in armed conflicts: UNHCR, the UN Children's Fund (UNICEF), and the World Food Programme (WFP). Under this arrangement, the UN's humanitarian agencies themselves would be absent when Chapter VII is in effect. If a peacekeeping operation changed to enforcement, they would withdraw.

The politicization of humanitarian action—or the perception of its politicization, which has the same impact—in Bosnia, Somalia, and Rwanda has altered civilian humanitarian orthodoxy. London's International Institute for Strategic Studies suggested some possible new principles that were based on an internal UN memorandum about humanitarian action when outside military forces are involved. The new bottom-line was the recommendation that civilian humanitarians "should not embark on humanitarian operations where, over time, impartiality and neutrality are certain to be compromised;" and, "[i]f impartiality and neutrality are compromised, an ongoing humanitarian operation should be reconsidered, scaled down or terminated."[79]

This argument would have been anathema to humanitarian practitioners only a few years ago, when there was an unquestioned imperative to respond to every man-made tragedy. But, as I have argued elsewhere, the "age of innocence is over."[80] The conclusion of a comprehensive evaluation of humanitarian conflict management in Somalia prescribes "tough love"—the heretical notion that the international community should have left when it became obvious that looting, corruption, and extortion of assistance effectively was fueling the war.

Although it may seem callous to walk away from suffering, it may prove to be the most humane option: "[I]t would likely have led either to improved protection allowing the continuation of aid or to an opportunity, with departure from Somalia, to channel scarce aid resources to other countries' emergencies."[81]

Like the military forces deployed for a humanitarian intervention, the proposed civilian delivery unit should form an integral part of a unified command that would report directly to the Security Council and not to the secretary-general. The troops authorized by the council and staff from the new humanitarian unit together would comprise a core of soldiers and civilians in possession of expertise and body armor—a "HUMPROFOR," or Humanitarian Protection Force.

The new UN humanitarian entity also should have ground rules for mounting and suspending deliveries. An essential element, for example, would be the explicit agreement by troop contributors that the UN-blessed interventionary forces would be bound by the Geneva Conventions and Additional Protocols. Instead of using customary international law and its incorporation into national military law, they would submit themselves to an international prosecution mechanism devised for the purpose.

This new unit's members would no doubt be more comfortable than the staffs of most UN organizations and international NGOs with the inevitable consequences of imposing either economic or military sanctions on vulnerable civilians as part of a political strategy. Assistance would go to refugees and internally displaced persons without regard to their precise juridical status. The new unit might be dominated by retired military personnel who would not reject out-of-hand the necessity to subordinate themselves and work side-by-side with military protection forces within a hierarchical and disciplined structure. In any case, they should be experienced in working with military forces and able to bridge the military-civilian cultural divide that has impeded effectiveness in many war zones. Moreover, a single structure, instead of the decentralized UN model, would make buck-passing, a standard clause in job descriptions, more difficult in active war zones.

Attaching this unit to the Security Council would insulate the office of the UN's chief executive from Chapter VII's finger-pointing and call to arms. The UN secretary-general should be kept available for more impartial tasks, and an especially important one will be administering failed states. This new unit attached to the Security Council would be a humanitarian adaptation of the precedent set by Rolf Ekeus. As executive chairman of the Special Commission on Disarmament and Arms Control in Iraq, he was appointed by and reports to the council rather than to the secretary-general. As part of the Chapter VII enforcement governing the terms of the cease-fire after the Gulf War, Ekeus is the Security Council's emissary. Boutros-Ghali remains a potential interlocutor for even a pariah regime or its successor.

Moreover, insulating purely humanitarian efforts would help reduce politicization. The staff of most UN organizations and the vast majority of NGOs are ill-equipped to function well when bullets are flying. And all are uncomfortable about their association with enforcement, which by definition contradicts the principles of impartiality and neutrality. UN and NGO humanitarian agencies should devote their limited human and financial resources to what they do better, namely emergency aid after natural disasters or cease-fires, as well as reconstruction and development.

Conclusion

The danger of prescription for contemporary history is evident. But the risk of not trying is even more perilous for a planet groping with the debris of micronationalism when the major power refuses to exercise leadership.

The November 1994 elections in the United States complicated relations between UN political and humanitarian authorities and the world organization's most powerful member state. With the United Nations bogged down in civil wars, there were growing political, economic, and military pressures in Washington and other Western capitals to avoid new engagements and to pull back from multilateralism.

The May 1994 Presidential Decision Directive (PDD) 25 was a harbinger of this reticence. This document about American participation in UN military efforts signaled a policy retreat from multilateralism by the first Clinton administration. Only three years separate the bullish optimism that guaranteed survival to the Kurds in northern Iraq and the utter indifference that not only ignored Rwanda's genocide in April 1994 but also prevented other states from acting to halt the tragedy. Proposals from the 104th Congress—in particular the House's National Security Revitalization Act (H.R. 7) and the Senate's Peace Powers Act of 1995 (S. 5)—suggested the further deterioration in Washington's attitudes toward the United Nations.

The United Nations was largely removed as a campaign issue when the Clinton administration announced abruptly that the United States would not support a second term for Boutros Boutros-Ghali. But the visible problems of the world organization, some would say its "death rattle," in the collective conflict management arena are far from finished.

Vigorous efforts at humanitarian conflict management contradict the military doctrines originally articulated by Secretary of Defense Caspar Weinberger, and subsequently by former Chairman of the Joint Chiefs of Staff General Colin Powell and others. According to post-Vietnam logic, the U.S. should not intervene unless it is committed to total victory with full support from the public and Congress for situations where massive firepower ensures attainable objectives, minimal American casualties, and a clear exit timetable. These are hardly characteristics of the threats of our turbulent times, when the unpredictable interplay of fragmentation and cheap weapons makes chaos commonplace. Or in the words of a leading student of media coverage: "[T]he new generation of conflicts can never be of the short, sharp, overwhelming kind that politicians and military planners now believe is vital to sustain a public consensus for involvement."[82]

The challenge is daunting—for the second Clinton administration in Washington's Beltway and for the United Nations in New York's Turtle Bay. Now that the champagne has been consumed for the world organization's fiftieth anniversary, even many confirmed internationalists are deeply pessimistic. However depressed by the problems and prospects for collective humanitarian conflict management in a changing world, they should take some solace from Dag Hammarskjöld who wisely described the UN as an institution created not in order to bring us to heaven but in order to save us from hell.

Notes

1. See Gaddis Smith, "Woodrow Wilson's Fourteen Points After 75 Years," Twelfth Morgenthau Memorial Lecture (New York: Carnegie Council on Ethics and International Affairs, 1993).

2. See George W. Downs, ed., *Collective Security Beyond the Cold War* (Ann Arbor, Mich.: University of Michigan Press, 1994); and Thomas G. Weiss, ed., *Collective Security in a Changing World* (Boulder, Colo.: Lynne Rienner, 1993).

3. "Humanitarian action" includes not only emergency delivery to victims in war zones but also the protection of their human rights. However, the focus of the present inquiry on the costs and benefits of military operations favors delivery because it is more quantifiable. For longer discussions, see Larry Minear and Thomas G. Weiss, *Mercy Under Fire: War and the Global Humanitarian Community* (Boulder, Colo.: Westview, 1995), and *Humanitarian Politics* (New York: Foreign Policy Association, 1995); and Thomas G. Weiss and Cindy Collins, *Humanitarian Challenges and Intervention: World Politics and the Dilemmas of Help* (Boulder, Colo.: Westview, 1996). See also Jonathan Moore, *The UN and Complex Emergencies* (Geneva: UN Research Institute for Social Development, 1996).

4. Raimo Vayrenen, *The Age of Humanitarian Emergencies* (Helsinki: World Institute for Development Economics Research, 1996).

5. Quoted by Alison Mitchell, "Clinton's About-Face," *New York Times*, September 24, 1996, A8. For a discussion of the impact of Somalia, see Tom J. Farer, "Intervention in Unnatural Humanitarian Emergencies: Lessons of the First Phase," *Human Rights Quarterly* 18, no. 1 (February 1996): 1–22; and Thomas G. Weiss, "Overcoming the Somalia Syndrome—'Operation Rekindle Hope'?" *Global Governance* 1, no. 2 (May–August 1995): 171–187.

6. These were first presented in Thomas G. Weiss, "The United Nations at Fifty: Recent Lessons," *Current History* 94, no. 592 (May 1995): 223–228.

7. For a discussion of the phenomenon of fragmentation, see Lori Fisler Damrosch, ed., *Enforcing Restraint: Collective Intervention in Internal Conflicts* (New York: Council on Foreign Relations Press, 1993); Michael E. Brown, ed., *Ethnic Conflict and International Security* (Princeton: Princeton University Press, 1993); Ted Robert Gurr and Barbara Harff, *Ethnic Conflict in World Politics* (Boulder, Colo.: Westview, 1994); Gidon Gottlieb, *Nation Against State* (New York: Council on Foreign Relations, 1993); and "Reconstructing Nations and States," special issue of *Dædalus* 122, no. 3 (summer 1993). For discussions of the difficulties of negotiating the end to such wars, see I. William Zartman, ed., *Elusive Peace: Negotiating an End to Civil Wars* (Washington, D.C.: Brookings Institution, 1995), and Fen Osler Hampson, *Nurturing Peace: Why Peace Settlements Succeed or Fail* (Washington, D.C.: U.S. Institute of Peace Press, 1996).

8. Boutros Boutros-Ghali, *Supplement to An Agenda for Peace: Position Paper of the Secretary-General on the Occasion of the Fiftieth Anniversary of the United Nations*, January 3, 1995, document A/50/60, S/1995/1, para. 77. This document was reprinted along with the 1992 *An Agenda for Peace*, in *An Agenda for Peace 1995* (New York: United Nations, 1995); paragraph numbers remain the same.

9. These dynamics are the subject of a forthcoming special issue of the *Third World Quarterly* 17, no. 3 (summer 1997), edited by Thomas G. Weiss, *Beyond UN Subcontracting: Task-sharing with Regional Security Arrangements and Service-Providing NGOs* (London: Macmillan, 1997).

10. David Rieff, "The Illusions of Peacekeeping," *World Policy Journal* XI, no. 3 (fall 1994): 3.

11. Boutros Boutros-Ghali, "Transcript of Press Conference," Press Release SG/SM/5518, January 5, 1995, 5. See also, Michael Barnett, "The United Nations and Global Security: The Norm Is Mightier Than the Sword," *Ethics and International Affairs* 9 (1995): 37–54.

12. See Jarat Chopra and Thomas G. Weiss, "Prospects for Containing Conflict in the Former Second World," *Security Studies* 4, no. 3 (spring 1995): 552–583.

13. See Thomas G. Weiss, "Humanitarian Action by Nongovernmental Organizations," in Michael E. Brown, ed., *The International Implications of Internal Conflicts* (Cambridge, Mass.: MIT Press, 1996): 435–459.

14. See Bertrand Schneider, *The Barefoot Revolution: A Report to the Club of Rome* (London: IT Publications, 1988).

15. See Peter J. Spiro, "New Global Communities: Nongovernmental Organizations in International Decision-Making Institutions," *Washington Quarterly* 18, No. 1 (winter 1995): 45–56; and Paul Wapner, *Environmental Activism and World Civic Politics* (Albany, N.Y.: State Univ. of New York Press, 1996).

16. See Lester M. Salamon and Helmut K. Anheier, *The Emerging Sector: An Overview* (Baltimore, Md.: The Johns Hopkins University Institute for Policy Studies, 1994).

17. Boutros Boutros-Ghali, "Foreword," in Thomas G. Weiss and Leon Gordenker, eds., *NGOs, the UN, and Global Governance* (Boulder, Colo.: Lynne Rienner, 1996): 7.

18. "NGOs and Conflict: Three Views," *Humanitarian Monitor,* Number 2 (February 1995): 32–33. See Ian Smillie, *The Alms Bazaar: Altruism under Fire—Non-Profit Organizations and International Development* (West Hartford, Conn.: Kumarian Press, 1995). See also a set of books by Michael Edwards and David Hulme, eds., *Making a Difference: NGOs and Development in a Changing World* (London: Earthscan, 1992); *Beyond the Magic Bullet: NGO Performance and Accountability in the Post-Cold War World* (West Hartford, Conn.: Kumarian Press, 1996); and *Too Close for Comfort? NGOs, States and Donors* (West Hartford, Conn.: Kumarian Press, 1997).

19. For a critique, see Thomas G. Weiss, "New Challenges for UN Military Operations: Implementing 'An Agenda for Peace'," *Washington Quarterly* 16, no. 1 (winter 1993): 51–66.

20. See George Soros, chairman of an Independent Task Force, *American National Interest and the United Nations* (New York: Council on Foreign Relations, 1996).

21. See Cindy Collins and Thomas G. Weiss, *A Review and Assessment of 1989–1996 Peace Operations Publications* (Providence, R.I.: Watson Institute, 1997), Occasional Paper #28.

22. Shashi Tharoor, "Forward," in Donald C.F. Daniel and Bradd C. Hayes, eds., *Beyond Traditional Peacekeeping* (London: Macmillan, 1995), xviii.

23. See Jay Luvaas, "Lessons and Lessons Learned: A Historical Perspective," Robert E. Harkavy and Stephanie G. Neuman, eds., *The Lessons of Recent Wars in the Third World: Approaches and Case Studies, Volume 1* (Lexington, Mass.: Heath, 1985): 68.

24. Joseph J. Collins, "Desert Storm and the Lessons of Learning,"*Parameters* 22, no. 3 (autumn 1992), 83–95; quote taken from 94.

25. Ian MacAlister, whose extensive work on disaster relief and nongovernmental organizations (NGOs), is currently researching institutional memory of NGOs that participate in complex emergencies. The Humanitarianism and War Project at Brown University will be attempting also to determine the role of outside applied research on institutional learning, if any, by civilian humanitarian agencies.

26. See, for example, William Durch, ed., *The Evolution of UN Peacekeeping: Case Studies and Comparative Analysis* (New York: St. Martin's, 1993) and *UN Peacekeeping, American Policy, and the Uncivil Wars of the 1990s* (New York: St. Martin's, 1996).

27. See, for example, Michael Doyle, *UN Peacekeeping in Cambodia: UNTAC's Civil Mandate* (Boulder, Colo.: Lynne Rienner, 1995); and Steven R. Ratner, *The New UN Peacekeeping: Building Peace in Lands of War After the Cold War* (New York: St. Martin's, 1995).

28. See, for example, Mats R. Berdal, *Disarmament and Demobilisation after Civil Wars* (Oxford, U.K.: Oxford University Press, 1996), Adelphi Paper #303.

29. See Trevor Findlay, ed., *Challenges for the New Peacekeepers* (Stockholm: Stockholm International Peace Research Institute, 1996); Michael Barnett, "The Politics of Indifference at the United Nations: the Security Council, Peacekeeping and Genocide in Rwanda," *Cultural Anthropology* (forthcoming, 1997); James O.C. Jonah, *Differing State Perspectives on the United Nations in the Post-Cold War World* (Providence, R.I.: Academic Council on the United Nations System, 1993) ACUNS Reports and Papers, No. 4. There are also articles addressing specific national policies on peacekeeping, such as the academic writing of Deborah L. Norden, "Keeping the Peace, Outside and In: Argentina's UN Missions," *International Peacekeeping*, no. 3 (autumn, 1995): 330–349; and the analyses of the U.S. Congressional Research Office, Joshua Sinai, ed., *United Nations Peace Operations: Case Studies* (Washington, D.C.: Library of Congress, 1995).

30. See, for example, J. Bryan Hehir, "Intervention: From Theories to Cases," *Ethics & International Affairs* 9 (1995): 1–14.

31. For example, in the case of Somalia, see operational problems cited by John G. Sommer, *Somalia: Hope Restored? Humanitarian Aid in Somalia, 1990–1994* (Washington, D.C.: Refugee Policy Group, 1994); Mohamed Sahoun, *Somalia: the Missed Opportunities* (Washington, D.C.: U.S. Institute of Peace Press, 1994); and Arnold and Stahl, "A Power Projection Army in Operations other than War," *Parameters* 23 (winter 1993/94): 4–26.

32. See such varied literature as Mats R. Berdal, *Whiter UN Peacekeeping?* (London: International Institute for Strategic Studies, October 1993), Adelphi Paper #281 ; Gwyn Prins, *The Applicability of the "NATO Model" to United Nations Peace Support Operations Under the Security Council* (New York: United Nations Association of the USA, 1996), a Paper of the UNA-USA International Dialogue on the Enforcement of Security Council Resolutions, No. 2 (July 1996); and John Mackinlay and Jarat Chopra, *A Draft Concept of Second Generation Multinational Operations 1993* (Providence, R.I.: Watson Institute, 1993).

33. Case studies published to date concern northern Iraq, Cambodia, Central America, former Yugoslavia, Liberia, Rwanda, Georgia, Haiti, Chechnya, and Nagorno-Karabakh. For these and other information, see http://www.brown.edu/Departments/Watson_Institute/H_W/H_W_ms.shtml

34. Document GAO/NSIAD–96–14, "Peace Operations: Effect of Training, Equipment, and Other Factors on Unit Capability."

35. See, for example, Chris Seiple, *The U.S. Military/NGO Relationship in Humanitarian Interventions* (Carlisle, Penn.: U.S. Army War College, 1996).

36. For a recent discussion of the rationalization of military assets for involvement in future conflicts, see Robert D. Kaplan, "Fort Leavenworth and the Eclipse of Nationhood," *The Atlantic Monthly* (September 1996): 75–90.

37. See John Mackinlay and Jarat Chopra, "Second Generation Multinational Operations," *Washington Quarterly* 15, no. 2 (spring 1992): 113–131. See also John

Mackinlay, ed., *A Guide to Peace Support Operations* (Providence, R.I.: Watson Institute, 1996), which contains up-to-date listing and discussion.

38. Boutros-Ghali, *Supplement*, para. 77.

39. Boutros Boutros-Ghali, "Transcript of Press Conference," 5 January 1995, Press Release SG/SM/5518, 5.

40. Boutros-Ghali, *Supplement*, para. 20.

41. For a wide-ranging collection of essays, see Gene M. Lyons and Michael Mastanduno, eds., *Beyond Westphalia? State Sovereignty and International Intervention* (Baltimore: Johns Hopkins University Press, 1995); Paul A. Winters, ed., *Interventionism: Current Controversies* (San Diego, Cal.: Greenhaven Press, 1995); and Marianne Heiberg, ed., *Subduing Sovereignty: Sovereignty and the Right To Intervene* (London: Pinter, 1994). The best bibliographic information and its interpretation is found in Oliver Famsbotham and Tom Woodhouse, *Humanitarian Intervention in Contemporary Conflict* (Cambridge: Polity Press, 1996). See also John Harriss, ed., *The Politics of Humanitarian Intervention* (London: Pinter, 1995); James Mayall, ed., *The New Interventionism: United Nations Experience in Cambodia, Former Yugoslavia, and Somalia* (New York: Cambridge University Press, 1996); and Jan Nederveen Pieterse, ed., *World Orders in the Making: The Case of Humanitarian Intervention* (London: Macmillan, forthcoming).

42. James F. Hoge, Jr., "Editor's Note," *Foreign Affairs* 73, no. 6 (November/ December 1994): v.

43. See Adam Roberts, "The Crisis in Peacekeeping," *Survival* 36, no. 3 (autumn 1994): 93–120; and Thomas G. Weiss, "Intervention: Whither the United Nations?" *Washington Quarterly* 17, no. 1 (winter 1994): 109–128.

44. For example, see articles "On Intervention" by Noam Chomsky, Christopher Hitchens, Richard Falk, Carl Coretta, Charles Knight, and Robert Leavitt in *Boston Review* 18 (December/January 1993–94): 3–16.

45. Alex de Waal and Rakiya Omaar, "Can Military Intervention Be 'Humanitarian'?" *Middle East Report*, nos. 187/188 (March–April/May–June 1994): 7.

46. See Richard A. Melanson, *Reconstructing Consensus: American Foreign Policy since the Vietnam War* (New York: St. Martin's, 1991).

47. For a reasoned presentation of some negative arguments, see Ernst B. Haas, "Beware the Slippery Slope: Notes Toward the Definition of Justifiable Intervention," in Laura W. Reed and Carl Kaysen, eds., *Emerging Norms of Justified Intervention* (Cambridge, Mass.: American Academy of Arts & Sciences, 1993): 63–87.

48. For a discussion, see Francis M. Deng, "Frontiers of Sovereignty," *Leiden Journal of International Law* 8, no. 2 (1995): 249–286.

49. See Nigel Rodley, ed., *To Loose the Bonds of Wickedness: International Intervention in Defence of Human Rights* (London: Brassey's, 1992), and Jarat Chopra and Thomas

G. Weiss, "Sovereignty Is No Longer Sacrosanct: Codifying Humanitarian Intervention," *Ethics and International Affairs* 6 (1992): 95–117.

50. Adam Roberts, "Humanitarian War: Military Intervention and Human Rights," *International Affairs* 69 (1993): 429–449; and Thomas G. Weiss and Kurt M. Campbell, "Military Humanitarianism," *Survival* 33, no. 5 (September/October 1991): 451–465.

51. See Kimberly Stanton, "Pitfalls of Intervention: Sovereignty as a Foundation for Human Rights," *Harvard International Review* XVI, no. 1 (fall 1993): 14–16.

52. See Mohammed Ayoob, *The Third World Security Predicament: State Making, Regional Conflict, and the International System* (Boulder, Colo.: Lynne Rienner, 1994); and Robert H. Jackson, *Quasi-States: Sovereignty, International Relations, and the Third World* (Cambridge, U.K.: Cambridge University Press, 1990)

53. See Ali A. Mazrui, "The Blood of Experience: The Failed State and Political Collapse in Africa," *World Policy Journal* XII, no. 1 (spring 1995): 28–34.

54. See Chaim Kaufmann, "Possible and Impossible Solutions to Ethnic Wars," *International Security* 20, no. 4 (spring 1996): 136–175.

55. For these and other disheartening statistics, see *The State of the World's Refugees 1995: In Search of Solutions* (New York: Oxford University Press, 1995); *1996 World Refugee Report* (Washington, D.C.: U.S. Committee for Refugees, 1996); *World Disasters Report 1996* (Oxford, U.K.: Oxford University Press, 1996); and Bread for the World Institute, *Countries in Conflict* (Silver Glen, Md.: Bread for the World, 1995).

56. Commission on Global Governance, *Our Global Neighbourhood* (Oxford, U.K.: Oxford Univ. Press, 1995): 90.

57. Gerald B. Helman and Steven R. Ratner, "Saving Failed States," *Foreign Policy* 89 (winter 1992–93): 3–20; and I. William Zartman, ed., *Collapsed States: The Disintegration and Restoration of Legitimate Authority* (Boulder, Colo.: Lynne Rienner, 1995).

58. See Winrich Kühne, *Winning the Peace: Concept and Lessons Learned of Post-Conflict Peacebuilding* (Ebenhausen, Germany: Stiftung and Wissenschaft, 1996).

59. For discussions of the difficulties of negotiating the end to such wars, see I. William Zartman, ed., *Elusive Peace: Negotiating an End to Civil Wars* (Washington, D.C.: Brookings Institution, 1995), and Fen Osler Hampson, *Nurturing Peace: Why Peace Settlements Succeed or Fail* (Washington, D.C.: U.S. Institute of Peace Press, 1996).

60. Michael Mandelbaum, "The Reluctance To Intervene," *Foreign Policy* 95 (summer 1994): 11.

61. For a review of these concerns, see Frank M. Snyder, *Command and Control: The Literature and Commentaries* (Washington, D.C.: National Defense University, 1993); *U.N. Peacekeeping: Lessons Learned in Recent Missions* (Washington, D.C.: General Accounting Office, December 1993), document GAO/NSIAD–94–9; and *Humanitarian*

Intervention: Effectiveness of U.N. Operations in Bosnia (Washington, D.C.: General Accounting Office, April 1994), document GAO/NSIAD-94-156BR.

62. Alain Destexhe, "Confronting the Genocide in Rwanda," *Foreign Policy* 97 (winter 1994–95): 10. See also his *Rwanda: Essai sur le Génocide* (Brussels: Editions Complexe, 1994).

63. See Thomas G. Weiss, ed., *The United Nations and Civil Wars* (Boulder, Colo.: Lynne Rienner, 1995).

64. See Thomas G. Weiss and Amir Pasic, "Reinventing UNHCR: Enterprising Humanitarians in the Former Yugoslavia, 1991–1995," *Global Governance* 3, no. 1 (January-April): 41–57.

65. See Antonio Donini, *The Policies of Mercy: UN Coordination in Afghanistan, Mozambique, and Rwanda*, Occasional Paper #22 (Providence, R.I.: Watson Institute, 1996).

66. See Larry Minear and Thomas G. Weiss, "Groping and Coping in the Gulf Crisis: Discerning the Shape of a New Humanitarian Order," *World Policy Journal* 9 (fall/winter 1992–93): 755–88.

67. Erskine Childers with Brian Urquhart, *Renewing the United Nations System* (Uppsala, Sweden: Dag Hammarskjöld Foundation, 1994): 114.

68. Commission on Global Governance, *Our Global Neighbourhood* ; Independent Working Group on the Future of the United Nations, *The United Nations in Its Second Half-Century* (New York: Ford Foundation, 1995); and South Centre, *For a Strong and Democratic United Nations: A South Perspective on UN Reform* (Geneva: South Centre, 1996).

69. See Jarat Chopra, *UN Transition Authority in Cambodia,* Occasional Paper #15 (Providence, R.I.: Watson Institute, 1994); Janet E. Neininger, *Peacekeeping in Transition: The United Nations in Cambodia* (New York: Twentieth Century Fund, 1994); Ratner, *The New UN Peacekeeping,* 137–206; and Doyle, *UN Peacekeeping in Cambodia.*

70. Paul Johnson, "Colonialism's Back—and Not a Moment Too Soon," *New York Times Magazine,* April 18, 1993. See also William Pfaff, "A New Colonialism? Europe Must Go Back into Africa," *Foreign Affairs* 74, no. 1 (January/February 1995): 2–6.

71. See, for example, Helman and Ratner, "Saving Failed States," and Peter Lyon, "The Rise and Fall and Possible Revival of International Trusteeship," *Journal of Commonwealth and Comparative Politics*, no. 31 (March 1993): 96–110.

72. Adam Roberts, "A More Humane World?" draft study for the Commonwealth Secretariat, dated December 1994, 20.

73. Paul Kennedy, *The Rise and Fall of the Great Powers* (New York: Random House, 1987).

74. Charles William Maynes, "A Workable Clinton Doctrine," *Foreign Policy* 93 (winter 1993–94): 3–20.

75. For an outspoken realist view, see John J. Mearsheimer, "The False Promise of International Institutions," *International Security* 19, no. 3 (winter 1994–95): 5–49.

76. Boutros-Ghali, *Supplement*, para. 86.

77. This argument was originally made in Weiss, "Overcoming the Somalia Syndrome."

78. For a discussion of expanding and making greater use of the ICRC, see James Ingram, "The Future Architecture for International Humanitarian Assistance," in Thomas G. Weiss and Larry Minear, eds., *Humanitarianism Across Borders: Sustaining Civilians in Times of War* (Boulder, Colo.: Lynne Rienner, 1993): 171–193.

79. International Institute for Strategic Studies, "Military Support for Humanitarian Operations," *Strategic Comments*, no. 2, 22 (February 1995). The ICRC is increasingly preoccupied by this subject. See Umesh Palwankar, ed., *Symposium on Humanitarian Action and Peace-Keeping: Report* (Geneva: ICRC, 1994).

80. See Thomas G. Weiss, "Military-Civilian Humanitarianism: The 'Age of Innocence' Is Over," *International Peacekeeping* 2, no. 2 (summer 1995): 157–174.

81. Sommer, *Hope Restored?*, 116.

82. See Nik Gowing, *Real-Time Television Coverage of Armed Conflicts and Diplomatic Crises: Does It Pressure or Distort Foreign Policy Decision?* (Cambridge, Mass. : Harvard University, 1994); Press, Politics, Public Policy Working Papers 94–1, 86.

About the Authors

Michael Barnett is associate professor of Political Science at the University of Wisconsin at Madison. He is the author of *Confronting the Costs of War* (Princeton, 1992), *Dialogues in Arab Politics: Negotiations in Regional Order* (Columbia, forthcoming), and *Governing Anarchy: Security Communities in History, Theory, and Comparison* (forthcoming), edited with Emanuel Adler. A former Council on Foreign Relations Fellow, he served at the U.S. Mission to the United Nations in 1993–1994 and has written widely on the topic of the United Nations and peacekeeping.

Andrew Bennett is assistant professor of Government at Georgetown University. He has written on Soviet and Russian foreign policy, regional conflicts, collective security, and burden-sharing. From 1994–1995, he served as Special Assistant to the Assistant Secretary of Defense for International Security Affairs.

Bruce Cronin is assistant professor of International Relations at the University of Wisconsin at Madison. He is currently researching transnational identity formation and the changing norms of sovereignty in world politics. He is co-author of "The State and the Nation: Changing Norms in the Rules of Sovereignty in International Relations" in *International Organization*.

Martha Finnemore is assistant professor of Political Science and International Affairs at George Washington University in Washington, D.C. She is interested in the ways in which normative and social understandings shape state interests and state behavior in international politics. She is the author of *National Interests in International Society* (Cornell University Press, 1996) and is currently writing a book about social and normative sources of change in patterns of military intervention.

Alan C. Lamborn is professor of Political Science at Colorado State University. He is the author of *The Price of Power: Risk and Foreign Policy in Britain, France, and Germany* (1991). His current research interests focus on the impact of varying assumptions about linkage politics and the process of strategic interaction on theories of world politics. With Joseph Lepgold he is presently completing *World Politics into the 21st Century: Unique Contexts, Enduring Patterns* (St. Martin's, forthcoming).

Joseph Lepgold is associate professor of International Affairs and Government at Georgetown University. He is the author of *The Declining Hegemon: The United States And European Defense, 1960–1990* (Praeger, 1990) and a number of articles dealing with various aspects of alliance politics and other international security issues. He is currently working on several projects that examine the link between international relations theory and practice, including the above-mentioned volume with Alan Lamborn.

Robert B. McCalla is an honorary fellow in the Department of Political Science at the University of Madison at Wisconsin where he was Assistant Professor of Political Science, 1989–1996. He formerly was a defense analyst at the Rand Corporation and a NATO Research Fellow. He is the author of *Uncertain Perceptions: U.S. Cold War Crisis Decision Making* (University of Michigan Press, 1992) and *"When Johnny Comes Marching Home": Environmental Change and Organizational Response in Military Organizations* (forthcoming).

Thomas G. Weiss is research professor and director of the Research Program on Global Security at Brown University's Thomas J. Watson, Jr. Institute for International Studies. He also serves as executive director of the Academic Council on the United Nations System. Previously he was executive director of the International Peace Academy and had held several UN posts (at UNCTAD, the UN Commission for Namibia, UNITAR, and ILO). He has authored or edited some twenty-five books on various aspects of international organization, conflict management, North-South relations, and humanitarian action including most recently *Humanitarian Challenges and Intervention: World Politics and the Dilemmas of Help*, with Cindy Collins (Westview, 1996); *The News Media, Civil War, and Humanitarian Action*, with Larry Minear and Colin Scott (Lynne Rienner, 1996); and *NGOs, the UN, and Global Governance* (Lynne Rienner, 1996), edited with Leon Gordenker.

Index